MW01659842

An Investigation into Christian SME Owner-Managers' Conceptualisations of Practice

Andrea Werner

DISSERTATION.COM

Boca Raton

An Investigation into Christian SME Owner-Managers' Conceptualisations of Practice

Dissertation.com
Boca Raton, Florida
USA • 2008

ISBN-10: 1-59942-675-7
ISBN-13: 978-1-59942-675-4

AN INVESTIGATION INTO CHRISTIAN SME OWNER-MANAGERS' CONCEPTUALISATIONS OF PRACTICE

A thesis submitted for the degree of Doctor of Philosophy

by

Andrea Werner

Brunel Business School, Brunel University
Uxbridge, West-London, UK

TABLE OF CONTENTS

LIST OF FIGURES AND TABLES

Acknowledgements

Writing this PhD thesis has been a long and strenuous yet very rewarding journey, a journey I could not have undertaken without the help of others.

First and foremost I would like to thank my supervisors, Dr Laura J. Spence and Prof John Hendry, for all their invaluable advice and support, and for their help whenever I got 'stuck'.

I am very grateful to Klaus-Dieter Trayser and the Plansecur Trust who provided a generous fund for my travel expenses and to the Brunel Business School who granted me a PhD studentship. Without their financial assistance it would have not been possible to do this PhD project.

I am particularly indebted to the 21 participants in the study, who very generously gave up some of their valuable time for me and who were willing to talk to me about a rather personal subject. Furthermore, I would like to thank all those numerous people who helped me gain access to the respondents.

There are many more that deserve thanks and praise for their help and support and I can single out only a few here. Special thanks go to my parents and to my sister for their love and for always being there for me. I would also like to thank all my housemates at 68 Granville Road for being great company and for making our house a real home for me. Furthermore, I am very indebted to Maria Penicud, Rosemary Jenkins and Dr Angela Ayios for their practical help; and to Sandra Münch and Uta Kreusel for their continuing support and encouragement.

Last but not least, however, my praise and thanks belong to God, who has kept and sustained me throughout this journey.

December 2006

1. Introduction

Social scientists have increasingly focused on the role of civil society as an intermediate institution between state and market and its potential to solve collective problems. This role is becoming more and more critical in the contemporary world, where free markets proliferate and the influence of the state as a moderating force on economic activity has been declining. In particular, a number of scholars show themselves concerned about the undesirable impacts that 'unrestrained' self-interested behaviour in the economic sphere can have on society, and they look to civil society arrangements as a means to counterbalance those potential 'excesses' of economic activity.

But how does civil society affect economic activity? This study seeks to shed light on this question by empirically investigating how individual economic actors might be influenced by the norms and values that are transmitted, generated and fostered through civil society activities and institutions. Singled out for investigation are owner-managers of small to medium-sized enterprises (SMEs), as due to the structure and set-up of SMEs they are thought to be in a good position to bring their norms and values to bear on their business. As an example, the study will focus on the influence of Christianity as one of the strongest and longest standing civil society institutions in Western societies. At the same time, secularisation and other societal processes in Western societies have affected the influence of Christianity on society, and hence it is interesting to explore the impact that Christianity still has in a contemporary context.

This study uses a socio-psychological approach and will investigate how the Christian context influences the way SME owner-managers who regard themselves as practising Christians conceptualise their worlds of business practice. The research is based on qualitative in-depth interviews with 21 conservative Protestant SME owner-managers from Germany and the UK and so embeds the research in a European context.

This thesis is structured as follows.

Chapter 2 will outline the context for the research in more detail by drawing on theoretical and empirical literature. It will make a case as to why it is important to empirically investigate civil society in relation to economic activity. It will further explain the approach that was chosen to investigate the phenomenon and give a brief outline of social theories that support such an approach. It will also explicate in more detail why the study focuses on SME owner-managers as well as outline some aspects of the Christian tradition that are relevant for this investigation. The chapter will moreover give a brief overview of empirical studies that have looked at the influence of religiousness and of adherence to the Christian faith on economic activity. The final section in chapter 2 will set out the aims of the study and outline some aspects of the national cultural contexts within which the study is embedded.

Chapter 3 will outline the methodological frameworks within which the study is located, explain the choice of an interview-based study and discuss some methodological issues. It will further explain how the study was carried out and discuss some issues that arose at various stages of the research process.

The next three chapters will present and analyse the research findings. *Chapter 4* will report on those Christian concepts on which the respondents drew to rationalise their actions. *Chapter 5* will examine some contexts that Christianity provides and their influence on the respondents' conceptualisation of practice. Finally, *chapter 6* will explore the different types of practices that the respondents linked with their faith and will also consider the presence of additional motivations.

In *chapter 7*, the research findings will be discussed further and suggestions for further research will be made.

2. Contextualising the research

2.1 Studying civil society's influence on economic activity

2.1.1 Why consider civil society

The idea to look at civil society and its potential to 'regulate' economic activity in such a way that it counterbalances the effects of unrestrained self-interested behaviour is not a new one. During the rise of industry and commerce in the late 19th century, Durkheim (1957) observed that economic activity seemed not really to be subject to any (restraining) moral influence (ibid., 10) and he feared that the pursuit of unrestrained self-interest in the economic sphere would have destructive consequences for society and, as a result, for individuals living in that society (ibid., 16). Durkheim drew a connection between his observations and classical economic theory, a theory that was largely accepted among his contemporaries (Hendry 2001), but of which he was rather critical. He critiqued the assumption of classical economic theorists that the economic sphere was an autonomous system that in its competitive set up would regulate itself and balance out self-interested behaviour (Durkheim 1957, 15) by arguing that such a set up would produce a "a chronic state of warfare and endless dissatisfaction amongst the producers" (ibid. 16). This he considered to have disastrous effects for society. Connected to this was his concern about the pronounced aim of the economic function to achieve an as large as possible productive output. He argued that productive output should not be treated as an end itself, and that the economic function should be considered only *one* among a number of societal functions that contribute to a harmonious social life and consequently to individual well-being. Durkheim contended that if the only way to achieve a high productive output was to disturb men's peace it was "not worth the cost" (ibid., 16).

His concerns about the potential negative consequences of 'unrestrained' self-interested behaviour led Durkheim to call for more moral discipline in the economic sphere and he suggested that this should be 'enforced' through voluntary societal arrangements – through what we would call today 'civil society' institutions. He particularly proposed that those engaged in economic activity should get together and form professional bodies. Those bodies would develop professional codes, which were to make economic activity subject to moral discipline and thus save it from its destructive tendencies (ibid., 23-25).

More than 100 years on, Durkheim's concerns are still echoed in the writings of present-day social economists, some business ethicists and sociologists (e.g. Daly and Cobb 1994, Lutz 1999, Ulrich 1997, Bellah et al. 1996, Bauman 1993) – although they have added some more contemporary concerns. Despite the fact that Western market economies have brought about an unprecedented level of material prosperity for their citizens over the last century, those scholars have voiced their concerns over a number of negative 'externalities' of 'unrestrained' economic activity, particularly over the effects on the natural environment. They have also focused on wider societal consequences that a pure self-interest based economic system can produce, such as social and economic inequality, and have examined its adverse affects on social cohesion and societal well-being. Finally, they have criticised the rising predominance of economic thinking in society, which leads to regarding societal actors merely as consumers or as human 'resources' and to focusing on economic growth as the sole criterion of societal well-being. Like Durkheim, those scholars have linked their concerns to classical economic theory and have criticised the fact that this theory – even though economists might treat it as only having a heuristic function - legitimises self-interested economic behaviour such as the maximisation of profits and the pursuit of economic efficiency without requiring economic actors to take any moral or social considerations into account.

Their concerns go hand in hand with the diminishing influence of quite an important institution that has - particularly since the end of World War II and particularly in (continental) Western European societies - provided quite an effective counter-balance to potential excesses of economic activities: the state. In the post-war era, Western European governments introduced legal and other regulatory frameworks that led to the formation of capitalist systems with a 'social conscience', such as the formation of the Social Market Economy (Soziale Marktwirtschaft) in Germany. In those societies it has been the function of the state to regulate numerous aspects of economic activity such as the labour market, the exploitation of natural resources and production standards, in order to channel economic activity in such a way that it produces beneficial outcomes for society. The state has further been ascribed the task of providing extensive welfare services, which are funded through a high level of taxation and which are meant to counter-balance inequalities in society and to fund collective goods such as education and health-care (Scharpf 2003, 372).

The role of the state as the effective provider of correctives, however, has been increasingly called into question. The fact that economic activity is tending towards internationalisation and global interaction - and this even more so since the end of the Cold War - has placed Western governments in a difficult position as they can impose their regulations only on a limited territory (ibid., 370ff). For example, large corporations can quite easily move production plants to other, less regulated countries to avoid national laws and regulations. This and the ability of private investors to move private capital across borders can threaten welfare budgets, taxation levels and other common-good orientated government policies (Held and McGrew 2003, 13). As a consequence, states are becoming more and more limited in their efforts to balance out potential negative consequences of economic activity.

At the same time, governments themselves have actively started to rid themselves of their 'welfare' responsibilities. They have - to varying degrees - actively adopted neo-liberal ideas and pursued free-market policies by deregulating markets, privatising public sectors, and encouraging foreign investment (Castells 2003, 326ff.) while at the same time curbing welfare provisions. There are several explanations as to why this has been happening. First, free markets, i.e. markets that are based on the self-interest of economic actors only, are "expected to operate economic and institutional miracles" (ibid., 327), particularly if governments face problems such as welfare overspending and high levels of public deficit. But Castells also argues that personal vested interests of political leaders may contribute to the favouring of free market policies (ibid., 328ff).

The increasing limitations and changing nature of the state, the proliferation of the free-market model, and the concern that self-interested economic behaviour does not always benefit society but may have harmful social consequences, have led scholars (and policy makers) - like Durkheim in his time - to focus on civil society and its moderating influence on economic activity (Münkler and Fischer 2002a and 2002b, Giddens 1998).

Some features of civil society

If we want to study the effect of civil society on economic activity, we need to understand a little more what 'civil society' encompasses. According to the working definition of the London School of Economics, civil society refers to "the arena of uncoerced collective action around shared interests, purposes and values" (LSE 2004). It is thus conceptualised against the more coerced structure of the state but also against the model of the market, which presumes that human action is guided by individual or private self-interest only (Münkler 1998). Yet civil society is not an autonomous societal sphere, but may interact with both the state and the market (LSE 2004) (see Figure 1). As such it is considered to have a moderating influence on both institutions (Hems and Tonkiss 2000, 5). At the same time, civil society is thought to have the ability to solve collective problems more effectively than the state or the market alone and is therefore also considered in this role of a 'collective problem solver' (Ostrom 1990; Putnam 2000; Hems and Tonkiss 2000, 5; LSE 2004).

This is particularly true for such civil society organisations or institutions whose explicit purpose is to alleviate certain problems in society. Here, the principle of subsidiarity is particularly important (Münkler and Fischer 2002b, 435). Civil society institutions that can tackle problems or challenges at the closest proximity to their origin are thought to be more effective than any bureaucratic state-led involvement can be. Moreover, they are able to identify and deal with problems that the state or the market might not be aware of or not take an interest in. At the same time, a number of civil society institutions such as environmental and humanitarian organisations or certain social movements work across national borders and so have the potential to solve societal problems on a more global scale (Held and McGrew 2003, 18).

Figure 1: Interactions between civil society, market and state

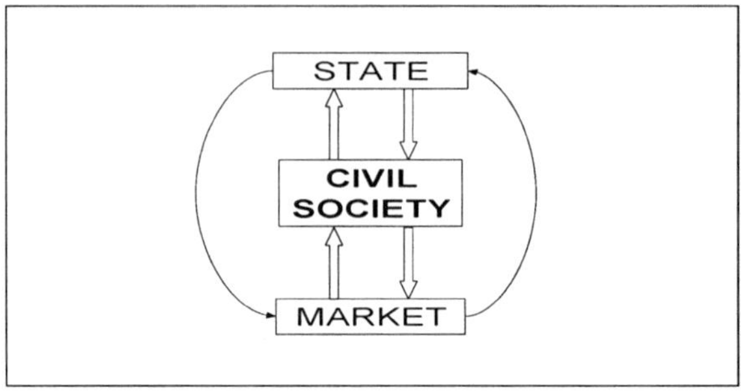

Other scholars draw attention to the values and norms that underlie any kind of civil society activity, i.e. any kind of associational activity or other forms of societal interaction or connectivity. Particularly Putnam (2000) explicates that continued interaction within social networks, whatever nature and purpose they might have, can lead actors within that network to develop 'civic virtues' such as norms of reciprocity, co-operative behaviour and mutual support.[1] This may not only be positive for the actors *within* the network, but might also influence the actors' behaviour beyond the network and thus have positive 'spill-over' effects on wider society (ibid., 20).

Yet we cannot naively assume that all civil society activities work for the good of society. First, there is the rather obvious objection that some civil society activities may be of a "nasty nature" and produce harm for wider society (Seligman 2000, 12, Putnam 2000, 21). Münkler and Fischer (2000a) also draw attention to the fact that civil society activities of societal actors are usually bound up with their own life-world, i.e. with their own interests. This personal interest might be necessary to sustain the actor's motivation, but in a wider societal context the pursuit of partial interests might lead, for instance, to group egoisms or conflicts with other groups.[2] At the same time, some social and political problems, for example, those where the effects are not personally and/or visibly felt, might not receive sufficient attention by civil society and might therefore not be tackled.[3]

Observers have, moreover, reported a rise in individualist behaviour among societal actors (e.g. Putnam 2000, Bellah et al. 1996), which might seriously diminish civil society's ability to solve collective problems and to be an effective counterbalance to self-interested market behaviour. Putnam (2000), for example, observed that in the United States people engaged less and less in civil society activities, from socialising with neighbours to actively participating in democratic processes, which in his view has led to an overall decline of 'civic spirit' or 'civic mindedness'. Offe and Fuchs (2001) and Hall (1999), on the other hand, who report from two European perspectives (Germany and the UK respectively), argue that there is not a decline in civil society activity as such but a change in the nature of civil society activities. Particularly focusing on associational activity, they argue that although the level of such activities has not declined, people – predominantly younger generations - are more likely to get involved in associational activities that foster their own individual interests and preferences, such as leisure activities, rather than in associations or organisations that are dedicated to a wider public interest or that require more of a sense of 'civic duty' (Offe and Fuchs 2001, 441; Hall 1999, 450, 457). There may be a number of reasons as to why people show more individualised behaviour. Putnam (2000) has pointed, for example, to the increasing spatial fragmentation between

[1] Other scholars argue that 'civic virtue' is actually a moral pre-requisite, a behavioural disposition for engaging in collective action, but that it requires civil society activities for 'civic virtue' to be fostered, re-produced and sustained (Münkler 1998).

[2] Particularly if one enlarges the concept of 'society' to the global community

[3] For example, long-term environmental consequences of economic activity or the existence of child labour in the Third World does not directly affect Western citizens in their day-to-day lives, and hence they might not feel strongly about doing something about those issues.

home and workplace or the invention of television. Other observers claim that the espoused individualism (and consumerism) of free-market ideologies have also adversely affected the problem-solving abilities of civil society (Fenton 2000, 161).

The ambiguous nature of civil society thus raises the important question whether and to what extent civil society does actually provide a counterbalance to potential negative side-effects of self-interested economic behaviour. This, however, is a question that may only be sufficiently explored through empirical studies.

2.1.2 Studying the influence of civil society on economic activity at the level of the individual

How can we investigate the relationship between civil society and economic activity empirically?

A number of researchers opt to study the phenomenon at an organisational level. Here we would have civil society organisations, for example, charities, NGOs, trade unions, pressure groups etc. on the one hand, and business organisations on the other. At this level, researchers might investigate how civil society organisations seek to hold corporations to account for their actions, for example, through 'stakeholder' dialogue and shareholder activism, and how effective they are in doing so (O'Rourke 2003, Burchell and Cook 2006). Others might study the effectiveness of social partnerships between civil society organisations and business organisations, which the former might seek to solve particular societal problems (Åhlström and Sjöström 2005).

This study, by contrast, will seek to investigate the influence of civil society on individual economic actors. In this case we do not consider civil society at an organisational level (only) but rather in terms of the (shared) norms and values that are transmitted, generated and fostered through civil society activity (Münkler 1998, Putnam 2000). In particular, the study will explore how membership of one specific civil society institution that espouses and transmits a certain set of norms and values might impact on the way societal actors carry out economic activities.

Two assumptions

If we want to study this phenomenon at the level of the individual societal actor, we will have to make two assumptions about the nature of human beings. Those two assumptions have been implicit in the arguments made above, but they will be made explicit here. We must assume that

1. Human behaviour is – at least to a certain degree – of voluntaristic nature.

In other words, we must presume that the actions of human beings are not causally determined by circumstances alone but that human beings have certain cognitive capabilities that mark them out as 'actors' or 'agents' who can take control over their actions. If this was not the case, the individual would not be a meaningful level for studying said phenomenon. At the same time, we must assume that

2. The personal norms and values that inform the actions of human agents are influenced by their interaction with their socio-cultural environment.

This means that we cannot assume an individualistic, self-contained or solipsistic view of human beings, where norms and values are considered the products of some inner cognitive processes that are based on 'inbuilt' mental mechanisms (Harré and Gillett 1994, 11). Kant, for instance, followed the first assumption and held that human beings inhabit a 'realm of freedom', which is not subject to causal (natural) laws but rather to cognitive capacities (Hughes et al. 2003, 122). But he was of the view that the mind was "an inner realm of rationally ordered operations using concepts in accordance with the laws of reason" (Harré and Gillett 1994, 74). Thus he regarded reason, the basis for cognitive processes, to be an inbuilt faculty of the mind.[4] Yet we must not regard the concepts and rules (including personal values and norms) that people use in their cognitive processes and that shape their behaviour as something 'closed', something that people inhabit independent of their interaction with their socio-cultural environment. Otherwise we would not be able to investigate the phenomenon that we have set out to study in a meaningful way.

Structuration Theory and Discursive Psychology

The two assumptions that have just been made are supported by a number of social theories. We will focus here on two theories in particular, as the researcher considers them to be appropriate frameworks for this study in more general terms as well as in terms of the methodological approach to the research (see chapter 3).

Giddens' theory of structuration (1984) focuses on the role of human agency in the production and reproduction of societal structures through social practices whereas Harré and Gillett's discursive psychology (1994) expounds how discourses shape human cognition. Although coming from different perspectives, a sociological and a socio-psychological respectively, and using different starting points for their arguments, those theories expound ideas that are compatible and complementary (Hendry 2000, 968, 971). We will now look at some of those ideas in more detail.

Harré and Gillett begin by criticising research traditions in psychology that assume a Cartesian worldview, i.e. an individualistic, solipsistic view of human beings where cognitive activity is thought to be based on 'inbuilt' mental mechanisms (ibid., 4, see also previous section). Building on the work of Wittgenstein (1953), Harré and Gillett argue that concepts, the basis of thinking, are expressed by words which are located in languages (1994, 21). But since language is a system of symbols or signs that is by implication shared with others[5], one cannot assume that human beings are "isolated cogniser[s] or interpreter[s] of the world" (ibid.) Human beings use language to jointly construct discourses within socio-cultural groups, and those discourses should, in Harré and Gillett's view, be regarded as an important part of the framework through which an individual interprets the world (ibid., 22).

Harré and Gillett hold that human beings are exposed to and inhabit a number of socio-cultural discourses that arise from the historical, political, cultural, social and interpersonal settings that individuals find themselves in. Each of these discourses, which embody clusters of signification as well as norms, rules, conventions etc. (ibid., 21, 25f.), have the potential to shape the individual's thoughts and behaviours. Harré and Gillett further point out that people adopt or commit themselves to certain positions in the discourses that they inhabit (ibid., 140), which might also be influenced by the interaction with other discourses. The cognitive 'task' of the individual consists then in 'managing' those interacting discourses and their positionings within those discourses (ibid., 26). This is particularly necessary when an individual perceives that some discourses in which they participate (especially when they encounter 'new' discourses) are in conflict to one another, as this might require negotiation, adjustment, repositioning if one wants to maintain coherence (ibid., 25). To what extent an individual can actually engage in such kind of mental activities depends however on the individual's ability to (discursively) reflect on the contexts that she finds herself in (ibid., 180). This ability, again, may be influenced by her social environment.

If we follow Harré and Gillett's theory, we can regard personal beliefs, norms and values that an individual might hold and that might influence their behaviour either as part of their discursive contexts or as product of the interaction between the different discourses that the individual is exposed to and inhabits. If we then regard a civil society institution (with its underlying and associated norms

[4] Kantian moral philosophers make a big point about the moral *autonomy* of human actors (e.g. Ulrich 1997). They hold that human actors should act morally independent of any social influences but only in reference to the 'dictates of their reason' ('reason' being an inbuilt human faculty). Such a view does not hold sway if one follows the social-constructionist view that is outlined here.

[5] That is, if one assumes that the primary purpose of language is the ability to communicate with others and to jointly make sense of the world.

and values) as a discourse or discursive context that the individual is exposed to, we may explore how participation in this particular discursive context may shape the individual's beliefs, attitudes and subsequent behaviour.

Giddens' expositions of his theory of structuration start with a critique of the structuralist traditions in sociology that regard human behaviour "as a result of forces that actors neither control nor comprehend" (Giddens 1984, xvi). In contrast, he argues that human beings are knowledgeable because they have reflexive capacities, i.e. they can reflect about the circumstances of their actions (ibid., xxii, 375). He further holds that human beings are 'real' actors or agents because they are the perpetrators of an action in the sense that they could have chosen to act differently (ibid., 9).

But Giddens argues that the knowledge that informs the practices of human actors in their various action contexts derives from "structural features of wider social systems", which are available to them depending on their location within a societal setting (ibid. 24); and that by drawing on those structural features human actors reproduce them through their actions. This is what Giddens means by the term 'structuration': The more often human actors draw on structural features across time and space and thereby reproduce them in their social practices, the more stabilised or institutionalised they become (ibid., xxxi). Structural features, however, refer to rules and resources, which enable as well as constrain social action (ibid., 25) and contain normative elements as well as codes of signification (ibid., xxxi).

Giddens further distinguishes between three levels of 'consciousness': discursive consciousness, practical consciousness and the unconscious. He argues that the knowledgeability or reflexive capacities of actors are largely carried in practical consciousness, i.e. on the level of tacit knowledge about "how to 'go on' in the contexts of social life" (ibid., xxiii).[6] Yet he holds that the line between the discursive and the practical is fluctuating and permeable (ibid., 4) and therefore practical consciousness is potentially open to discursive reflection (ibid., 26, 328) – unlike the unconscious, which is often barred by repression (ibid., 4, 375).[7]

Within the Giddensian framework personal values and beliefs might be regarded as deriving from those "structural features of wider social systems" that human actors draw on in their social practices. We may thus regard a civil society institution as such "structural feature" that is available in the individual's societal setting and that contains rules and resources which might inform the individual's values and practices. Giddens further draws attention to the fact that values and norms are often embodied or routinised in the actor's day-to-day conduct and therefore held unconsciously. But as the practical consciousness is regarded to be accessible to the discursive consciousness human actors will be able to verbally reflect about what they are doing and about the values and norms that might play a role there when they are asked to do so. This, however, opens up the possibility that the reasons actors might offer discursively for what they do may diverge from the actual reasons that made them act in a certain way (ibid. 4), which needs to be taken into account when one studies the possible impact of values and beliefs on human behaviour.

In summary, both Giddens' theory of structuration and Harré and Gillett's discursive psychology support the assumptions that we must make if we want to study the influence of civil society on economic activity at the level of the individual. Both theories grant that human beings have cognitive abilities - knowledgeability (Giddens) or discursive capabilities (Harré and Gillett) – that enable them to take some control over their actions. At the same time, they propose a social-interactionist view, i.e. they hold that the practices or the cognition of human beings can be understood only through their interaction with the 'structural features' or the 'socio-cultural discourses' that are part of their socio-cultural settings. This view may be applied to an economic actor's interaction with a civil society institution. Thus both theories form a suitable conceptual basis for investigating the phenomenon.

---

[6] Discursive consciousness refers to the ability of human actors to reflect discursively about social conditions and particularly about the conditions of their own action (Giddens 1984, 374).

[7] According to Giddens, the knowledgeability of actors is bounded on the unconscious and also on unacknowledged conditions/unintended consequences of action (Giddens 1984, 282).

2.1.3 Studying owner-managers of small and medium sized enterprises

It would have been possible to study the influence of civil society in relation to different groups of individual economic actors: Chief Executive Officers, middle managers, employees, but also consumers or investors. The researcher chose, however, to particularly focus on owner-managers of small and medium sized enterprises (SMEs) and this section will outline why SME owner-managers are a worthwhile and interesting group to investigate.

First, a more general argument concerning research on SMEs. Even though an increasing number of researchers are taking an interest in small firms, most research in business ethics focuses on large corporations (Spence 1999).[8] Likewise, researchers that investigate the influence of civil society on business activity tend to focus more on larger firms (e.g. Burchell and Cooke 2006, O'Rourke 2003). Yet more than 99 per cent of all businesses are classed as small and medium sized, they account for more than 50 per cent of employment and about half of the turnover (SBS 2005, Günterberg and Kayser 2004). Those figures indicate that SMEs have quite an important role to play in the economy and that they therefore deserve attention by researchers.

Now to some arguments specifically regarding SME owner-managers. The first argument relates to the owner-manager's ability to bring his values and norms to his business activities. In section 2.1.2 it was argued that we must make the basic assumption that human beings are not solely driven by their circumstances but that they have abilities that enable them to take control over their actions, if we want to study the level of the individual in a meaningful way. Yet in 'real' life the actions of human beings may be constrained by a number of circumstances.[9] Quinn, for example, points out that managers in large organisations may be constrained "by imposed systems and established norms" (Quinn 1997, 120). SME owner-managers, by contrast, are thought to be in a better position than those managers to bring their ideas, norms and values to bear on their business activities, as SMEs are legally independent and ownership and control usually coincide in SMEs (ibid., Spence 1999, 164). That means that owner-managers will not have to deal with tensions that arise from being an 'agent'[10] who acts on behalf of a large number of absent shareholders (ibid.).[11] Interestingly, even one of the main proponents of the free-market ideology, Milton Friedman (1970), granted owner-managers the right to bring their own personal norms and values to the business, whereas he denied this to managers who run a company on behalf of its shareholders (Quinn 1997, 121).

The second argument relates to the assumption that personal norms and values are influenced by a person's interaction with her socio-cultural environment. As with any societal actor we can assume that an SME owner-manager is exposed to a number of different socio-cultural environments and that a number of their personal norms and values derive from their interaction with such environments. Quinn (1997), for example, investigated potential links between SME owner-managers'active membership of specific civil society institutions, such as the church and the local community, and their ethical attitudes in their business context in a quantitative study (see section 2.3.2). However, the extent to which an SME owner-manager might be influenced by socio-cultural contexts may not only arise from his interactions with those contexts in his personal life but also from his capacity of running an SME. Due to their size and set-up, SMEs are considered to be embedded in, interact with and be influenced by a number of different social and economic networks as well as by wider cultural, geographical and political environments (Curran and Blackburn 2001, 6-7, Perry 1999). We may

[8] This still seems to hold true in 2006. If one goes through the table of contents of business ethics journals, one will find that empirical studies that look at large firms by far outweigh empirical studies focusing on small firms.

[9] Giddens argues that social constraints are not to be equated with the dissolution of individual action as such. For example, social constraints do not eliminate the reflexive monitoring of conduct, which marks out human beings as 'actors' (cf. Giddens 1984, 15).

[10] 'Agents' do not refer here to the Giddensian concept of agency.

[11] At the same time, this relative freedom can be restricted by external factors such as the obligation to pay off bank loans, difficult economic circumstances or the fact that the activities of SMEs are more likely to be "dictated by the market" (Curran and Blackburn 2001, 7). An SME owner-manager may also be constrained if he is not the sole owner of the business but has, for example, a number of co-owner-managers.

therefore assume that the values and norms of owner-managers can also be influenced by interactions with those networks and socio-cultural contexts within which their businesses are located.[12]

In addition, the study of SME owner-managers is also interesting in that small businesses have different characteristics to large businesses; i.e. a small business is not just a small 'large business'. Spence (1999, 165) argues that the size and set-up of SMEs entails that owner-managers often have close individual contact with employees, customers and suppliers. She further states that SMEs are characterised by a high degree of informality, i.e. that owner managers tend to rely on informal control-mechanisms in the every-day running and monitoring of the business rather than on bureaucratic mechanisms. Both the personal interaction with stakeholders as well as the preference for informal control-mechanisms may also impact on the way the SME owner-managers seek to bring their personal values and norms to bear on their business, in contrast to managers of large organisations.

In sum, SME owner-managers are, first, thought to be in a good position to bring their values and norms to bear on their business because of the ownership structure of SMEs. We may further assume that through their personal and business-related interactions with various socio-cultural environments SME owner-managers might derive a number of their norms and values from those environments. Those two features characteristics of SME owner-managers concur with the assumptions that we have made in section 2.1.2. Therefore we can assume that SME owner-managers are a group of economic actors that are relatively likely to reveal the influence of civil society on economic activity if such influence exists. Furthermore, the relational and informal characteristics of SMEs add another interesting angle to the investigation of the research problem.

We will now turn to the civil society institution that was singled out for investigation.

[12] This contrasts with the set-up of a large enterprise. The larger a business is, the more it is able to escape the restraints of socio-cultural influences.

2.2 Christianity, civil society and economic activity

2.2.1 Christianity as a civil society institution

One may choose from a range of civil society institutions to investigate civil society's influence on economic behaviour: from more business-related institutions such as professional bodies or business groups, to more 'general' groups such as community groups, charities, or groups that are related to leisure activities (such as choral societies or sports clubs). This study, however, focuses on a more general, yet rather 'strong' civil society institution in the Western world: Christianity.

Although Christianity is treated by some scholars as standing outside civil society - which is then conceptualised as a secular phenomenon (Hems and Tonkiss 2000, 9 in reference to Alexander 1998) - others have recognised and studied the contribution that the Christian religion has made as a civil society institution (e.g. Putnam 2000, Bellah et al. 1996, Offe and Fuchs 2001, Hall 1999). As examples of the positive contribution to society, scholars have pointed to the numerous social services that Christians have provided over the centuries and still continue to provide, such as schools, hospitals, homeless shelters, housing programmes, poor relief charities, self-help groups etc., and to the contribution of Christians to social movements, such as the abolitionist movement in the 19th century, and the civil rights movement and the right to life movement of the 20th century (Putnam 2000, 66; Sandel 1998, 213).

This engagement of Christians is clearly linked to some core (ethical) values that the Christian faith espouses, as it encourages believers to go beyond their own self-interest (Putnam 2000, 67, Offe and Fuchs 2001, 445, Bellah et al. 1996, ix). Christ's commandment to love God and one's neighbour, which is at the heart of Christian ethics, means that - arising from their relationship to the transcendent - believers should not concern themselves only with their own good but also with the good of others. The Parable of the Good Samaritan, through which Jesus answers the question 'Who is my neighbour', moreover makes clear that this love for one's neighbour means to care about all individuals not just fellow kinsmen or fellow believers (Bellah et al. 1996, xxx).

We may apply here the social-interactionist view of the relationship between civil society institutions and societal actors (see section 2.1.2) as follows. The other-regarding values that are embedded in and linked to Christian doctrine are transmitted through the community of faith, through teaching, rituals, Christian texts and so on, and might so influence the values and norms of those who interact with the Christian faith in that way in different spheres of their lives. Those values and norms might translate into specific civic engagement but might also, more generally, influence the way believers interact with others in society. The continued interaction with the community of faith may also strengthen and sustain those 'Christian' values that the individuals have come to hold.

The community of faith context is also important when we consider the link between civil society institutions and economic activity. The faith community may provide not only a context in which people are being encouraged to get civically engaged or which informs their societal interactions in general (including interactions in the economic sphere). It may also provide business people with the opportunity to develop a spiritual perspective on business activity through religious texts, specific teaching etc. (Rossouw 1994, Verstraeten 1998).

Some scholars have recorded case studies where Christians are thought to have translated Christian convictions into business practices and two examples will be mentioned here. The first example is Scott Bader Ltd in the UK. After having started the business in 1920, the founder Ernest Bader felt an increasing tension between his Christian faith and capitalist principles. This led him to reform the ownership pattern of his business and he transferred gradually all his shares into a 'Commonwealth' which is communally owned by the Scott Bader employees (Blum 1968). By making employees co-owners of the business, Bader wanted to "present an alternative to a war-based capitalist economy on the one hand and to Communism on the other" (ibid. 10). Another example is the 'Economy of Communion' or 'Economy of Sharing' movement, which developed out of the Focolare Movement - a global, ecumenical Christian movement - and to which SMEs around the world adhere. 'Economy of Communion' businesses adhere to business guidelines that are based on biblical principles and address, among other things, interpersonal relationships, the environment, health and physical fitness, wisdom and learning. They also share their profits according to a "three parts rule". That means, that one third of their profits are to be reinvested in their firms at their own discretion, one third is to be given to the poor and the final third is to fund education for a "culture of giving" (Gold 2000).

Yet despite the positive actual and potential contributions that Christianity can make as a civil society institution, it is not clear – as with civil society in general (see section 2.1.1) - whether it always will make a 'positive' contribution. We will turn now to some developments related to Christianity that might call its potential to make a 'positive' contribution into question.

Privatisation of faith

Generally, scholars have observed a decline in church membership and a slump in church attendance over the last few decades in Western societies (Putnam 2000, 72; Offe and Fuchs 2001, 433; Hall 1999, 429). As a result, the day-to-day actions of Western citizens as a whole are less likely to be explicitly informed by Christianity than in the past - although Christian norms and values might still be held in a secularised form.

But even more importantly, scholars have pointed to some developments relating to Christianity in Western societies that suggest that people might treat their faith more as a personal, private matter rather than something that informs their participation in public life.

Some scholars, among them a number of business ethicists, have argued that secularised, modern societies allow religious believers to treat their faith only as a private matter (e.g. Herms 1991, Rossouw 1994, Fort 1999, MacIntyre 1988). Religious beliefs may inform a Christian's personal morality but should have no place in the believers' participation in public life including participation in economic activity. The public sphere should rather be 'value free' or 'ideologically neutral' as it needs to accommodate people who do not subscribe to religious worldviews.[13] As a result, believers are thought to find it difficult to voice opinions on public matters that are based on religious beliefs, as references to religious beliefs might be regarded as 'irrational', i.e. they would not meet the public criterion of 'objective rationality' (Herms 1991, Rossouw 1994).[14] What worries scholars, however, is that in the case of economic activity the criterion of 'objectivity' often relates to the (allegedly) 'value-free' neo-classic economic theory (Herms 1991), and that with a withdrawal of Christian input this societal sphere might lose an important force that might channel economic activity in a way that it is beneficial and not harmful for society.

This concern about the impact of societal secularisation processes on Christianity as a civil society institution is mirrored by observations about what is actually happening in the Christian community of faith. The three observations that are listed here are related but they cover slightly different angles.

Bellah et al. (1996, pp. 230) observed how Christians might privatise their faith. They found, while studying a particular conservative Protestant (evangelical) church, that the Christian commandment to 'love and care for others' was primarily applied to the community of faith but not to the wider community, which was of interest only as a target for missionary outreach. They further observed that moral injunctions of the Christian faith were applied to the believers' personal morality only, i.e. a morality that relates only to one's personal conduct and family life and not to wider social commitments. In other words, even though moral values played an important role in the church's

---

[13] This argument might also be made to accommodate people of other religious worldviews. But the demand for value neutrality seems to be more driven by secularism than by multi-culturalism.

[14] A related problem is that, according to the liberalist ideal, modern societies should not espouse any 'substantive' ideas about the common good. The emphasis is solely on just and transparent procedures (procedural justice), which is supposed to ensure that every view is heard and taken into account (Schuppert 2002, Münkler and Fischer 2002a). Political scientists recognise the danger that all views might be treated as equally valid and thus in a democratic society the view that gets the majority vote wins. To counteract this, they follow the Habermasian discourse ethic and argue that one has to give reasons that legitimatise their viewpoints in the context of the common good (Schuppe 2002). Again, reasoning based on a religious worldview might be regarded as inferior, as it makes too many 'irrational' (substantive) assumptions, which secular rationality cannot understand.

teaching and in the life of the faith community, they were not translated into engagement with and for wider social issues.[15]

Other (non-academic) observers report on a similar phenomenon within the Christian community. They argue that a number of believers tend to compartmentalise their lives into a 'sacred' and into a 'secular' realm (Greene 2003). As a consequence, Christians might regard only those social actions as spiritually significant that they can readily link with their faith, such as engagement in church activities, evangelising or perhaps engagement in the right to life movement. They would not bring a faith perspective to their participation in other spheres of public life.

Finally, scholars point to the fact that Christian believers might link their faith with spiritual experience rather than with injunctions for one's 'public' morality (Fort 1999, Bellah 1996, 232). This may be the result of Protestant doctrine, which places a particular emphasis on the individual experience of salvation and an individual relationship with God (Offe and Fuchs 2001, 445; Bellah et al. 1996, 232), but may also be influenced by wider cultural tendencies of individualised and consumerist behaviour (see section 2.1.2). As a result, the Christian faith might be primarily regarded by believers as something that brings spiritual fulfilment and psychological comfort rather than as an inspiration to 'make a difference' in the world. Similarly, the community of faith may be considered a place that helps to meet the believers' individual spiritual, psychological and social needs rather than a place that has a mission to 'transform' society.

The fact that believers might privatise their faith does not only have consequences for their 'civic engagement' in society in general, but even more so for their engagement with economic activity. The theologian James Childs calls this a 'shareability gap' and he argues that among many Christians there is a "long-standing dualistic assumption that spiritual life and business life belong to separate worlds" (1995, 8). In other words, Christians might not seek to influence economic activity as they might not consider it relevant from a spiritual point of view. Rossouw underlines this by his observation that churches very often use the expertise of their members who are in business but only very rarely provide spiritual and theological guidance for the same people and their life in business (1994, 567). He also points out that Christians who are involved in business activities might often be "forced to live a schizophrenic life – having one understanding of reality, identity and morality in the workplace, and an altogether different understanding, identity and morality in the church" (ibid., 568 in reference to Schlender 1982).

The Protestant Work Ethic

Apart from more contemporary developments within Christianity that might prevent Christians from engaging in the public sphere in general and from engaging with economic activity from a spiritual point of view in particular, there has been a historical development within Christianity which has been thought to prevent Christians from going beyond their self-interest and which directly relates to economic activity.

Catholic and a number of Protestant traditions (e.g. the Lutheran tradition) have generally condemned 'unrestrained' accumulation of wealth and sought to conceptualise economic activity in the context of a wider human and societal good. Catholic traditions, for instance, often refer to the idea of the 'common good' within which economic activity should be embedded (e.g. Aquinas 1969, Argandoña 1998) whereas the Lutheran tradition has conceptualised economic activity as a service to others or to society (Childs 1995, Pawlas 2000). In both cases, those who engage in economic activity are asked to go beyond their self-interest and also consider the good of the neighbour or the community.

By contrast, Calvinist and Puritan strands in Protestantism are assumed to have produced a 'work ethic' that is more congenial to the self-interested behaviour that classical economic theory espouses.

[15] Putnam reported on similar findings in his study (Putnam 2000, 77). Even though it is helpful to point out such tendencies, one should not generalise from these observations, i.e. assume that all evangelical churches are like the one described by Bellah et al. Evangelical Christians in the U.S. are getting increasingly engaged in wider social issues (Luo 2006, Roels 1997), and social reality might thus be more complex and things might be different in other evangelical churches.

Those traditions, which are also referred to as 'ascetic Protestantism', have received a lot of attention from scholars such as Weber (1930) and Tawney (1938), as those traditions are thought to have contributed to the rise of modern Capitalism.

Two elements in Calvinist and Puritan teaching are regarded to have led to the rise of the 'Protestant Work Ethic': the teaching on work as a vocation or calling and the teaching on predestination. Unlike most pre-reformist thought, work was considered by Calvin a place that was spiritually significant, a place that was assigned to believers by God, a place in which they were to live out a spiritual vocation and 'carry out the will of God' (Hughes et al. 2003, 99; Geldard 1992).[16] At the same time, the Calvinist tradition taught the doctrine of predestination, which said that God had predetermined whose soul will be saved and who will go to heaven. This produced quite considerable anxiety among believers and so, Weber argued, they tried to prove their salvation by working diligently and striving to be successful in their work, as material success was considered a sign – but no ultimate proof - of being among the elect (Hughes et al. 2003, 100; Frey 1998). The belief that one had to do well in one's calling also led to the view that one had to take up every economic opportunity that arose (and was regarded as God given) and not be constrained by traditional obligations (Hughes et al. 2003, 101). Particularly Tawney observed in his study on non-conformist Christians in the 18th century that they gave a lot of attention to the importance getting the most financially through their work, although they did not indulge in luxuries but saved the money and invested it back in the business or gave it away (Banks 1998). As a result, even though Calvinist or Puritan Christians were not interested in the accumulation of wealth for its own sake – and actually often lived an 'ascetic' lifestyle - their behaviour is thought to have contributed to the rise of 'capitalist' attitudes such as the continuous search for commercial opportunities. At the same time, scholars argue that the focus on one's individual salvation would have pushed considerations for the good of others more and more in the background (Pawlas 2000, 77).

The thesis of the Protestant Work Ethic has been met with lots of criticism and controversy. Some scholars point out that it was not so much the teaching of Calvin itself that gave rise to such behaviour, but the psychological impact that this teaching had on the believers (Hughes et al. 2003, 102, Razzell 1977). Others point out that theologians in the Calvinist and Puritan traditions allowed the adoption of more commercial attitudes as well as self-interested economic behaviour within careful conditions – unlike other Christian traditions – but that they always considered economic behaviour in the wider context of the common good or social justice (Geldard 1992, Frey 1998, Banks 1998). Frey (1998), who examined the writings of a number of Puritan theologians, argues, for instance, that exclusive self-interest was considered to be a manifestation of sin, that believers had to display the virtue of moderation, and that wealth had to be used in service to the common good. Frey further points out that the Protestant Work Ethic survived as a secular ethic beyond the Puritan era. This secularised ethic made economic success an end in itself, not a sign of conformity with divine will and appreciated the Protestant virtues of honesty, hard work etc. because of their utilitarian value (ibid., 1574). Thus the capitalist spirit that is associated with the 'Protestant Work Ethic' should rather be regarded as part of a 'Post-Protestant Work Ethic'.

Nevertheless, Van Buren and Agle (1998) argue that the 'Protestant Work Ethic' still continues to exist as a religious belief among Christians (particularly in the U.S. American context) – even though it has no direct biblical warrant – and might influence their workplace behaviour. Bellah et al. (1996, x) point to another element that is part of ascetic Protestantism and that they consider to be influential in contemporary American culture: the belief that the 'saved' can take care of themselves and that one has therefore no obligation to look after others in society. This, so Bellah et al. argue, might even lead to excluding the poor from the social body altogether because they are considered morally unworthy, with 'unworthiness' being determined by their lack of economic success.

The two 'faces' of Christianity, the strong injunctions that command believers not to seek only their own good but also the good of others, on the one hand, and the privatised, individualised and self-interest focused expressions of the Christian faith, on the other, makes it an interesting civil society institution to study. Before we set out how the influence of Christianity on business behaviour will be

[16] An idea that was also promoted by Luther, albeit with a different emphasis (see section 4.1).

examined in this study, we will look at some studies that have already been carried out in the business ethics field.

2.2.2 Previous research on the influence of religion on economic activity

A number of researchers have sought over the last few years to empirically examine the influence of Christianity on economic activity, although they have done so with quite different research questions in mind. This section provides a brief overview and a critical evaluation of those studies.

The most striking aspect about those studies is that most of them were conducted in the United States. This may be explained by the fact that the role of religion is in the United States (still) more accepted in the public sphere than in other Western countries, e.g. Western European countries, where secularism seems to have 'progressed' more and researching religion might be less acceptable. At the same time, the predominance of U.S. based studies points to the need to investigate the influence of religion on economic activities in other national contexts.

Even though some of those studies focus on religiousness rather than specifically Christianity, most of the different religious affiliations that they investigate are Christian ones, with a few also including Judaism and other religions (e.g. Longenecker et al. 2004). Hence they mirror the religious make up of the U.S. population.

Quite a few of those studies used quantitative methods, with which they sought to measure relationships between variables, for example, between personal religiousness and ethical judgments in business situations (Clark and Dawson 1996, Longenecker et al. 2004); religiousness and unwillingness to engage in unethical behaviour (Kennedy and Lawton 1997); religious practice, Christian beliefs and attitudes towards Corporate Social Responsibility (Agle and van Buren 1999). The first three studies mentioned were scenario-based studies and used different scales and questionnaires to measure people's religiousness. Agle and Van Buren used a slightly different approach. They identified beliefs that Christians potentially hold through a review of Christian literature (concerning stewardship, wealth distribution, other-regarding values etc.) and that may influence Christians in their managerial decision-making (Van Buren and Agle 1998). They then tested whether those beliefs, as well as religious practice, correlated positively with attitudes towards Corporate Social Responsibility (Agle and Van Buren 1999).

As a result of the quantitative approach, the research findings were usually phrased in very general terms: "People that show a high degree of intrinsic religiousness found actions described in scenarios to be less unethical" (Clark and Dawson 1996); "Little relationship between religious commitment and ethical judgment was found when responses were compared on the basis of broad faith categories – Catholic, Protestant, Jewish, other religions, and no religion. However, respondents who indicated that religious interests were of high or moderate importance to them demonstrated a higher level of ethical judgment ... than others in their evaluations. Evangelical Christians also showed a higher level of ethical judgment." (Longenecker et al. 2004), or "Religious practice and Christian beliefs have a weak relationship to attitudes towards CSR" (Agle and Van Buren 1999).

Apart from the obvious fact that if one compares those studies the results are not conclusive, Weaver and Agle (2002, pp.79) criticise such quantitative studies as a) they often use undergraduate and MBA student samples b) they mostly focus on attitudinal measures of business ethics, which may suffer from social desirability biases, especially if both they and the religiosity measures are assessed at the same time and c) use widely varying definitions and measurements of religiosity (intrinsic vs extrinsic, religious affiliation etc.) that often do not sufficiently yield motivational and cognitive differences.[17] Following these criticisms, one might question the suitability of quantitative research in general in an area such as this. In other words, how likely is it that researchers sufficiently captures a complex phenomenon such as religion in its impact on economic activity if they seek to produce

[17] Longenecker et al. (2004) have sought to address some of those criticisms by a) focusing on business managers and professionals and not students b) trying to measure the respondents' religiousness through a more sophisticated scale. Yet their study is still a quantitative and does not sufficiently uncover the complexity of the phenomenon.

generalised statements through large scale surveys? Therefore such quantitative studies provide only limited understanding of the relationship between religiousness and business activity.

Still, two more quantitative studies must be mentioned, as the chosen group of economic actors there was more similar to the one that the author has chosen. Ibrahim et al. (1991) focused on companies in the U.S. that described themselves as "Christian-based" companies. Their aim was to find out to what extent those companies showed similar behaviours towards different stakeholder groups and they sent out open-ended surveys to such 'self-described' companies. Although they found that a number of practices were shared among the majority of the respondents, such as seeking customer satisfaction, prompt payment of bills, and proselytising stakeholders, they also found differences when they compared different industries.[18] Again, such surveys might give some insights into the practices of such companies (or reports thereof), but using a large sample and seeking to produce generalised statements is unlikely to unravel motivations that underlie those behaviours.

Lastly, Quinn (1997) sought to identify to what extent active involvement in civil society institutions influenced ethical attitudes of SME owner-managers. In addition to the positive fact that this is a study that is located within a U.K. context, it also – unlike the other studies – takes into account that religion is just one factor among others that might influence economic actors. The study found that religion had a higher influence on the owner-managers' ethical attitudes than involvement in the community, which again had a higher influence than involvement in business groups. Aside from the fact that this study had a rather weak empirical basis for a quantitative investigation (41 respondents), again this kind of study does not give much in-depth insight into nuances of the relationship between religion and economic behaviour.

A more interesting methodological approach, an approach that moves away from survey data and quantitative analysis, is found in Lee et al.'s (2003) study on Christian executives in Hong Kong (again, another national context!). They based their study on Niebuhr's 'Christ and Culture' typology (1951), which was later modified by van Wensveen Siker (1989) into a 'Christ and Business Culture' typology. This typology has five categories, with the two extremes 'Christ against Business Culture', where Christianity and business are in complete opposition, and 'Christ of Business Culture', where Christianity and business are in complete agreement (i.e. Christian principles always work for one's self-interest). The remaining three categories 'Christ and Business Culture in paradox', 'Christ above Business Culture' and 'Christ the Transformer of Business Culture' respect the differences between Christianity and business and seek out different ways to reconcile the different principles (compromising, integrating and transforming respectively). Lee et al. carried out interviews with over 100 Chinese Christian executives, in which they sought to elicit 'critical incidents' that featured significant encounters between faith and work. The data analysis revealed that across the sample all five types of 'Christ and Business Culture' were identified in the respondents' rationalisations of their actions. This approach provides rather interesting insights, particularly as it acknowledges diversity among Christian business people in the way they rationalise the link between their faith and their business practices. On the negative side, this study 'imposed' a framework on the data and did not explore in-depth underlying beliefs and values of the reported practices.

Finally, there are two more qualitative U.S. based studies that focus particularly on Evangelical Christians[19] that deserve mentioning.

Nash (1994) set out to investigate in an interview-based study how evangelical CEOs brought their faith to their business. Her aim was two-fold. First she wanted to investigate whether the unfavourable image that the evangelical faith enjoyed in America held true with those CEOs, and secondly she wanted to stimulate discussion about the role of faith and economics, particularly among Christians (ibid., 272).[20] In particular she sought to explore how those evangelical CEOs dealt with the following

---

[18] Ibrahim pursued his interest in 'Christian-Based' companies further by investigating whether they yielded a better long-term performance than their secular counterparts (Ibrahim and Angelides 2005).

[19] Evangelical Christianity may be understood as a particular brand of 'conservative' Christianity that is widely spread in the United States and predominantly found in Protestant denominations. Nash defines the evangelical strand of Christianity by outlining three features: 1. A felt sense of sin and redemption that has resulted in an ongoing personal relationship with Jesus Christ. 2. An obligation to bear witness to Christ's love and to the divine nature of the Trinity. 3. A belief that all aspects of life are subject to scriptural authority (1994, 5-6).

[20] As such it is written in popular style and not as a strict academic study.

'tensions': the love for God and the pursuit of profit, love and the competitive drive, people needs and profit obligations, humility and the ego of success, family and work, charity and wealth; and faithful witness in the secular city. In her interviews with over 85 CEOs she identified three types: the 'generalist', the 'justifier' and the 'seeker' (ibid., 40). A generalist would be of the conviction that there was never a real problem between faith and the requirements of business lives and skate over apparent inconsistencies. A justifier would similarly ignore conflicts between biblical principles and business requirements and regard his economic success as a justification of his faith. The seekers, by contrast, would be acutely aware of dilemmas between faith and business and be prepared to address them. A seeker would confront those conflicts or tensions "through prayer and the perspective of faith and seek out a course of action consistent with Christianity" (ibid. 45). Nash argued that seekers would adopt from their faith a relational and holistic perspective that would shape their leadership style (ibid., 271).

Nash's study gives some interesting insights into the relationship between faith and business activity, as, like Lee et al. (2003), she maps out the diversity among her respondents. At the same time, it is rather apparent that she writes from an U.S. American background where the 'tensions' between corporate activity, with its focus on profit-making and growth, and the other-regarding values that are embedded in the Christian faith are probably more evident than in other national contexts.[21] This may explain why she conceptualised her interest in the relationship between faith and business as 'conflicts' and 'tensions'. Furthermore, even though her sample contained CEOs from different sizes of business she does not particularly address potential differences between owner-managed and other businesses or between CEOs of small and large enterprises. Such differences might be particularly important, however, as Weaver and Agle (2002, 86) point out that those managers that seek to 'climb the ladder' of success within a (larger) corporation may lay their personal values aside while doing so and might not revert back to them once they have reached the top of the ladder, even though a top-managerial position might give them greater opportunity to follow their personal values.

Roels (1997), lastly, reports on her personal observations of evangelical business people that run small to medium-sized companies to give some insight into what Christian concepts are likely to be of relevance for those people. She observed that the business ethics of evangelical business people had primarily four emphases: 'piety', which relates to Bible study and prayer as the "sources for business integrity and daily motivation"; 'witnessing', which relates to the overt sharing of their faith; 'tithing' which means that they will give ten per cent of their profits away to Christian or other charities, and 'neighbourliness', which might relate to helping people in the local community or in the community of faith. This study comes closest to what the author is seeking to achieve with this study as it also observed a similar group of economic actors, even though Roels' insights are rather anecdotal in nature and she does not investigate in detail how these concepts are adopted by these people. She, moreover, seems to miss out on some aspects. For example, she suggests that evangelical business people should learn to draw on other Christian traditions and, for example, consider the concept of stewardship. Yet this concept is known among evangelical business people as other studies indicate (Nash 1994, 47, 271).

The rather different and diverse set-ups of those studies in terms of their research questions, their methodological approaches, their national and cultural contexts, and their research 'subjects', makes engagement with them rather difficult. Yet those studies confirm that there is no straightforward answer as to how Christianity influences economic activity - even though there are indications that it can make a 'positive' impact - and that Christians may apply their faith to their business practices in rather different and diverse ways. Those studies leave a lot of scope for more in-depth research into the 'why' and 'how' of the relationship between Christianity and economic activity and for investigating the phenomenon in other national contexts. The following section will set out in more detail how this study approaches the phenomenon and will highlight how this approach is different to those of the other studies and will therefore be able to make an 'original' contribution.

---

[21] As state and national culture do not have as much a moderating influence on business activity as in Western European countries.

2.3 Setting up the research

2.3.1 What this study seeks to achieve

This investigation is framed by the general problem of the influence of civil society on economic activity. As explained in the preceding sections, this study seeks to explore the phenomenon at the level of the individual actor by focusing on the influence of membership of a particular civil society institution. As an example, the study investigates how adherence to the Christian faith might impact on SME owner-managers' behaviour.

As already indicated in the preceding section, the researcher is rather critical of quantitative studies that seek to explore the influence of religiousness on economic activity. She follows Weaver and Agle (2002, 77) who argue that the influence of religion on business behaviour is a rather complex matter as religion itself is rather complex phenomenon and other factors might have an impact too[22] and that quantitative studies are unlikely to be able to sufficiently explore those complexities (see also their critique of quantitative studies in section 2.2.2). She therefore decided to investigate the problem by using a qualitative, interpretative approach in the spirit of Weber's 'verstehen' method.

She further decided to explore the phenomenon from the owner-managers' point of view, through conducting interviews (see section 3.1.2). [23] This has implications for the formulation of the research questions.

Section 2.1.2 mentioned two social theories, Giddens' (1984) theory of structuration and Harré and Gillett's (1994) discursive psychology, which were identified as a suitable framework for the research problem. Whereas the former has a more sociological focus, as it is interested in the production and reproduction of societal structure in the social practices of societal actors, the latter takes up a socio-psychological perspective by focusing on the role of interacting discourses in the shaping of individual cognition. Harré and Gillett's approach is obviously more in line with the decision to study individuals' point of views and the researcher will thus follow more closely the ideas that the discursive psychology approach espouses.

In such socio-psychological analysis the primary focus is on how human beings conceptualise their practices while at the same time it is assumed that such conceptualisations might also translate into actual practices. Christianity is thus considered a particular discourse or discursive context that the chosen group of economic actors inhabit and that may (or may not) play a part in the way they conceptualise their business practices. The socio-psychological perspective takes further into account that the economic actors that are the focus of the investigation inhabit other discourses which might equally influence the conceptualisation of their business practices and might also interact with the Christian discourse: the 'economics' discourse through their own participation in economic activity, but also other socio-cultural discourses.

Following the socio-psychological approach, the aim of the study is to explore the following questions:

- How do Christian SME owner-managers draw on the Christian discourse in relation to their business activities? Which beliefs, values and norms play a role and why?
- How do they link those beliefs, values and norms with actual practices?
- How do other socio-cultural discourses interact?

[22] Weaver and Agle (2002) are particularly interested in organisational culture as mediating influence. This seems to be particularly important if one seeks to study the ethics of Christian managers in large organisations.

[23] Weaver and Agle (2002, 91) point out some drawbacks of interview-based research such as social desirability biases and self-deceptions, and suggest, for example, to interview persons that are close to the subjects. This option will be discussed in section 3.1.2, which will also explain in more detail the researcher's decision to focus on interviews only.

The questions to those answers might then allow some careful conclusions to the question of how Christianity impacts on the actual business practices and whether and how it might 'make a difference'.[24]

The focus of the study is on Christians only and no comparison is made to any other group, as it is the primary aim to gain an in-depth understanding of what 'is happening' within this particular group.[25]

2.3.2 How is this approach different?

This socio-psychological approach is different to previous studies that have sought to investigate the relationship between Christianity and economic activity as follows.

Unlike Lee et al. (2003), who 'imposed' a particular typology on their interview data, this study seeks to draw out the Christian (and other) beliefs, values and norms that lie beneath the respondents' practices, in other words, it seeks to investigate in-depth the underlying cognitive structures that are related to the Christian framework of belief and that the respondents link with their practices.

By doing so, the study did not, like Van Buren and Agle (1998), 'pre-establish' what values, norms and beliefs Christians are likely to hold but rather pursued an inductive approach and identified the relevant Christian concepts and beliefs from the interviewees' responses to more 'general' questions (see section 3.2.2).

Unlike most studies that have investigated the phenomenon, this study also focused on other 'discourses' that may play a part in the respondents' conceptualisation of practice and that may interact with the Christian discourse.

Lastly, the researcher did not start like Nash (1994) with the assumption that there are 'tensions' between Christianity and business activity but rather sought to investigate whether and how Christian discourse may influence the way profit is pursued.

2.3.3 The European context

It was mentioned in section 2.2.2 that the majority of the empirical research on the influence of religiousness on business activity has been conducted in a U.S. American context. By contrast, this study was carried out within a European context, more particularly within the two national contexts of the U.K. and Germany, and hence makes a contribution to the study of the phenomenon by providing a different national-cultural perspective.

The researcher chose those two particular countries because she had the opportunity to access respondents in both contexts due to her language abilities and cultural familiarity and wanted to take advantage of this opportunity. At the same time, the choice of the two countries would enable her to explore possible cross-national differences.

Both countries would have been classed in the post-war era as 'welfare' states, i.e. states in which the governments provide extensive welfare provisions to its citizens by redistributing the wealth that was generated in the economy and so differ from the societal set-up of, for instance, the United States. At the same time, even though the economies in both countries are based on the capitalist system, economic activity has been organised rather differently historically (Lane 1992, Charkham 1994, Donnelly et al. 2001). Despite the danger of simplification and over-generalisation and – particularly in the case of Germany – the possibility that things have been changing over the past few years, some features of those different systems will be outlined in the following.

Observers generally regard economic activity in Germany as a more 'cooperative' (Charkham 1994, 8), 'communitarian' (Lane 1992, 76) activity, which next to the pursuit of self-interest also accepts obligations and responsibility to society. As an example, Charkham cites the fact that a lot of

[24] Although it is not intended to judge the accounts against some type of performance.

[25] A comparative study would be an interesting subsequent phase to this study but would go beyond the scope of *one* in-depth study.

German companies train more people than they need as a conscious attempt to produce more well-trained people for the country (Charkham 1994, 8). The sense of cooperation is also evident in the high degree of employee co-determination and consultation, which has been made mandatory through law (Lane 1992, 74, Donnelly et al. 2001, 6). For example, boards have to consult employee representatives (works councils) over decisions that affect the future of the organisation and employees sit on the supervisory board of companies.

It is further argued that German managers seem to be more concerned with long-term planning, involving for example investment in long-term research and development and employee training, rather than the production of short-term results (Charkham 1994, 8). This emphasis on the long-term has been underpinned by the ownership structure of German firms. Ownership has been relatively concentrated, with banks often being long-term institutional shareholders in large corporations and taking an active, long-term interest in the well-being of firms (Lane 1992, 69). Although this has been changing in the last few years due to pressures arising from the internationalisation of capital markets (Donnelly et al. 2001, 32), the long-term involvement of banks had made German firms less dependent on the short-term demands of the stock market.

Furthermore, the state provides uniform regulatory frameworks for firms (Lane 1992, 67), for example, a number of environmental regulations. Lastly, the German system has been marked by a dense network of trade associations and Chambers of Industry and Commerce, which have statutory status (ibid. 66), and through which economic activity is also geared towards 'cooperation'. In these networks, firms engage in a number of collaborative activities that also produce 'collective' goods, for example, through joint engagement in research and development activities. Chambers of Industry and Commerce are also involved with the vocational education system, by certifying and ensuring the quality of vocational courses, which are jointly provided by firms and state colleges and regulated by the state (ibid. 70).

If economic activity in Germany has been regarded as being strongly embedded in societal institutions and as a more 'cooperative' activity geared towards the long-term, economic activity in Britain has been regarded as being less embedded in societal institutions, as relying on arms-length market relations as coordinating mechanisms, and as having a more short-term perspective (ibid.). Economic activity in the U.K. is not as comprehensively regulated as in Germany, and business behaviour that takes a wider societal interest into account is often based on the principle of voluntarism (ibid., 68, Donnelly et al. 2001). Furthermore, in Britain Chambers of Commerce do not enjoy statutory status and trade associations are often not subject to uniform regulation, which means that that the latter two organisations are less effective in structuring economic activity and producing 'collective' goods than their German counterparts (Lane 1992, 73, 84). At the same time, economic activity is often focused on the short-term, as the stock market – which is used by large firms as the main means of raising capital – demands high, short-term returns on capital (ibid., 68).

Even though not all differences described might be relevant to owner-managed SMEs, we may assume that the national context can also influence SME owner-managers' conceptualisations of their worlds of practice in one way or another.

Whereas the economic systems are distinct enough to expect some differences between economic actors due to their nationality, the religious landscape in both countries is rather similar, i.e. has a similar make up and diversity. This enables the researcher to treat the respondents in terms of their Christian identity as one group rather than as two distinct groups.

In brief, both countries have a long-standing Christian tradition and were influenced by the Reformation, which led to the establishment of Protestant main stream denominations.[26] Furthermore,

[26] Unlike countries like France and Italy, where Catholicism is the predominant Christian denomination. The Catholic church is still quite prominent in Germany - about half of those who claim affiliation to the Christian faith are Catholics - whereas in the U.K. Catholicism is less prominent. Affiliation to the Catholic faith is about 9 per cent in the U.K. and somewhat over 30 per cent in Germany (National Statistics 2000, EKD 2004). Those differences, however, are not relevant for this study, as it focuses on Protestant Christians (see section 3.2.1). Furthermore, the mainstream Protestant churches in both countries are set up somewhat differently as a result of their respective reformation histories and differ in style of worship. However, the underlying theologies, apart from some doctrinal details, are rather similar and affirm, at least in their original set-up, 'orthodox' Protestant beliefs.

as a result of Protestant renewal movements over the centuries (and still continuing today), both countries have a number of free churches (Methodist, Baptist etc.), with Germany also having free-church like groups (Pietists) within the mainstream churches.

At the same time, both countries have been considerably affected by secularisation processes, so that the doctrine and teachings of the church are no longer regarded to be relevant by the majority of the people (Hendry 2004, 126). Even though the majority of the population in each country - about 65-70 per cent - still claims to be affiliated to the Christian religion (National Statistics 2001, EKD 2004), church attendance has been in stark decline, and thought to have slumped to under 10 percent.[27] If we regard church attendance as an indicator for committed religious practice, we may conclude that about one tenth of the population in each country are practising Christians.

Lastly, in both countries the mainstream churches – who have been hit hardest by the slump in church attendance and membership - have also been adopting different 'strategies' over the last few decades to make Christianity relevant to society. Some strands, particularly in Germany, have adopted a more liberal theology, which is influenced by enlightenment thought and which, to put things simplistically, questions and reinterprets the 'irrational' elements in the Bible such as the miracles and the resurrection of Christ and often interprets the Christian message in purely ethical rather than spiritual terms (Gaffin 1998). Other strands, particularly in the U.K. but also to some extent in Germany, have embraced 'evangelicalism', i.e. a return to conservative biblical doctrine and spirituality and the emphasis on a need for a personal relationship with God, often coupled with a conscious attempt to reach out to non-Christians and (re-)attract them to the Christian faith. Somewhere between the liberal strands and the evangelical strands within the mainstream churches, however, are also strands that might be regarded as 'traditional', i.e. as retaining conservative Christian doctrine but not being as 'intense' and outreach-focused as the evangelical strands – although boundaries between those different strands might at times be blurred.[28]

The researcher chose to focus in her investigation on practising Christians that would in both countries come from more 'conservative' Protestant backgrounds (see section 3.2.1). This choice was determined by the researcher's familiarity with conservative Protestantism.[29]

Having outlined the set-up for this study, the following chapter will discuss some methodological issues before we turn to the presentation and analysis of data.

[27] The National Centre for Research found in 1999 that in the U.K. about 12 per cent of those who claimed affiliation to a religion attended religious services at least once a week (National Statistics 1999), which means that about 8 to 9 percent of the population regularly attend religious services. The researcher assumes – based on her own observations – that attendance figures in Germany are similar.

[28] Liberal strands can also be found in a few free churches. However, free churches are usually considered to have a conservative doctrine, with a number of them describing themselves as 'evangelical'.

[29] Having grown-up in such an environment herself.

3. Methodology

3.1 Choosing methodological frameworks and research method

3.1.1 Choosing the epistemological framework

In his work 'The Structure of Scientific Revolutions' (1996), Thomas Kuhn challenged the common assumption that natural science researchers investigated phenomena in the natural world in an 'objective', 'value-neutral' way. He demonstrated that scientific 'facts' were always intertwined with the theories and beliefs that the relevant scientific community held by pointing out, for instance, that new discoveries were often resisted by scientists if they did not fit into their theoretical and belief systems.

Researchers who investigate social phenomena, by contrast, have tended to be more aware of the fact that scientific research cannot be objective and value-neutral (Denzin and Lincoln 2002). They have recognised that social science research is guided by the 'worldview' of the researcher, i.e. by their epistemological and ontological assumptions about the social world as well as by philosophical and ideological assumptions (Christians 2002, 149, Lincoln and Guba 2002).

As it is thus inevitable that the researcher brings her assumptions about the world to the research it is important that those assumptions are spelt out (Christians 2002, 149), as they will have consequences for how the research is carried out and how data is analysed.

Section 2.1.2 cited some social theories, Giddens' (1984) structuration theory and Harré and Gillett's (1994) discursive psychology, which the researcher identified as a suitable general framework to investigate the research problem, i.e. how a specific civil society institution may influence individual economic actors. Given the many assumptions that are made in those theories about the nature of human agency and its links to societal structure, those theories can also be regarded as broad epistemological frameworks. The researcher particularly considered Giddens' structuration theory a suitable epistemological framework for the research, as it is a widely known social theory. Giddens' theory, however, was considered a suitable framework not only because it captures the research problem appropriately in its assumptions about the link of agency and structure (see section 2.1.2), but also because the researcher considered the assumptions made in the theory to be in line with her own 'worldview'.

This particularly applies to the assumption that human beings are knowledgeable actors, i.e. that they can reflect about the circumstances of their actions (Giddens 1984, xxii) and are perpetrators of an action (ibid., 9). The researcher's worldview is informed by the Christian faith, and she considers Christianity a belief system that holds, among other things, that human beings have a 'free will' and that consequently a large part of human behaviour is of voluntaristic nature. Therefore the researcher agrees with the stance of the Giddensian framework that human behaviour should not be regarded as a "result of forces that actors neither control nor comprehend" (Giddens 1984, xvi), but as something that human beings can – at least to some extent - control and comprehend.

Thus the researcher identified the Giddensian framework as a suitable epistemological framework as it a) captures appropriately the research problem and b) is in line with her worldview.

3.1.2 Choosing research methodology and method

Having spelt out the epistemological framework, the next logical step would be to identify suitable methods for investigating the research problem. Commonly, researchers distinguish between quantitative and qualitative research methods (Silverman 2000, 1) and a researcher should reflect about what each type of method can achieve. Quantitative approaches are usually adopted when the researcher wants to make quantifiable, 'easy-to-generalise' statements, whereas qualitative methods are used when the researcher is concerned with gaining an in-depth understanding of a particular social phenomenon (ibid.)

We will first look at the 'quantitative' option. The choice to adopt quantitative methods often goes hand in with the adoption of a positivistic approach to research (Hussey and Hussey 1997, 47). A positivistic approach assumes "that there is an objective truth existing in the world, which can be revealed through the scientific method where the focus is on measuring relationships between variables systematically and statistically" (Cassell and Symon 1994, 2). The measuring of relationships is usually done by the formulation of hypotheses that are deduced from theories and that make law-like, causal predictions about human behaviour, which are then tested on a relatively large sample (ibid.; Harré and Gillett 1994, 3). In this, the positivistic approach resembles rather closely the approaches that scientists apply in the natural sciences. The positivistic approach, however, makes rather different epistemological assumptions than the Giddensian framework, and therefore a positivistic analysis cannot be used for this study. There are a number of reasons as to why the positivistic approach is in conflict with the chosen epistemological framework.

More generally, there are grounds to question the claim that the positivistic 'scientific approach' can uncover 'objective' truth. It was stated above that 'scientific' research – particularly social science research but even to some extent research in the natural sciences – cannot uncover 'objective' realities as the research is always bound up with the beliefs of the researcher and/or the relevant scientific community. Those beliefs might either form part of the researcher's ideological commitments or worldview or might be implied in the theoretical frameworks that the researcher uses to inform her research.

A more specific point is that in seeking to uncover causal 'mechanisms', positivist social research often treats human beings as 'objects' and does not sufficiently take the complex and dynamic nature of human actors including their mental capacities into account (Harré and Gillett 1994, 6, Giddens 1984, 347, Christians 2002, 149). For example, if the research 'objects' had more knowledge about the phenomenon that the researcher seeks to investigate and that relates to their own circumstances, they might be able to reflect about it and actively influence the research outcome (ibid.). Here the positivistic paradigm is very obviously in conflict with the Giddensian framework. As we have seen, Giddens makes a great point about the knowledgeability of human actors (1984, xxii) and he rejects the positivistic paradigm by arguing that there can be no universal laws in the social sciences "because the causal conditions involved in generalisations about human social conduct are inherently unstable in respect of the very knowledge (or beliefs) that actors have about the circumstances of their own action" (1984, xxxii).

However, the Giddensian framework would allow the use of quantitative methods that are not tied to a positivistic framework (Giddens 1984, 333). For example, in the context of this research it would have been possible to conduct open-ended surveys or semi-structured interviews with a large number of Christian SME owner-managers. The data could have then provided insight into the business practices of Christian SME owner-managers (or reports thereof) in the form of some generalised trends and tendencies, similar to the study done by Ibrahim et al. (1991), and the researcher could have provided some general explanations as to why Christian owner-managers tend to behave in this way.

Yet the researcher was more interested in gaining a detailed and nuanced in-depth insight into the research problem and not in producing some generalisable, quantified statements (see section 2.3.1). In the spirit of Weber's 'verstehen' approach (Hughes et al. 2003, 123), she wanted to understand how Christianity might impact the behaviour of owner-managers and thus she decided to pursue a more qualitative, interpretative approach to explore the research problem.

A qualitative approach is not tied to specific methods, and the choice of a suitable qualitative research method was largely guided by pragmatic considerations. The researcher could have, for instance, carried out an ethnographic study, involving a 'mix' of qualitative methods such as interviews – with both Christian SME owner-managers and people who are close to the owner-managers and who can therefore provide some insight into their behaviour[30] -, focus groups or even participant or non-participant observation. Such an approach could have provided her with a rather 'comprehensive' picture as to how Christianity might have an impact on Christian SME owner-managers' behaviour by taking different viewpoints into account. Such an ethnographic study, however, would have been difficult to conduct. People's religious faith is a sensitive matter (Weaver

[30] Weaver and Agle (2002, 91) suggest that interviews with persons who are close to the 'subjects' would be a suitable strategy to seek to understand links between religiosity and ethical behaviour in a business setting.

and Agle 2002, 91) and it might have been rather difficult to get 'comprehensive' access, particularly to observational studies and to interviews with owner-managers' 'stakeholders'. The time-frame of the research project also played a part in the decision not to opt for a comprehensive, ethnographic approach.

Therefore the researcher decided for pragmatic reasons to restrict herself to one particular research method. She decided to conduct qualitative, semi-structured interviews with a sample of about 20 Christian SME owner-managers, as she felt that it would be easier to access Christian owner-managers if she asked them for personal face-to-face interviews only, and also felt that a pure interview-based approach would more easily fit into the given time-frame. As a result, she would restrict herself to investigating the research problem from the Christian SME owner-managers' point of view only and would formulate her research questions from a socio-psychological perspective (section 2.3.1). At the same time, the interview-based approach made it possible to conduct research across a somewhat larger sample than would have probably been possible with an ethnographic approach.

3.1.3 Embedding interview-based research into a suitable methodological framework

Yet the decision to carry out an interview-based study entailed some further methodological issues: What insights can be gained from the research data? And how should the data be analysed?

In an interview-based study, research participants produce personal accounts of, say, certain practices that they engage in, experiences that they have had or events that have been taking place in their lives. A number of researchers have suggested that such data does not give so much insight into the actual practices and real subjective experiences of the respondents as such but rather into the discursive practices and discursive resources that the respondents use and draw on when talking about those practices, experiences and events (e.g. Potter and Wetherell 1987). Thus interview data should be treated as discourse and should be analysed accordingly.

Among the many available discourse anlaysis frameworks, the researcher chose one that would provide insight into the problem that she had set out to investigate, that was in line with the socio-psychological approach that she had adopted (see section 2.3.1), and that was coherent with the chosen epistemological framework: Watson and Harris' (1999) *discursive framing* approach.

Watson and Harris assume that the world which exists outside of us becomes a 'reality' to which we can relate only if we bring language to bear upon it. In other words, language or talk is the necessary means both to make and to understand the 'realities' of the world around us (1999, 20). However, how human beings make sense of the world around them depends on the discursive resources that are available to them in their culture (ibid. 6). Their arguments here closely resemble Harré and Gillett's arguments about the role of socio-cultural discourses that human beings are exposed to and inhabit in the shaping of their cognition (1994, 25; see sections 2.1.2 and 2.3.1).

Discursive framing is defined by Watson and Harris as "a process whereby human beings draw on sets of linguistic resources, categories, and concepts made available in their culture to make sense of a particular aspect of their lives and are thereby influenced in the way they conduct themselves in that part of their life."(ibid., 6). They hold that interviews can be used to gain insight into how human beings make sense of particular aspects of their lives (ibid., 20). In the interview process respondents talk about the aspects of their lives that the researcher is interested in, and the way they talk about it or frame their accounts discursively, gives an insight into how they use culturally available discursive resources to conceptualise those aspects of their lives. A sense-making process is usually considered to be a retrospective activity (Weick 1995, 24) because human actors seek to make sense of an aspect of their lives through recounting experiences, events and practices that have already occurred. Yet Watson and Harris hold that those discursive resources that respondents use to make (retrospective) sense of a certain aspect of their lives also influence the way "they conduct themselves in that part of their life" (see definition above). In other words, they hold that one can, through a sense-making process that takes place in an interview situation, also draw some conclusions as to how those discursive resources might influence the respondents' behaviour in the present and perhaps also in the future.

Watson and Harris acknowledge that the accounts created in an interview situation are a social construction, produced jointly by the researcher and the respondents. But as the interviews revolve around phenomena that exist outside the interview situation, those accounts are not an outcome of the interview situation alone but they may give an insight into the respondents' lives beyond the interview situation (ibid., 20).

Of course, respondents may be selective in their accounts and as they usually have access to different sets of discursive resources, they might frame events differently in different situations, which may make it difficult to judge which discursive resources are actually more relevant to the respondent (ibid., 21; see also section 3.1.4). Moreover, there is also the possibility that the language people use to explain their behaviour – even if they seek to be truthful in their accounts - may not always correctly describe what actually prompts them to engage in such behaviour, for example, if they do not have access to those discursive resources that would provide a more appropriate explanation for their behaviour (Harré and Gillett 1994, 178). Another possible 'gap' is between 'conceptualisation' and 'practice'. Even if the way the respondents conceptualise their practices provides them with a strong motivation to act in a particular way, they might not always do so, for example, because of the 'weakness of the will'. All this makes talk a rather uncertain phenomenon but it might serve as an indicator (Alvesson and Karreman 2000a, 152) that provides "uncertain, but often interesting clues for the understanding of social reality and ideas, beliefs, values and other aspects of 'subjectivities'" (Alvesson and Karreman 2002b, 1146).

If we relate the discursive framing framework to the research problem that this study seeks to investigate, we can assume the following: Christianity can be regarded as a discursive resource that, among others, is culturally available to the respondents and that contains concepts and categories that are meaningful to the respondent. Therefore they may draw on the different categories and concepts that Christian discourse provides to make sense of various aspects of their lives – in this case their activities as SME owner-managers – and their conduct in this area of their lives might also be influenced by those discursive concepts that derive from Christianity. Of course, such interviews would also give insight into how other discursive resources might influence their conceptualisation of practice.

3.1.4 Some further methodological issues

It was argued in section 3.1.1 that social science research can never be objective and value-neutral as researchers always bring consciously or unconsciously their 'worldview' to the research. This 'subjectivity' on the part of the researcher does not only influence the choice of the epistemological framework, but also the way the research is carried out and the presentation of the data.

A particular aspect of the researcher's subjectivity in this study was that the researcher is a Christian herself and this inevitably affected the research. Her Christian identity gave rise to a personal interest to investigate the impact of Christianity on business activity and thus the very choice of the research subject resulted from the researcher's 'subjectivity'.

Her personal engagement may have furthermore affected the way the research was carried out. Critics might argue that member-status creates a bias on the side of the researcher towards her research subject. Johnson argues, however, that member-status and lived experience is no longer stigmatised among social scientists and it is becoming more and more accepted that researchers investigate "phenomena about which they have prior or current member-based knowledge" (2002, 107). Johnson further suggests that member-status gives the researcher the chance to access phenomena to which 'outsiders' would have no access or would find more difficult to access (ibid. 108), and so membership status is actually considered to be of advantage. A further potential advantage is the ability to develop a trust-relationship with the respondents through shared membership – which in interview-based research might encourage the respondents to produce more open and honest accounts. And finally, member-based knowledge potentially enables the researcher to understand and interpret the respondents' use of community-specific 'language'. Of course, there are also potential difficulties with shared membership. One that is commonly cited relates to the so called social desirability effect, that is that respondents might give answers that they believe the interviewer would like to hear

(Bryman 2001, 123). This effect can occur in any interview situation, but in the case of shared membership status it relates to the fact that because of the shared identity between interviewer and interviewee the latter might ascribe more of his attitudes and behaviours to his group-based beliefs and values than is actually the case (Alvesson and Deetz 2000, 73).[31] This needs to be taken into account in the data analysis. The researcher will highlight in section 3.2 where – in her view - in the research process member-status proved to be an actual advantage and where it proved to be an actual disadvantage.

The subjectivity of the researcher further impacts on the way the data is analysed and presented.[32] Symon and Cassell argue that data analysis in qualitative research is an interpretative process on the side of the researcher "which precludes the very idea of a 'scientific objectivity'" (1998, 6). Furthermore, the way the researcher selects and organises the data material for data presentation, using her own judgment and theoretical knowledge, makes the study a 'crafted artefact', a rhetorical construction (Watson and Harris 1999, 21). Because of the 'artfulness' of qualitative social science research (ibid.) positivistic criteria of 'reliability' and 'validity' cannot be applied to judge the 'quality' of the research (Symon and Cassell 1998, 6, Denzin and Lincoln 2002, 21). Still, the researcher can strive to provide an account of the research as truthful as possible, so that it provides credible insight into the phenomenon that she has been investigating, which might help other interested individuals – other academics, practitioners etc. - to understand this particular phenomenon or related phenomena better (Watson and Harris 1999, 21-22). This, so the researcher hopes, has been achieved with this study.

[31] Alvesson and Deetz give an example of how a feminist female researcher that emphatically interviews women may make her respondents "express pro-feminist opinions or feminism-supporting accounts of experience than would otherwise be the case."

[32] This is the case with any social science researcher, not only with those researchers that have shared member status with the research subjects.

3.2 Carrying out the research

3.2.1 Sample selection

The researcher decided to carry out the interview-based study among a sample of about 20 Christian SME owner-managers as this seemed to be a 'manageable' sample size. For reasons outlined in section 2.3.3 it was further decided to conduct the research in the U.K. and in Germany with about 10 respondents respectively in each country.

It was important to the researcher to identify respondents whose commitment to the Christian faith would go beyond 'nominal' commitments, i.e. who would consider their religious faith an important part of their lives, as something that forms a large part of their identity. Gorsuch and McPherson (1989) use the term 'intrinsic religiousness' to describe those expressions of faith where religion is treated as an end in itself and impacts on the person's life in a significant way. Given the national contexts in which this study is located, the respondents would come from those ten per cent of the population that could be regarded as practising Christians (see section 2.2.3). Practising Christians may come from all kinds of denominations and theological strands, and – for reasons of familiarity – the researcher focused on those Christians who come from those Protestant denominations and traditions that could be loosely labelled 'conservative'. This means that those groups - despite some differences in doctrine and style of worship - take a conservative stance towards Protestant Christian doctrine and the authority of the Bible. The people who took part in this study came from 'traditional' and 'evangelical' strands of Protestant mainstream and free churches (see Table 1) and would describe themselves as practising Christians. As such, some respondents would either come from those backgrounds because they grew up in them and continued to find the Christian faith as personally relevant for their lives. Others would report that they had (re-)'discovered' the Christian faith at a particular point in their adult life (see Appendix I).

As the researcher was based in the U.K., the interviews in Germany had to be conducted within a restricted time-frame. The researcher decided to carry out the German interviews first and then to try and find a matching sample in the U.K. She felt it was important to at least attempt to find a matching sample, as sector-specific features may play some role in the way owner-managers conceptualise their business practices (Curran and Blackburn, 2001:16-19).

For pragmatic reasons[33] the researcher decided to concentrate her field work in Germany to one larger city, and eight out of the ten respondents were based in that city (the exceptions were D5 and D10). This city happened to have quite a few Christian networks – general networks as well as specific business networks – and this helped the researcher enormously to identify suitable respondents, mostly with the help of the 'snowballing' technique. 'Snowballing' means that a researcher makes initial contact with a small group of people who are relevant to the research topic and who can then direct the researcher to other contacts (Bryman 2001, 98-99). In the case of this study, initial contact was made with the co-ordinators of those networks, who then directed the researcher to SME owner-managers who they knew in one way or another through those networks. In the case of the two 'exceptions', D5 was approached through a personal contact and D10 was approached through contact with another Christian business network.

Given the difficulty and effort that was involved in trying to identify research participants in Germany whilst based in the U.K., the researcher could not be too 'choosy' about the make up of the sample but accepted most of the candidates that were suggested to her. As a result the respondents in the sample represented a range of sectors and company sizes (see Table 1).

Having completed the first round of research in Germany, the researcher sought to find a research sample in the U.K. that corresponded to the sector make up of the German sample. Unlike in the case of Germany she did not have to restrict herself to one geographical area, but was able to travel to different parts of the U.K., which helped her to find suitable participants for a corresponding sample.

---

[33] I.e. due to monetary and time constraints.

Table 1: Summary of participants[34]

	Main line of business	Employees	Church affiliation[35]
D1	Pharmacy	10	United State Church (evangelical)
D2	Property Management	4	Pietistic Church Fellowship
D3	Mobile Home Rental	0	United State Church (evangelical)
D4	Heating and Plumbing Installation and Service	65	Pentecostal
D5	Printing	20	Independent Free Church/Moravian
D6	Decorating and Special Surface Coatings	3	United State Church (evangelical)
D7	Optician	7	United State Church (evangelical)
D8	Industrial Building Services (specialising in demolition work)	20	United State Church
D9	Safety Analysis Projects and Software Development	10	Pietistic Church Fellowship/ United State Church
D10	Manufacture of Measuring Instruments	11	Lutheran State Church
UK1	Project Management in the Ceramics Industry and Manufacture of Birthpool Liners	1	Anglican
UK2	Manufacture of Metal Parts	70	Anglican
UK3	Estate Agent	4	Anglican (evangelical)
UK4	Car and Van Rental	18	Pentecostal
UK5	Heating Installation and Service	5	Anglican (evangelical)
UK6	Civil Engineering	100	Anglican
UK7	Engineering	25	Anglican/Pentecostal
UK8	Industrial Design	14	Baptist
UK9	Building Services	2	Anglican (evangelical)
UK10	Pharmacy	7	Methodist/ Congregational
UK11	Optician	7	Independent Free Church/Methodist

The respondents in the U.K. were contacted via 'snowballing' through personal contacts and some were accessed through a Christian business directory. Even though the U.K. sample was not exactly identical to the German one, it had a similar range of sectors and company sizes (see Table 1).

In both countries, but particularly with the German sample where research participants had to be contacted from a 'distance', the member-status clearly helped the researcher to access the respondents. Her introduction as a 'fellow Christian' often made either the initial contact persons or the respondents themselves quite willing to help her find contacts or to grant an interview respectively.

If one looks at the different company sizes that were represented in the sample, the question may be asked whether the firms may not be more appropriately labelled 'small' businesses as opposed to 'small and medium sized' businesses. According to the definition of the Department of Trade and Industry in the U.K., small businesses have 0-49 employees and medium-sized businesses 50-249 (SBS 2005).[36] Curran and Blackburn (2001, 10), however, suggest that the classification of SMEs

[34] More detailed information on the respondents can be found in Appendix I.

[35] As shown in this table, some respondents claimed affiliation to more than one denomination. The first denomination mentioned denotes their main/current affiliation. 'Evangelical' is only denoted where the respondents explicitly pointed out that their church was evangelical.

[36] 1. The EU definition for SMEs adds yet another category: firms that have fewer than 10 employees are classed as 'micro-firms' (Curran and Blackburn 2001, 1) 2. For reasons of sensitivity the researcher did not enquire about the respondents' turnover, which is another factor that classifies SMEs.

varies in each sector. And, indeed, when respondents with, say, 20 employees were asked whether they would consider their business small, medium-sized or large compared to other businesses in the same sector, a number of respondents said that they ran a medium-sized business. Furthermore, in Germany SMEs are categorised somewhat differently. A business that has 0-9 employees is classed a small business, whereas businesses that employ 10-499 employees are classed as medium-sized (Günterberg and Kayser 2004). Hence the researcher considered it still appropriate and justified to call the respondents in her sample SME owner-managers.

All of the respondents were male, apart from UK11. The age of the respondents ranged from early forties to mid sixties. This gender and age related make up of the sample was not the product of a deliberate decision but was simply a consequence of the other selection criteria.[37]

Lastly, the make up of the German sample incidentally highlighted the fact that one cannot generalise about the conceptualisations of practice of a group of people just because they are exposed to the same kind of religious teaching or to a certain religious group identity. As the majority of the German sample was based in one city, it happened that four respondents (D1, D3, D6 and D7) attended the same church but the way they conceptualised their worlds of business practice was quite different from each other. Another set of respondents (D2, D3, D4 and D8) were members of the same Christian business group, but again, their accounts differed a lot in the way they engaged with Christian concepts and ideas. In other words, this 'peculiarity' of the research showed that each Christian individual engages with their faith in unique ways and that their engagement might depend on a number of different factors, not just affiliation to a particular church or a particular Christian business group.

3.2.2 Research design and data collection

The researcher decided to conduct two interviews with the respondents. The rationale behind this decision was, firstly, that this might enable the researcher to develop a better trust relationship with the respondents, which might lead the respondents to provide more 'open' accounts. Secondly, the double visit was also to enable the researcher to probe more deeply into details of how the respondents link their faith with their business practices. Thirdly, as this study was the first interview-based project for the researcher, she felt that a double visit would enable her to learn how to conduct effective interviews and improve her interviewing skills.[38]

For the first visit, the researcher developed a semi-structured questionnaire with open-ended questions. Such a questionnaire is usually regarded as an 'anchor', i.e. a set of initial questions that will allow the researcher to follow up any interesting leads that might occur during the interview (Wengraf 2001, 59). The questionnaire had three parts.

In the first part the respondents were asked to give some background information with regards to the company and their church background. The questions about the background of the company were not only asked to obtain some 'factual' information but were also meant to set the respondents at ease and to 'get them talking', as the topic was thought to be of more 'harmless' nature. The questions concerning the church background were to give some insight into their particular faith tradition(s) and also into the extent to which the respondents were involved with their church.

In the second part they were asked several questions concerning the link between their faith and their business (How do you bring your faith to your business? Are there any conflicts between your faith and your business? etc.) and concerning their relationships to their various stakeholders (To whom do you feel responsible?). Here it was important to the researcher to ask very broad open-ended questions. This was to encourage respondents to come up with their own accounts, and only when their account 'dried' up, the researcher asked more specific questions, for example, questions about specific stakeholder relationships.

---

[37] See Appendix I for more detailed information on the respondents.

[38] The respondents were initially asked to grant one interview. At the end of the first interview they were asked whether they were willing to do a second interview. A few respondents were visited three times as the researcher felt that the previous two interviews had not yielded enough information (see appendix I).

In the third part, finally, the respondents were asked about their relationships to their wider environment. They were asked specifically about their charitable giving and their civic engagement, but also about their perceived role in society and how they related to wider societal developments.[39]

All interviews were conducted in the respondents' mother tongues (as the researcher speaks both languages) and the respondents were assured that their accounts would remain anonymous. The interviews were recorded on tape and transcribed (see section 3.2.3).

In the second interview, which took place about half a year after the first one (see Appendix I), the researcher used the transcript of the first interview to formulate some follow-up questions, for instance, where the respondents had said something interesting, which had not been picked up by the researcher. The respondents were also given space to talk about recent business-related developments and events with the aim to elicit some potentially valuable information.

On the whole, the strategy to pay double visits proved very valuable, as both interviews together provided quite a rich and complex picture of how the respondents perceived their relationship between their faith and their business practices. Particularly the ability to follow up leads from the first interview was very effective, as it enabled the researcher to gain more insight into the respondents' motivations or to elicit more detailed accounts of certain attitudes or behaviours that they had mentioned. Sometimes the respondents even mentioned things in the second interview that they had not done before. This helped the researcher on occasion to correct some impressions that she had gained from the first interview.

The member-status of the researcher definitely impacted on the way the respondents produced their accounts. Most of them used very community-specific language with which they framed their accounts - e.g. they frequently referred to spiritual concepts and beliefs - which they would probably not have done had they talked to a non-religious interviewer. Section 3.1.4 already mentioned some potential 'pros' and 'cons' of shared membership. Here the fact that the respondents used such strong religious framing can either be interpreted as something positive or as something negative. On the one hand it might be regarded as something very positive, an 'opening-up' on the part of the respondents or a willingness to talk about an aspect of their lives to which outsiders may have no or little access. At the same time, as already stated in section 3.1.4, respondents might give answers that they think the researcher would like to hear – the so-called social desirability effect. Yet the researcher did not feel that this presented a big problem for this study. First, the researcher was primarily concerned about conceptualisations rather than practices. Therefore statements along the lines "I always behave in such and such way because I'm a Christian" with which respondents could have presented themselves in a good light were only of secondary interest to the researcher, although she tried to challenge respondents in the interviews whenever such statements were made. At the same time, the data reflected a wide diversity of conceptualisations, which indicates that the respondents were not interested in finding out about the researcher's preferred concepts and give an account accordingly. Moreover, the interviewees themselves often offered additional or alternative explanations for their behaviour where other motivations than Christian ones could have played a role. The existence of other motives was also taken into account in the data analysis (see section 3.2.3).

3.2.3 Data transcription and analysis

All interviews were transcribed by the researcher herself. The transcriptions follow spoken word and repetitions, pauses and some other extra-linguistic phenomena were also transcribed to give some insight into how the accounts were produced. Although in hindsight the researcher feels that she would not have needed to transcribe all 'uh's and 'um's, as the focus of the analysis was more on the

[39] At the time the questionnaire was developed the researcher had still focused more on *practices* than *conceptualisations* – as the original research question that she had set out to explore was 'What do Christian SME owner-managers contribute to the common good?'. As a result, both the second part and the third part of the interview were initially designed to yield information about the respondents' practices and how they related to the 'common good'. However, the researcher realised that the produced accounts gave more insight into conceptualisations than practices and were analysed accordingly.

discursive resources rather than on the use of extra-discursive resources, it nevertheless makes the quotations more 'real'.

With the German interviews, the main challenge was how to translate colloquial German into colloquial English. As discursive resources play an important role in the data analysis, every effort was made to produce an as accurate as possible rendering of the German original. Some of the translations might sound rather clumsy but the researcher felt that it was better to opt for a literal translation as a means to maintain the meaning of the original rather than to provide a linguistically correct translation.

The reference numbers for the German interviews start with 'D' (for 'Deutschland'), the ones for the British interviews start with 'UK'. The subsequent number indicates the chronological order in which the first interview round was carried out. Small letters 'a' and 'b' (in a few cases also 'c') denote the first and second (or third) visit respectively. In the analysis chapters the respondents will be referred to with their reference number (e.g. UK2, D7) to maintain the anonymity of the respondents.

In the quotations in the data analysis chapters, any emphases that the respondents made are highlighted in bold; and italics are used when the researcher wants to draw attention to particular words or phrases that the respondent used.

Analysing the data by using the discursive framing approach was a rather difficult and lengthy process and involved repeated reading of and 'meditating' over the transcripts.

The researcher gradually identified five different 'frames' with which the respondents rationalised and explained their actions, all of which were linked to distinct theological concepts. Reading up on those concepts in theological literature helped the researcher in turn to conceptualise the frames more clearly.[40] The first data analysis chapter (*chapter 4*) gives an account of those frames.

The researcher felt, however, that those frames or concepts did not capture all aspects of the Christian influence on the respondents' conceptualisation of practice. This led her to identify three contexts that were related to the Christian faith and that played an important additional and/or complementary role in the conceptualisation of the respondents' business practices. Those contexts are the focus of the second data analysis chapter (*chapter 5*).

Lastly, the researcher decided to focus in a third data analysis chapter (*chapter 6*) specifically on the different kinds of practices that the respondents reported. She sought to determine here to what extent Christianity may 'make a difference' in the respondents' behaviour but also wanted to show how the respondents' practices might have been influenced by the presence of other socio-cultural discourses.

Given the complexity of the data, the themes that are addressed in the three data analysis chapters inevitably overlap at times and therefore the chapters contain a number of cross-references.

[40] The theological concepts that are described in chapter 4 follow a conservative interpretation of Christianity – to be in line with the respondents' identity.

4. How Christian concepts provide the frame for action

This chapter reports on the concepts in Christian discourse that the respondents drew on in their accounts and that formed the background against which they explained and conceptualised their actions. From the analysis of the interview accounts the use of five main concepts emerged, each of which is different in motivation and reasoning as they presume distinct understandings of the relationship between the respondents' faith and their actions. Thus each concept represents loosely a type of identity that the respondents take on when they conceptualise their actions (Weick 1995, 24). The people in the study often referred to more than one of those concepts in their accounts. Hence the concepts are not to be regarded as a strict typology, but rather as different frames that the respondents applied in their accounts.

The five concepts/frames identified were:

- **Calling.** This concept referred to the respondents' belief that they followed a calling or a vocation in their business, which was given to them by God (section 4.1).
- **Stewardship.** This concept was linked to the respondents' belief that God had entrusted the business to them or that God was the Lord of their business, from which they derived some responsibilities with regards to their business (section 4.2).
- **Witness.** Here the respondents regarded themselves as bearing witness of the Christian faith through their actions and they explained what that meant for them in the context of their business (section 4.3).
- **Holiness.** This concept referred to the belief that the lifestyle and actions of a Christian are to be morally blameless and/or be a reflection of Christ, and the respondents explained what implications that had for them in the context of their business (section 4.4).
- **General Christian moral tenets.** Using this frame, the respondents conceptualised their actions by drawing on general moral tenets that the Bible provides and by saying that they should act in a certain way in their business because they were Christians (section 4.5).

The following sections will look at each concept/frame in turn. Each section first outlines the concept's origin in Christian teaching and tradition. Then it investigates how the respondents interpreted and engaged with the concept and how the respondents linked those frames with practices. The sections will conclude with some observations and comments about the use of the concept.

4.1 Calling

The concept of calling has been a key concept in Christian teaching and tradition, carrying a number of different meanings. In a very general sense it refers to the belief that a Christian is called to follow Christ and to live in fellowship with him (Matthew 9:9, 1 Corinthians 1:9), and called to eternal life (1 Timothy 6:12). In a more specific sense, it refers to the belief that God calls believers to serve Him by carrying out particular tasks or fulfilling a particular role, often with a specific spiritual connotation.[41] The concept of calling, for example, is often invoked when believers consider becoming full-time ministers.

In church history, this narrower interpretation of calling as a purely spiritual vocation was particularly criticised by the Protestant Reformers. Writing against the background of medieval Christianity, Martin Luther criticised the fact that calling was considered relevant only for the religious professions such as priests, monks and nuns. He then extended the concept of calling to all so-called 'stations' in every believer's life, i.e. parenting, marriage, work and citizenship, with a specific emphasis on work. Luther argued that by serving others through one's work believers were in fact serving and glorifying God and actively participating in and contributing to God's Kingdom. Thus he conferred spiritual significance to the 'mundane' workplace (Childs 1995; Pawlas 2000). The concept of calling in relation to work was also promoted in the Calvinistic and Puritan tradition. Although Calvin held similar ideas to Luther about calling (Atkinson 1988, Davies 1983, Geldard 1992), the Calvinistic and Puritan tradition is perceived to have conceptualised calling primarily in terms of 'carrying out the will of God' in the workplace rather than in terms of 'serving others' (see section 2.2.1).

In the context of the study, calling was identified as a frame when respondents talked generally about 'God wanting me to be in this place' or 'God wanting me to do this' in relation to their business. In that sense, calling may be understood as the frame that 'sets the scene for action' and that may motivate people to engage in specific practices.

Several people in the study engaged with the concept of calling, and although all of them talked of a sense that God wanted them to be in the place of work they were in, they differed enormously in the way they interpreted this concept, both in content and strength of motivation. In this section we will look at those diverse interpretations of the concept of calling and what they entailed in terms of the respondents' practice.

4.1.1 "That's where you're supposed to be"

A number of respondents used the concept of calling to simply confirm that where they are was the right place for them to be.

UK3, for example, who became a Christian in his adult years, sought external confirmation as to whether there was any tension between him being an estate agent and a Christian, or whether he should follow a more spiritual vocation.

> In in fact after all these years, I can say that there, I've worked out that there isn't any conflict. Um, when I first became a Christian I would spend the first five years wondering whether I was gonna be a missionary, you know. ... And it was about five years before someone said 'Well, where were you when you were called?' And I said 'Well, I was here selling houses.' 'If you've got nothing to the contrary, that's where you're supposed to be.' 'Oh, really?' [laughs]
> (UK3a, estate agent)

[41] The stories of the Old Testament where people were called by God to carry out a specific task, for example, God's call to Moses and Joshua to lead the people of Israel to the Promised Land (Exodus), often serve as role models to illustrate the concept of calling.

This was echoed by D7, who had a similar conversion experience and would also have preferred to become a minister. He said that he kept asking himself whether running his business is the right thing for him to do.

> And um, quite often I tend to say 'Lord is this place where you want me or do you want me somewhere else?' And, I've been asking myself this question again and again. This this is quite important to me.[42]
> (D7a, optician)

He also reported that he had had a real struggle to bring his conception of a Christian lifestyle to the business.

> I've always tried to imitate St. Francis; that was always the path I wanted to take, in my heart and mind. ... And he, well, he preferred to live in poverty, to look after the frail and weak. Um, and so be totally available to God. And I was struggling with that for a long time. So much so that I thought 'You're not really, you need to integrate this somehow' [into his working life]. And this has been a process.[43]
> (D7a, optician)

He, too, had come to realise that his work in his business did not conflict with his life as a Christian. He said that he believed that, for now, God wanted him to run the business.

> I don't have to tear myself apart anymore *because I'm certain that God has put me here*. And then I can do my work, you know, in all humility. ... So that has, that has changed somewhat, I realised: 'You are right here for now. And that's fine - you do your work here, I've put you here.' ... In the end, there's not much money left anyway. So [laughs] it's a similar end result.[44]
> (D7b, optician)

Having worked out that being owner-managers did not contradict their faith, UK3 and D7 also reported how they thought their faith might link with their business lives. As we shall see in sections 4.2 and 4.3, both referred to different ways of being a witness in their business and D7 also referred to some stewardship responsibilities.

D5 talked slightly differently about the notion of God putting him in a specific place. For him it was first a sense of duty to his family that had made him to take over the business, but he also said that he recognised this to be the place God wants him to be.

> But, I'd say in my current, and ... in our company we're all a bit puritan, we take our duties very seriously. So we all kind of feel that you've got to work where God has placed you. I found that quite difficult at first, that I, I have a degree in graphic design and

[42] Und ähm [Pause] da habe ich oftmals auch die Tendenzen zu sagen ‚Also Herr, ist es wirklich der Ort hier, wo du mich noch haben möchtest oder woanders?' Und, also die Frage stelle ich mir schon immer wieder. Die die ist auch wichtig für mich.

[43] Ich hab' mich so nach meinem Weg, ich habe immer eher versucht, so diesen Franziskus mh –weg so einzuschlagen, das war so vom Kopf und vom Herz her immer mehr so meine Richtung. ... Ja. Und ähm er war auch so auf der Linie, eher so in die Armut zu gehen, also sich wirklich um die äh Schwächeren oder die Schwachen zu kümmern. Ähm, um ganz für Gott dazusein. Und das habe ich lange nicht auseinanderbekommen. Soweit, dass ich dachte ‚Mensch, du bist jetzt irgendwie außerhalb, aber diese Punkte musst du doch noch irgendwie mit reinkriegen.' Und das war auch ein Prozess.

[44] Also dieser dieser große Spagat ist dann nicht mehr. Mh, *weil's mir einfach klar ist, dass ich von Gott dahingestellt bin*. Und dann kann ich ja auch meine Arbeit, ich sag's mal jetzt so, aber in Demut trotzdem machen. ... Also mh, nee das das hat sich ein bisschen, das hat ein Stück weit andere Akzente bekommen, zu sehen 'Nee, da bist du jetzt richtig für einen gewissen Zeitraum.' Und das ist gut und da mach das, ich hab' dich dahin gestellt, mach' das mal' Letztendlich ist es ja auch so, dass nicht so viel übrigbleibt. Also [lacht] so insofern ist das Ergebnis ja ähnlich.

really wanted to be a graphic designer or something like that, I wanted to do book design. But then I forced myself to be reasonable and take over the (family) business.[45]
(D5a, printing)

He considered it important to live out his calling, believing that God was able to use him in his capacity as an owner-manager as well.

> *What is important for a Christian? That he lives out his calling. That he knows he is in the right place. So that he does, I think, wherever God wants him to be.* I think that's a lot more important. ... Because, well, later it became clear to me that God also uses our natural gifts ... I think you've got your natural gifts and you should be careful about staying in God's will in our lives with your natural gifts. And [pause] He wanted me to be a small tradesman. [laughs] So here I am.[46]
> (D5b, printing)

Yet for D5 calling had a specific spiritual connotation, as he saw the point of running the business in his ability to use his profits to support Christian causes and also use part of the business to serve the Christian market.

> And, it has a point. First, perhaps we really will start a (Christian) publishing company. If we could kick start something like that, I'd be really pleased. And then there is also, a (NAME OF MISSIONARY ORGANISATION) group have set up here recently and they want to start a college for missionaries. ... And missionaries always need a flock of people who fund them. And you've got more chance to help if you've got a business. Of course, you can give a lot more money if you own a company than if you're just earning a salary. That gives me a buzz.[47]
> (D5a, printing)

---

[45] Aber ja, da würd' ich schon sagen, dass dass ich mit meiner momentanen, und, ... in unserem Betrieb, sind wir natürlich alle ein bisschen ein bisschen Puritaner, sind richtige Pflichtmenschen. Ja, wir sind also alle ein bisschen davon äh geprägt, dass man das zu machen hat, wohin einen Gott gestellt hat. Und das ist auch am Anfang mir relativ schwer gefallen, dass ich mal, ich hab' mal Grafik studiert und hatte mal so'n so'n Kick freier Grafiker zu werden oder irgend sowas, also Buchgestaltung. Und hab' mich dann doch mit Vernunft und Gewalt ein bisschen gezwungen, die Firma zu übernehmen.

[46] *Was ist wichtig für einen Christen? Dass er in seiner Berufung lebt. Dass er dass er weiß, dass er am richtigen Fleck ist. Also dass er das macht, denke ich, wo Gott ihn hinhaben will.* Das ist, meine ich, extrem viel wichtiger. ... Weil ja auch, das ist mir erst später klar und wichtiger geworden, dass eben Gott durchaus unsere natürlichen Begabungen benutzt. ... Nicht. Ich denke, dass dass man einfach seine natürlichen Begabungen hat und darauf achten muss, dass man mit seinen natürlichen Begabungen in dem Willen Gottes für sein Leben bleibt. Und [Pause] Er hat mich hier als kleinen Handwerker gerade haben wollen. [lacht] Na gut, da hat er mich nun.

[47] Und siehe, es hat ja auch einen Sinn. Erstens, vielleicht kommt es ja vielleicht wirklich nochmal zu zu einem (christlichen) Verlag. Dass sich auf der Schiene was tut, das würde mich sehr freuen. Dann hat's ja auch den Sinn, wir haben jetzt seit seit neuestem in (ORTSNAME) 'ne Gruppe von (NAME VON MISSIONS-GESELLSCHAFT), die hier gerne ein ein Missionszentrum aufbauen wollen. [E]s müssen ja um jeden Missionar 'rum eine ganze Herde von Leuten sein, die ihn finanzieren. Und wenn man das also im von von der Möglichkeit ... ist natürlich 'n Betrieb eine feine Sache. Du kannst natürlich mit so 'nem Betrieb, wenn du für eine Sache was spenden willst, ganz anders in die Schachtel langen, als wenn du bloß dein Gehalt hast. Das ist schon was feines.

4.1.2 Called to be an "ambassador for Christ"

For D9, too, the concept of calling had a more spiritual connotation. Considering himself an "ambassador for Christ" in his working environment, he did not relate this to his work, but to sharing his faith in the social context of his business.

> And well about witnessing, my colleagues know I'm a Christian. So every now and then I invite them to outreach events and they are quite tolerant of this. But over the last ten years nothing much has happened. But three or four years ago I had to decide on whether to quit the company. I'd got the chance of a professorship at (PLACE NAME). *But somehow I felt that I uh had been put into the company to be an ambassador for Christ.* And I'll have to wait and see what comes from it.[48]
> (D9a, security analysis)

4.1.3 Called to "live out the Christian faith in the workplace"

In contrast to D9, UK7 interpreted the concept of calling in quite a different way. He did not think that evangelising was a call that he should follow in his business, but he emphasised the 'living out' aspect of his faith.

> ... I (don't) feel a great need to evangelise in the workplace and so on. That's not me. I don't think that's my call. *But to live out my faith in the workplace is my call.*
> (UK7a, engineering)

Having been an active Christian for most of his life and, at the same time, having held top management positions or running companies in the engineering sector, he explained that it took him a long time to understand the connection between his working life and his Christian ministry, which then enabled him to say that he was following his calling in the workplace.

> *UK7:* Um, but my, I mean, I was still a Christian. Don't misunderstand me. And I wouldn't have done, I wouldn't have done anything in business terms that was wrong or what my father and grandfather would have called 'unrighteous' ... I would never have done that. But personally, um I had this driving ambition to get to the top. Um, um we were we were wealthy, (had) a lot of money. And a lot wealthier than I am today [laughs] in financial terms. ... Uh, and, I mean, I was, at the same, I was the head of um the um Adult Christian Education Programme in our church. You know, I I've had a Bible teaching ministry going back longer than that. But I made, I, really looking back on it, I made no connection with, between theology and what I did at work.
> *Interviewer:* So it was like living in two different worlds?
> *UK7:* Yeah, very much so. You know, almost complete separation of the sacred and the secular. I didn't see them as having much relevance to each other. I mean, I passionately believed in both and as I said, would never have done anything um unrighteous at work. But I didn't see, even with the level of Bible knowledge that I have, I mean, I didn't see any great connection between that and world of work. So I suppose the biggest single um change for me over that 20 year period is that I now see the two as not just connected but as one whole. They are the same thing. You know, there is not a sacred part of my life, and a secular part of my life. (UK7b, engineering)

---

[48] Und äh im Zeugnis ist es so, dass meine Kollegen wissen, dass ich Christ bin. So ab und zu lade ich sie mal zu Einsteigerveranst- -veranstaltungen ein und irgendwie haben sie das jetzt auch wohl akzeptiert. Allerdings hat sich da im Laufe der letzten 10 Jahre, wo ich das mache, nicht allzu viel getan. Ich hab' aber mal vor drei, vier Jahren vor der Entscheidung gestanden, ob ich das mit der Firma bleiben lasse, da hatte ich 'ne Möglichkeit, in (ORTSNAME) 'ne Professur zu kriegen. *Und dann hatte ich irgendwie den Eindruck, dass ich äh als Botschafter Christi äh praktisch in diese Firma nun reingestellt sei.* Und was daraus wird, muss ich sehen.

He stated that he now actively tried to live out his calling by bringing his Christians principles and values to the engineering company that he started and co-runs with a non-Christian. He framed most of his actions in terms of stewardship responsibilities – financial, social and environmental - which we will look at in section 4.2 (see also section 6.1.6 and 6.2.1).

UK7 also reported that his calling extended into the civic sphere by being involved in industry-related and professional bodies, where he promotes renewable energy. This civic engagement was accompanied by his decision to no longer take up church leadership roles, as he believed that he was more effective integrating the 'sacred' with the 'secular' outside of an immediate church-context.

4.1.4 Called to "serve the community"

The 'living out' aspect of the Christian faith was also emphasised by UK11 and UK10 in their accounts, although with a different focus. They both reported that they felt they were called to serve the community with their businesses, even though they had arrived there by different routes.

UK11 said that the trigger to start her own business was when she felt she could not maintain her work ethic with her former employer, a large optical chain. She recounted how she decided to open a shop in a town which had not had an optician.

> *UK11:* And I was getting tired of being told what to do.
> *Interviewer:* Why?
> *UK11:* I was being, particularly, there were uh, they wanted to pay us more if we gave somebody a pair of glasses or change somebody's glasses or something than they would if we didn't change them. So they were paying us by results. Results being dispensings. And as a joke I said to somebody one day 'Uh, I'm gonna go and open up in (PLACE NAME)' And I'd never wanted my own business.
> (UK11a, optician)

As she picked the location of her business, it was clear to her that she would not be able to run her business in the same way as other independent opticians may do.

> (PLACE NAME), I don't know why I picked (PLACE NAME), there wasn't an optician there. And it's quite a big town. Its uh, its catchment, we reckoned, was about 13,000. And everybody from that area used to go to either (PLACE NAME) to the opticians or (PLACE NAME). *Because it's a rundown area, no other optician would open there. You know, they are too much, sometimes, into selling designer frames and that sort of thing. And that's not what you do in (PLACE NAME).*
> (UK11a, optician)

In retrospect, she sensed that it was not only her own decision to open her business in this particular place but that God had led her to do this.

> I mean, I wouldn't be there if I wasn't a Christian. If God hadn't led me to (PLACE NAME) there wouldn't be an optician's in (PLACE NAME).
> (UK11a, optician)

All these circumstances and factors created a strong sense in her that God had put her in this place to serve the community. She explained this when asked what she thought she contributed to the common good.

> The common good? Well I think I serve the community. That sort of thing. I think that's quite significant with my business, because there isn't another optician in that community. *Um, so I feel particularly that I've been put there to serve the community, provide them with a service they wouldn't have had otherwise.* (UK11b, optician)

"Providing a service to the community" had a wide range of connotations for UK11. She stated that on the one hand it gave her a sense of satisfaction as she was now able to make her own decisions in terms of how the customer was treated and what services she offered. An important aspect for her was that she had the freedom to "do what I know is right rather than giving people glasses that don't need them or changing glasses that don't need changing". In terms of services, she said that, for example, she had made a decision to provide free glasses to people on low-incomes by stretching their benefit vouchers in a way that the clients did not have to pay anything on top; and that she offered home visits to elderly, housebound people. At the same time, she stated that 'serving the community' also created a number of responsibilities and obligations for her, for instance, the responsibility to be available to her customers and also to live up to the trust that people placed in opticians to do their best for them.

Unlike UK11, whose call more or less just 'happened' arising from her circumstances, UK10 said that he had felt for a long time that God was calling him to be a pharmacist.

> But also um my interests there and my skills were were very much science-based. And um I came to to faith at about 17 um, and did think quite hard about what I was gonna do as a career. *And I really felt I wanted that was gonna help people.* So um and *felt that uh to a large extent that God was calling me to to do pharmacy*, which is why I ended up doing pharmacy.
> (UK10a, pharmacist)

Also being a part-time, non-stipendiary minister, he said that he regarded both his work for the church and his business as one calling which "just happens to have two facets". To him doing pharmacy – and working for the church – came "from, really from from the ministry of loving people. And caring for them."

Like UK11, he said that "by owning your own business you have that option of of actually beginning to control everything really", which enables him to live out his calling of loving and caring for people. For him

> ... the purpose of the business isn't to make money. Um, although it's helpful to me, enough money to have to live, um but it does mean that the emphasis on anything that I do there doesn't have to be money-related as with all mixed up with the business. Um, and it means that um, you know, I've decided to offer services that, you know, I make no money out of, but that's that's my decision.
> (UK10a, pharmacist)

The decision not to "always search ... the bottom-line profit" and "chase ... the last penny" but to focus on the service he is offering, affected the way he conceptualised his business practices in a number of different ways. He talked about offering free home delivery services to housebound customers, not refusing to serve drug addicts but actively working with them, offering special advisory services, but generally taking time to "interact with the customers and advise them".

'Serving the community' also had a meaning for him beyond the interaction with the customer. He stated that it had also meant for him to subsidise one of his two shops for a period of time when circumstances did not allow him to run the shop profitably.

> When we started there, um the government contract at that time was quite quite good and and and it was quite profitable. Um, they changed the contract two years after I bought the shop, which was not so good, so the profit margins decreased quite noticeably. And then about a year after that they uh or was it two years after that they moved a lot of people out of the area as they were uh upgrading the premises of all the accommodation in the area.... Um, so I was losing money for about two years. But fortunately at that time I'd opened the other shop and that was just starting to pick up. *Um, and so the profits from that shop really subsidising the the first shop. And we decided that that was the way to do it, um because if you had withdrawn from the area um the area would have been without the services that it had for quite some years. Um and their health provision would have suffered quite heavily.* (UK10a, pharmacist)

UK10 also reported on community-related civic engagement as part of his service to the community. He said that he felt that he had had an obligation to join a panel that made decisions about building developments in the local area.

> As as a Christian pharmacist, as as and also as a minister um I've had concerns the community, which go completely outside of the business, um in in terms of the way the developers and the councillor think about developing the area which would have probably fractured the local community. Um, and certainly causing divisions.
> (UK10b, pharmacist)

He said that a number of his customers had raised concerns about the impact of the building development on the local community, and that they had turned to him for help as they felt that because of his educational status he would help them to get their concerns heard. He felt that he could not refuse to help, also because of his belief that Christian had the task to care for and love other people.

> Because, I mean, you know, as a Christian part of your mission is to to care for and love other people. And um, and therefore caring for those people you want things to be good for them. Um, and, you know, ... justice to be done for them. Because some of the things that were being proposed were were unjust. Um, and and they weren't getting sufficient representation.
> (UK10b, pharmacist)

He further mentioned that he felt he also had to represent the interests of the more vulnerable people in the community on the panel.

> But also, I mean, there are drug addicts in the area and prostitutes in the area. A lot of the community don't like those people for obvious reasons. Um, but they are part of the community just as much as we are. And they, they don't have a voice. Um, because they certainly won't go to the meetings. Um, and I feel I've got responsibility to speak for them as well.
> (UK10b, pharmacist)

4.1.5 Observations

The concept of calling is often used within a religious context (e.g. Sauser 2005), although non-religious people in the Western world might sometimes refer to it as well. Perhaps as a legacy of the Christian tradition on which Western society is based, they might say things like "This is my calling/vocation" when they rationalise life choices that they have made, usually in line with their abilities and/or preferences.

However, it is the religious context which makes the concept of calling important for Christian believers, as it is not (only) about what they want to do but about what they believe God wants them to do. Not all people in the study engaged with the concept of calling, but everyone who did considered the question of what God wanted them to do in their business context, even though they showed a remarkable diversity in how they interpreted the concept.

Two respondents, UK3 (estate agent) and D7 (optician), considered their business activity in the light of their general calling as Christians to follow Jesus Christ, although they did so in slightly different ways. They both asked themselves whether running a business was a worthwhile thing to do or whether they should follow a more 'spiritual' call, but D7 particularly related a spiritual calling to a Franciscan lifestyle of poverty and service. Both reported, however, that they had come to the conclusion that God had called them to run the business, and that they had worked out how their faith and their business fitted together. Although they did not interpret the concept of calling in a Lutheran sense, i.e. that they were called to run their businesses in order to serve others, they talked about being a witness in their workplace in various different ways, and D7 also made some allusions to the stewardship concept.

In D5's (printing) account we find some notions of calling that are ascribed to the Calvinistic or Puritan tradition, as he talked of being "Puritan", "taking one's duties seriously" and of his concern to "stay in God's will with one's natural gifts". The Puritan tradition conceptualises calling less as 'serving society/serving one's neighbour' - as the Lutheran tradition does - but more as 'obedience to God' (Hughes et al. 2003, pp. 99). It is therefore perhaps not surprising that D5 filled calling with more spiritual connotations, as he primarily referred to his ability to raise money for Christian causes with his business and to his ability to serve the Christian market with his printing business. Hence the community of faith and their causes, but not the wider community, were the primary beneficiaries of how he wanted to live out his calling,

For D9 (security analysis), also, calling had a more spiritual notion. D9 felt that his specific calling related to openly sharing his faith in the context of his workplace by, for example, inviting his colleagues to Christian outreach events. His belief that he was "an ambassador for Christ" was a version of the narrower interpretation of the concept of calling, which relates to 'spiritual' responsibilities only and not to responsibilities related to business activities. In such cases, the concept of calling has relatively little direct impact on specific business practices.

A third set of respondents, however, related the concept of calling to their general approach of how they wanted to run their businesses, and this led them to conceptualise a number of their business practices in a way that they benefited others. In that way they came closer to the Lutheran conception of calling, in which work is perceived to be a divine call to 'serve others'. This notion was found particularly in UK10 (pharmacy) and UK11's (optician) accounts, as they believed that they were called by God to "serve the community" through their businesses. 'Serving the community' meant for them, for example, not to charge for certain services and it also affected the way they dealt with vulnerable and disadvantaged customers. The fact that both their professions have a 'caring image' may have made it easier for them to regard their work in their business as a calling from God. At the same time, both stated that they believed that what they did in their business went beyond the requirements of their professions. UK7 (engineering), on the other hand, very strongly believed that he was called by God to live out his faith in the workplace. He translated his calling into a wide range of stewardship responsibilities, which included socially and environmentally responsible practices. Although he did not explicitly frame his practices in terms of 'serving society/the community' a number of what he conceptualised as his stewardship responsibilities were clearly meant to benefit wider society as well.

UK7 and UK10's belief of being called by God to their respective places of work carried a particularly strong force for them, as not only did it have implications for their business practices, but also for their engagement in the civic sphere. UK7 reported to be engaged in learned societies to promote renewable energy and environmental sustainability. And for UK10 it meant to represent the concerns of his customers – and thus of the community - in a panel that decided about building developments in the area. In addition to that, UK10 reported that he used to run one of his shops like a charity for a period of time when circumstances did not allow him to run the shop profitably, because he wanted to ensure that the community was still provided with pharmaceutical services.

The way Christian owner-managers engage with the concept of calling may depend, among other things, on their understanding to what extent the 'worldly affairs' that they are involved in also carry spiritual significance. In other words, it depends on whether business activity as such is considered an activity that God takes a particular interest in, or whether God is thought to be primarily interested in activities that readily link with the Christian faith such as faith community activities or evangelising (see discussion in section 5.3).

Another factor that might influence the interpretation of the concept of calling is the national context. None of the German respondents talked as passionately about their calling to their respective business activities as UK7 and UK10 did. The reason for this might be that the notion of 'serving others/serving society' through work (including business activity) is already very much embedded in the German national culture, and Christian owner-managers in Germany may not need to revert to an explicitly spiritual frame like calling to rationalise their business activities as service to society. D9 (security analysis), for example, who interpreted calling in a more narrow sense, might have not extended the concept of calling to his business activity, as, so he said "security is something that society demands".[49] And so working according to high and responsible standards may have arisen for him naturally from a societal expectation but not from an explicit spiritual motivation.

In conclusion, the concept of calling carries potentially a strong force for believers to engage in certain practices that are related in one way or another to the world of work. But whether those practices actually make a 'difference', i.e. whether they also benefit others in society, depends on the believers' interpretation and application of the concept. The concept seems to make most impact on business practices if believers feel called to 'live out Christian values in business' or feel called to 'provide a service for the community' with their business.

[49] Sicherheit ist etwas, was die Gesellschaft einfordert.

4.2 Stewardship

The concept of stewardship in the Christian tradition is based on the understanding that "everything comes from God as a gift and is to be administered faithfully on his behalf" (Hillyer 1988). Thus, believers are considered to be stewards over God-given resources; they are put into a position of trust and are accountable to God (Carey 1992). The concept refers to a number of different 'resources', from stewardship over natural resources or creation, to stewardship over 'personal' resources such as money, time, gifts and talents, to stewardship over the resources of society. In the context of the faith community, the concept may further refer to stewardship over the Gospel and the resources of the church (Hillyer 1988).

In the study, stewardship was identified as a frame that people used when they believed that *something*, i.e. the business, gifts and talents etc., or *someone*, e.g. their employees, had been entrusted to them by God; or when they believed that Christ was the actual Lord of their business, such as UK7 did.

> Um, I feel, that my my primary responsibility is to God. *I believe very strongly in in Lordship of businesses.* Um, and to me to say uh that Jesus is Lord of all is not um is not just something I say but something I believe and practice.
> (UK7a, engineering)

People who used the frame engaged with it in very different ways, ranging from a vague sense that God had entrusted something to them, to strong conceptualisations of what stewardship is supposed to mean. To unravel the concept of stewardship, we will first look at the sense of responsibility and accountability that the concept invoked for the respondents, then look at some examples of how respondents interpreted stewardship as a comprehensive concept for their business, and then finally give an account of the different practices that the respondents linked with the stewardship discourse.

4.2.1 Responsible and accountable to God

The respondents who engaged with the stewardship discourse said that they felt responsibility and accountability to God for what they did in their businesses, as the following quotes illustrate.

> I mean, you know, I feel a responsibility to God to look after (the business), I mean, He gave me it I guess.
> (UK11a, optician)

> I am convinced that when we die we'll stand before Jesus. ... We'll be asked how we treated the people who were entrusted to us. We'll be asked about how we used the talents and gifts we were given.[50]
> (D10a, manufacture of measuring instruments)

> Responsible like a good steward. I'm a steward over what God has entrusted to me. And I'll have to make the most of it. I'll have to make the best of it.[51]
> (D4a, heating and plumbing)

> *D6:* But as I said, my primary responsibility is to God.
> *Interviewer:* What does responsibility to God mean in concrete terms?

[50] Ich bin davon überzeugt, dass wir in der Ewigkeit vor Jesus mal stehen werden. ... Wir werden gefragt werden, wie die Menschen, die uns anvertraut worden sind, wie wir mit denen umgegangen sind. Wir werden gefragt werden, wie die Talente und die Gaben, die wir bekommen haben, wie wir die genutzt haben.

[51] In der Verantwortung wie ein guter Verwalter. Ich bin ein Verwalter, von dem ähm was Gott mir anvertraut hat. Und da habe ich zu wuchern. Und hab' das Beste draus zu machen.

D6: Well, whatever job I do, it's just a job at the end of the day whether I'm self-employed or in a management position. *That I've been given something that I should, deal with it carefully, should deal with it responsibly.*[52]
(D6a, decorating and special surface coatings)

This sense of responsibility and accountability was framed with phrases such as "look after the business", "deal with carefully and responsibly", "make the most of" or "use". It seems that by doing so the respondents referred to two broad aspects of what "administering God-given resources faithfully" might entail. They referred 1) to the responsibility to utilise and manage available resources in the business to their best effect and/or 2) to social responsibilities that come with running the business. D10's quote illustrates this very well. His perceived responsibility to "use one's talents and gifts" refers to the former aspect whereas his perceived responsibility regarding the treatment of his employees may refer to the latter.

4.2.2 Guiding the focus of the business

For some respondents, being a steward clearly meant that they needed to be in business for reasons that go beyond the profit-motive. UK7 made a rather strong statement on this, following his exposition on Christ being the Lord of the business (see above).

> My fundamental belief (is) that (if the only thing you're concerned about) is is the financial returns, I don't think you have any right to be in business. *You are a steward.*
> (UK7a, engineering)

Being a good steward meant for him to look after every aspect of the "triple-bottom line".

> If you if if you are a good steward of your, of your business then you will be looking at the well-being of the environment, the well-being of your of of the people in the business. As well as looking after, um, amounts of money on a on a profit and loss statement or your balance sheet.
> (UK7a, engineering)

D7, similarly, said that the focus in his business was on things that went beyond the profit-motive. He reported that he had been focusing a lot more on the profit-motive before he became a committed believer (in his capacity as the junior owner-manager in the family business), but that his focus had changed because he now believed that the business was entrusted to him by God. In the following quotation he regarded specifically the interaction with his customers as well as social responsibilities to his employees as his stewardship responsibilities.

> *D7:* Yes, well, I know what it's like to be focused on all those other things, *but that was before God entrusted me with it [the business] again.* ... It was like everything had to be bigger, better, faster, higher, more expensive. I now know there's nothing in it. And so I focus on other things now, you know.
> *Interviewer:* So what do you focus on now?
> *D7:* Well I guess it's that when people who come here feel at home, um that they realise that they're important to us. Um, let's say, that many of them will feel blessed. Well it's not particularly to do with starting intense conversations, also about other things, but simply through the way I deal with them. That they notice that things are a bit different

[52] *D6:* Aber wie gesagt, grundsätzlich Verantwortung natürlich als allererstes erstmal Gott gegenüber.
Interviewer: Wie würden Sie das formulieren, was das heißt, Gott gegenüber Verantwortung, konkret?
D6: Dass ich, äh ja dass die die, den Beruf, den ich ausübe, das ist ja letzten Endes ein Beruf, ob ich selbständig bin oder in leitender Funktion oder äh wie auch immer. *Dass ich da damit ja eine etwas in die Hand bekommen habe, womit ich halt behutsam umgehen muss. Verantwortungsbewusst umgehen muss.*

here. Um, that's one thing that's important to me. Another is that we don't have to get rid of staff. ... So that as far as possible things stay stable. Some of our staff have been here for a long time, and um, if we had to make people redundant, one of our employees for example, he wouldn't get another job because of his age. So that this is covered. And, I have to say, it's worked so far.[53]
(D7a, optician)

Lastly, in D10's account we can see how his belief that God had entrusted his employees to him (see section 4.2.1) also guided his deliberations on what the focus of the company should be.

What's it about? Is it about ... *doing something together with other people? Or is it about making money?* But if you want to do something with other people, your finances have got to be strong, you've got to make the necessary profits to fund this. So, you know, these things go hand in hand – they complement one another.[54]
(D10a, manufacture of measuring instruments)

4.2.3 Good stewardship a prerequisite for a Christian owner-manager

D5 engaged with the stewardship concept in quite a different way.

D5: (T)o make it known that you, as the boss, run the company as a Christian, that you as a Christian, of course it's true for everyone that whatever you've got has been lent to you by God and you are the steward. You're a steward, always. But your company has really got to be tip top if you want to spell that out to other people.
Interviewer: What do you mean by tip top?
D5: 'Earning the right to be heard.' People will fall around on the floor, won't they, if the boss says "Hallelujah, this firm is the Lord's" when in reality it's about to go bankrupt, or things are out of control or everybody is backbiting. So if I wanna say that my firm belongs to God, then I need to make sure that it is in a condition that doesn't bring shame upon God, if it is to be His company.[55] (D5b, printing)

---

[53] *D7:* Ja, weil ich ähm eigentlich bevor ich *das hier alles nochmal so anvertraut* bekommen habe, die andere Seite auch so intensiv gelebt habe. ... Da war es so, dass es höher, schneller, breiter, besser, teurer und so weiter sein musste. Und dass es das nicht ist, dass weiß ich jetzt. Und insofern mh habe ich da jetzt andere Schwerpunkte. Ganz klar.
Interviewer: Was sind da jetzt Ihre Schwerpunkte?
D7: Schwerpunkte sind, dass mh Leute tatsächlich auch, die hier 'reinkommen, mh, dass sie sich wohlfühlen, dass sie wissen, dass dass sie uns wichtig sind. Ähm, ich sage auch einfach mal so, dass dass viele einfach auch gesegnet werden. Also, das das hat nicht unbedingt jetzt damit zu tun, dass man äh jetzt so intensiv das Gespräch sucht, auch über andere Themen, sondern einfach durch die Begegnung. Dass sie merken, dass da ein bisschen was anders ist als sonst. Mh, das ist mir wichtig. Zum einen. Zum andern ähm, dass wir personell nicht abbauen müssen. Dass wir die Möglichkeiten, die wir jetzt einfach so haben. ... Ähm, dass das möglichst stabil bleibt. Einige Mitarbeiter sind schon ganz lange da, und ähm, selbst wenn wir jetzt abbauen müssten, die eine ein Mitarbeiter zum Beispiel, der würde gar nicht in seinem Alter auch mehr unterkommen. Also dass das abgesichert ist. Und, ich sag' mal, das funktioniert bisher.

[54] *Worum gehts? ... Mit Menschen gemeinsam was tun? Oder geht es darum Kohle zu verdienen?* Äh, wobei, wenn man mit Menschen was tun (will), muss man wirtschaftlich auch stark sein und muss entsprechende Finanzen auch erwirtschaften, um das, was wir uns vorgenommen haben, auch finanzieren zu können. Also, ich sag jetzt mal, das ist schon 'ne ziemlich komplementäre Sache, die ineinander geht.

[55] *D5:* Um sozusagen als Chef das öffentlich zu machen, dass du den Betrieb als Christ führst, dass du als Christ, natürlich ist das für jeden so, du hast das, was du besitzt, von Gott geliehen zur Verwaltung. Du bist Verwalter, in jedem Fall. Aber das, das so deutlich zu sagen, kann man eigentlich nur, wenn der Betrieb in einem, gewissermaßen Top-Zustand ist. Nicht.
Interviewer: Was ist damit gemeint, Top-Zustand?
D5: ‚Earning the right to be heard.' Ähm, ja. Das Recht erreichen, gehört zu werden. Ähm, ein Betrieb, der kurz vor'm Abkratzen ist, oder in dem's drunter und drüber geht und in dem die Fetzen fliegen, wenn der Chef dann

He believed that he had to manage the company well, in order to claim in front of his employees and other people that he was God's steward. Otherwise, he said, he would bring God into disrepute and would not be able to be upfront about his running the company as a Christian. We find here an indication that he combined the stewardship discourse with the witness discourse, which we will look at in section 4.3. Being asked what a "tip top condition" entails for him he referred to the financial structure of his business, the atmosphere in the company and his responsibility to pay good wages to his staff.

> Well, you know, the firm needs to have proper control of its financial situation, there shouldn't be any problems looming in this area. The staff should be at peace with one another. And the social issues, well you know, you should pay at least, and I already do that, you should pay at least good wages for the area. Uh, as far as possible pay good wages for the area so that people don't feel exploited. Have the company on a sound financial footing. I can't talk about God's blessing if my company capital is negative. That's simply not on. I could be personally of the opinion that God's been blessing me, but I'd have no proof of it on my balance sheet.[56]
> (D5b, printing)

4.2.4 Different understandings of what stewardship entails

As we have seen, people had different connotations with regards to the stewardship concept, which also led them to frame different practices in the stewardship discourse. Sometimes the respondents had developed particular conceptualisations as to what stewardship entailed for them, but others connected the stewardship discourse in a more random way with their practices. We will outline here the themes that the people in the study specifically connected with the stewardship discourse.

Affecting business conduct

For some respondents, being a steward had an impact on their business conduct, particularly in their relationship to their customers, as UK11 and D4 stated.

UK11 said that "looking after the business" meant for her to run the business in a way that would be approved of by God.

> *UK11*: I mean, you know, I feel a responsibility to God to look after it, I mean, He gave me it I guess.
> *Interviewer:* How, in what ways?
> *UK11:* Well, I wouldn't want to do anything that I felt He wouldn't approve of, I guess. Um, so I want to run the business in the way that I think He would want me to.
> (UK11a, optician)

---

sagt 'Oh, Halleluja, dieser Betrieb gehört dem Herrn', dann lachen die sich schlapp. Nicht. Es muss also, wenn ich davon rede, dass meine Firma Gott gehört, muss die Firma auch einen einen einen Zustand haben, dass der Gott keine Schande macht, wenn sie ihm dann schon gehören soll.

[56] Die Firma muss in 'nem, sagen wir mal, finanztechnisch ordentlichen Verfassung sein, also nicht nicht kippeln. Es möchte einigermaßen Friede unter den Mitarbeitern herrschen. Es möchte äh die die sozialen Sachen, also man muss zumindestens in, an dem Punkt bin ich im Prinzip schon, ähm, man muss zumindestens im Umfeld ordentlich zahlen. Äh, nach seinen Möglichkeiten gut zahlen, so dass es also angemessen für die Gegend ist, dass die Leute sich nicht ausgebeutet vorkommen. Eine finanziell seriöse Konstruktion des Betriebes. Also nicht, ja, ich kann nicht von Gottes Segen reden, wenn ich negatives Eigenkapital habe. Das geht einfach nicht. Dann kann ich persönlich zwar der Meinung sein, Gott segnet mich, aber ich kann es nicht belegen auf meiner betriebswirtschaftlichen, auf meiner, in meiner Bilanz.

Being asked to give an example, she talked about treating her customers equally well and doing the best that she can.

> *One thing I've been thinking about is treating everybody equally.* So it's easy in our job, you know, somebody comes in who looks well, ... like they got plenty of money, it would be very easy to treat them differently to somebody who comes in, who obviously isn't going to spend very much money. So I just thought about it yesterday, about making sure to give everybody the same care no matter what they're gonna spend on their glasses. *And I think that would be something that God would disprove of, to discriminate between people.* And in other ways as well, you know, when somebody comes in and you think 'Oh no, not them again' 'Oh no, not them again.' It's that smelly lot. [laughs] And um, yeah, treating everybody (equally) and fairly. Um, I'm trying to think of anything else [pause] *It is really to do the best you can. Sort of cutting corners or not bothering, always working to the best of your ability.*
> (UK11b, optician)

Likewise, D4 regarded his company's conduct as a stewardship responsibility. He specifically referred to honesty in his relationship to his customers.

> We get contracts because uh customers know we we don't defraud them. And that's a very important factor. Um, because I've, I'm a steward.[57]
> (D4a, heating and plumbing)

Gifts and talents

A recurring theme for the people who drew on the stewardship discourse was the use of gifts and talents.

Some respondents believed that their business was the place in which they should utilise the gifts that they thought were given to them by God. UK9, for example, said he was running a building services company because God had given him the gift of working with his hands.

> *I I enjoy working with my hands because God's given me a gift of creation, creating things with my hand.* I love it, I love working with my hands.
> (UK9a, building services)

But the respondents mentioned gifts and talents not only in relation to themselves but referred to it quite frequently when they talked about their employees.

For UK7, considering and understanding his employees' gifts and talents was a natural part of managing the business.

> And first of all you have to understand that they are the right members for the team. Um, and that has to do with their, um with their attributes, their characteristics. Um, *in Christian terms what we would call their gifts and talents.* Um, and these need to be complementary in a team.
> (UK7b, engineering)

For D10, considering the gifts of his employees formed part of his management practice, too, and he even expressed this in his company's mission statement. This mission statement stated that the "external focus" of the business was to provide good customer service. This was however linked with the following "internal focus" relating to his employees.

---

[57] Es ist so, dass eben wir Aufträge bekommen, weil äh Kunden auch wissen, wir wir betrügen sie nicht. Und das ist für mich ein ein ganz wichtiger Faktor. Ähm, denn ich hab als erst-, bin ein Verwalter.

> Our internal focus is that our company is to be a place where employees can develop their gifts and use them for the benefit of our customers.[58]
> (D10a, manufacture of measuring instruments)

But he considered the development of gifts not only to be something that benefited the customer and, as a result, the business, but he also linked it with a concern about the personal development of his employees.

> Well, the business should be a place where they can develop their gifts. That's one possibility. [pause] Most of them take advantage of it, too. And that means seeing where their potential is, what are their strengths, what are their weaknesses. *That employees have the chance to build on their strengths. To get a sense of achievement from it. So that they can develop personally.*[59]
> (D10a, manufacture of measuring instruments)

This concern for the personal development of employees also played a role in difficult management decisions, even though a concern for the well-being of the business may have had an impact there, too.

> I also have to put a stop to things when someone hasn't got the gifts for a particular job. It doesn't help to say to him 'Well, it'll work out OK somehow, we'll help you' and so on. Uh, if he's not in the right place, i.e. if God hasn't given him the appropriate gifts for the job then he'll not benefit at all. He's unhappy, frustrated and sees that he's not successful. The others have to carry him and so on. The others (are also unhappy) because they have to carry him, uh, it simply doesn't make sense.[60]
> (D10a, manufacture of measuring instruments)

More responsibilities to employees

Some respondents referred to other stewardship responsibilities that related to their employees.

D4, for example, took a more paternalistic stance towards his employees. In his accounts he repeatedly emphasised that he regarded it as his responsibility to make sure that his employees do their work well and conduct themselves well when they do their work. At the same time, he also recognised – like D7 (section 4.2.2) - a responsibility to keep them in employment.

> A responsibility towards my staff and their families, uh, and that means ensuring that they have a livelihood. And that they do a proper job. And that we've got enough work coming in. ... *And uh this responsibility, I try to make it clear to my staff that I have a responsibility towards them and of course also to God.* If I didn't have this uh but was

---

[58] Und dann der Schwerpunkt, der nach innen gerichtet ist. Danach soll das Unternehmen (ein Ort sein), in denen Mitarbeiter ihre Gaben entwickeln und zum Wohle unserer Kunden einsetzen können.

[59] Ähm, das Unternehmen soll ein ein Lebensraum sein, wo sie ihre Gaben entwickeln können. Das ist eine Möglichkeit. [Pause] Die allermeisten nutzen das auch. Und das heißt zu schauen, wo sind Potentiale drin, wo sind Stärken, wo sind Schwächen. Und dass die Mitarbeiter die Möglichkeit haben, ihre Stärken auszubauen. Um einfach auch darin ein gewisses Erfolgserlebnis zu haben. Also (sich) als Menschen weiterentwickeln zu können.

[60] Es muss auch ganz klar ein Schnitt gemacht werden, wo jemand einfach für eine bestimmte Tätigkeit die Gabe nicht hat. Es nützt dem jetzt auch nichts zu sagen ‚Na gut, es geht schon, wir tragen das schon durch.' und so weiter. Äh, wenn derjenige nicht an der richtigen Stelle ist, das heißt, wer nicht entsprechend den Gaben, die er von Gott bekommen hat, dann bringt demjenigen das gar nichts. Der ist unzufrieden, der ist frustriert, der merkt, er hat keinen Erfolg. Die anderen müssen ihn durchschleppen und so weiter. Die anderen (sind unzufrieden), weil sie ihn durchschleppen müssen, äh, das bringt gar nichts.

only answerable to myself, then that would be selfish, because I'm always answerable to God first. Next come my employees. And these two things combined shape my identity. And the way I live.[61]
(D4a, heating and plumbing)

Others emphasised the financial obligation that they have to their staff. As we have seen, for D5, paying good wages formed one important part of his stewardship responsibilities. D10, similarly, explained his obligation of paying a proper wage to his employees by referring to what the Apostle Paul says about the good management of one's household (1 Timothy 5:8).

> "Whoever does not provide for his house, uh his household, is worse than a heathen." ... It's very important to God that we take our responsibility to provide for them seriously. St Paul says that we'll run into huge problems with God if we pay an unjust wage or no wage at all. These things are pretty practical, if you'll interpret them that way.[62]
> (D10b, manufacture of measuring instruments)

Responsibility to use financial resources wisely

Stewardship meant for some respondents to deal wisely with their financial resources. As we have seen earlier, D5 talked about the company being "in proper control over its financial situation".

We also saw that one of UK7's stewardship responsibilities had a financial or economic angle, namely "to look after looking after, um, amounts of money on a on a profit and loss statement or your balance sheet." He underpinned this with a number of other financial principles, one of which was self-financing.

> And uh for instance, we operate, we operate the business with no debt. We don't have an overdraft. And we have a policy of um of paying our um creditors as soon as we can. Um, we have a policy of of chasing our debtors very very quickly. We bring money into the business quicker. And we we do self-financing. We meet regularly to go over the the management accounts and a central part of that is our is our debtors and creditors um policy. And we won't allow, we we have a strict policy of of paying in 30 days where where we can. And in 60 days if we if we struggle. Uh, because of, because other people don't treat us that way, you know.
> (UK7a, engineering)

Responsible to care for creation

UK7 was the only respondent in the sample who specifically regarded the way natural resources are treated as a specific stewardship responsibility that was related to his business.

---

[61] Meinen Mitarbeitern gegenüber die Verantwortung und für ihre Familien, äh dafür zu sorgen, dass sie in Brot und Arbeit stehen. Und dass sie ihre Arbeit eben eben ordentlich machen. Und dass wir auch dann auch genügend Arbeit haben. ... *Und äh diese Verantwortung äh versuche ich auch den Mitarbeitern klarzumachen, dass ich diese Verantwortung, die ich ihnen gegenüber habe natürlich auch Gott gegenüber habe.* Und wenn ich das nicht habe, ähm, sondern dass ich mir selbst gegenüber verantwortlich bin, ähm, dann ist es halt eben 'ne egoistische Sache, weil ich bin an erster Stelle immer Gott gegenüber verantwortlich. Und dann meinen Mitarbeitern. Und aus dieser Situation entsteht eine eine Verbindung, die äh die mich die mich ausmacht. Und in der ich lebe.

[62] So, 'Wer sein Haus äh, wer seine Hausmitglieder, die im Hause wohnen, nicht versorgt, ist schlimmer als ein Heide.' ... Das heißt also die Verantwortung, die wir haben in der Versorgung, da legt Gott großen Wert drauf. Einen ungerechten oder keinen Lohn zu zahlen, kriegen wir Riesenprobleme mit Gott, sagt uns der Apostel Paulus. Ja, also solche Dinge sind schon sehr sehr konkret, wenn man sie als solche nehmen will.

> Um, and uh I would describe [pause] um sustainability in a Christian sense, as as caring for God's creation. Um, I believe we're here as as stewards. We don't own anything on this planet. It's not ours. But we've been put in the position of stewards. And uh uh and sustainability in effect, is another word for stewardship.
> (UK7a, engineering)

His awareness of his responsibility to 'care for creation' had led him to make renewable energy projects one focus of his business and to formulate extensive environmental policies for the other areas in which his business operates.

By contrast, D10 and D5, who also drew very heavily on the stewardship discourse, took a different line when they were asked about their responsibilities to the environment. D10 framed his environmental responsibilities mainly in terms of the protection of his employees and the people who lived around them and did not go beyond that.

> *Interviewer:* Do you do anything for environmental protection?
> *D10:* Yes, in principle. We've implemented working practices so that corrosive fluids for stainless steel and so on that need to be disposed of, that they're properly contained. That's a health and safety matter. Uh, I don't know, health and safety is equally important or more important. Both basically protect people, the environment, you know.[63]
> (D10a, manufacture of measuring instruments)

D5, finally, said that his faith did not play much of a role in terms of caring for the environment and disassociated the things he might do for the environment from his faith.

> *Interviewer:* What role does environmental protection play in your company?
> *D5:* In the company? Well, as far as my faith goes, not much. I mean, I separate my rubbish and that type of thing [laughs]. But I'm rather suspicious about environmental protection – it's almost as though it's a new religion. ... And Germany is the star pupil anyway as far as looking after the environment is concerned. Right? We've got to be, I can't just go and dump 10 kilos of dye somewhere in the countryside. You have to dispose of it properly - as hazardous waste. ... (But) at the moment I'm thinking about installing photovoltaic panels for electricity production. Then I'd score some points with the 'green' Christians [ironic]. But, I've looked at this in terms of cost saving; installing photovoltaic panels would probably be really efficient because I've got a south-facing flat roof. But that hasn't got a great deal to do with my Christian faith. This is more to do with considering technological options if I do something here.[64] (D5a, printing)

---

[63] *Interviewer:* Spielt bei Ihnen Umweltschutz 'ne Rolle in der Firma?
D10: Ja, also erstmal prinzipiell ja. Das ist äh also äh Arbeitsanweisung, dass also Beizpasten, Beizbäder für Edelstahl und so weiter, die zu entsorgen sind, dass die also nicht in die Umwelt gelangen dürfen und so weiter.Da gibt's also entsprechende Arbeitsschutzbelehrung. Äh, ich weiß jetzt nicht, auf gleicher Stufe oder auf höherer Stufe steht im Prinzip für mich der Arbeitsschutz. Also beides ist im Prinzip ein Schutz für den Menschen, Umwelt, wie auch immer.

[64] *Interviewer:* Inwieweit spielt Umweltschutz eine Rolle in Ihrem Unternehmen?
D5: Im Unternehmen? Also im vom vom vom christlichen Glauben her eher wenig. Ich meine, ich trenne meinen Müll. Und ich [lacht], all solche Sachen, das ist klar. Aber äh ich bin im Bezug auf den Umweltschutz insoweit ein bisschen misstrauisch, als das ja natürlich bei uns zur neuen Religion wird, ja. ... Dann ist Deutschland natürlich umweltschutzmäßig sowieso der der Musterschüler. Ja? Das kannst du dir gar nicht leisten, ich kann doch nicht daher gehen und kann 10 Kilo Farbe irgendwo in die Natur schmeißen. Ich muss das doch als Sondermüll entsorgen. ... (Aber) ich überlege zur Zeit, ob ich mir hier 'ne Photovoltaik-Anlage draufmache. Da könnte ich wieder bei den grünen Christen äh Punkte sammeln [ironisch]. Aber, ich hab' mir das ausgerechnet, 'ne Photovoltaik-Anlage würde sich wahrscheinlich richtig rechnen, weil ich ein wunderschönes Süd-Flachdach habe. Also dass, aber das, das hat mit meinem christlichen Glauben eher weniger zu tun. Sondern das sind mehr technische Spielereien, dass ich was mache.

4.2.5 Observations

Compared to the other concepts that will be described in sections 4.3 to 4.5, stewardship appears to be a concept that is more specifically related to the world of work, as the respondents referred to the effective and responsible use of resources that they work with or to responsible behaviour that resulted from their belief that the business was entrusted to them. Stewardship in that sense is not a uniquely religious concept, as some non-religious business people may also talk about responsible use of resources and refer to the stewardship concept.[65]

What distinguishes it as a religious concept, however, is the respondents' belief that God has entrusted the business to them or that Christ as the Lord of all is also Lord of their business. Allport argues that "the thought, feeling and behaviour of individuals are influenced by the actual, imagined or implied presence of others" (1985, 3 cited in Weick 1995, 39). In the case of Christian stewardship, this 'other' refers to God or Jesus Christ whose presence in the thoughts of the respondents creates a strong sense of responsibility and accountability, and thus a strong motivation to act in a certain way.

Stewardship as a faith-related concept is not unique to Christianity. The concept is also known in Judaism and Islam, and it was identified as one shared principle among Jewish, Christian and Muslim business leaders in the Interfaith Declaration of Business Ethics (Webley 1999). Stewardship, sometimes also called trusteeship, may thus be more peculiar to monotheistic faiths, where believers relate to an omnipresent God who is regarded as the provider of all resources and to whom believers feel accountable. On the other hand, each faith tradition will interpret the stewardship concept in a way that it becomes a meaningful concept for their respective followers, by linking it to faith-specific beliefs and ideas with which the believer is familiar or to which he can relate.

The respondents differed in the way they translated the stewardship concept into practices, and the reasons for this may vary. Some respondents reported that they had been exposed to specific Christian teaching concerning the relationship between faith and business, which may have shaped their understanding of what stewardship may entail: financial stewardship, responsibilities relating to their employees, and stewardship over creation. A specific biblical concept to which respondents repeatedly referred and which they related to their business practices was that of 'gifts and talents'. They either referred to their responsibility to use their own gifts to their best effect or to utilise or develop their employees' gifts.[66]

But most respondents 'picked and chose' when it came to translating the different aspects of stewardship to their business practices. D10, for example, regarded the utilisation of his own and his employees' gifts and talents as well as paying his employees on time as stewardship responsibilities, whereas D5 considered it important "to have the company on a sound financial footing", to pay his employees well and to ensure that his staff were at peace with each other. The respondents' own plans and preferences, as well as the presence of other discourses may have had an influence on what they considered their stewardship responsibilities. D5's interpretation, for example, was probably also influenced by his belief that the company also served as a witness of God to others (see section 4.3),

---

[65] References to stewardship can be found, for example, in corporate codes of ethics. Anglo-American's 'Good Citizenship Principles' say this about environmental stewardship: "We recognise the need for environmental stewardship to minimise consumption of natural resources and waste generation and to minimise the impact of our operations on the environment." (Anglo-American, p.4). Microsoft's 'Standards of Business Conduct' talks about stewardship over company assets: "We are responsible stewards in the use, protection, and management of Microsoft's assets." (Microsoft)

[66] The concept of talents and gifts goes primarily back to two passages in the Bible. 1 Peter 4:10 says "As each has received a gift, use it to serve one another, as good stewards of God's varied grace." (English Standard Version) The passage may primarily refer to using one's gift within the community of believers, but may also be applied in a wider societal or business context. The other passage that is often interpreted as talking about the utilisation of one's gifts and talents is 'The Parable of the Talents' (Matthew 25:14-30). The parable is about a man who entrusts each of his servants a different amount of talents (here: a unit of money) before he goes on a long journey. On coming back he commends those servants who worked with their 'talents' and multiplied them and severely rebukes the servant who hid his 'talent' and did not put it to work. Particularly the reformer Calvin promoted the concept of gifts and skills in contrast to Luther, who focused more on people's 'stations' (Banks 1998).

hence his emphasis on making sure that nothing "is out of control" and no one "is backbiting" in his company.

Other respondents, who did not report on being exposed to specific teaching on stewardship but who nevertheless felt that God had entrusted the business to them, related the concept to responsible business practices that they personally considered to be important. UK11, for example, felt that her responsibilities to God were to treat her customers equally and to always give her best. This may have also been affected by the presence of other discourses, in her case, specifically by the co-presence of the 'called to serve the community' discourse (see section 4.1.4).

Another factor that may influence the different interpretations of the stewardship concept is the national context. UK7, as the only British respondent who primarily engaged with the stewardship concept, emphasised repeatedly how important it was also to consider oneself a steward of the environment and reported how this led him to formulate a number of environmental policies for his business. His German counterparts, by contrast, did not have this strong motivation to consider environmental responsibilities from a stewardship point of view in the depth and breadth as he did. This may be due to the fact that high environmental standards are embedded in the German culture both through legal standards and as a cultural value, so that a Christian owner-manager may not perceive the need to invoke a specific religious discourse, such as the stewardship discourse, in order to engage in environmentally friendly practices. D5 illustrated this in his account. He mentioned that he engaged in environmentally friendly practices either because he was required to do so by law, because he simply did what a German citizen normally does, or because he had a personal interest in environmental technology. Yet he consciously rejected doing this out of an explicit spiritual motivation.

An alternative explanation for the inclusion or exclusion of the environmental aspect in the respondents' stewardship responsibilities is that the respondents might have had a different understanding about the spiritual significance of the natural environment, i.e. whether the 'material' world is regarded to be significant from a faith perspective (see discussion in section 5.3).

A number of the stewardship principles and practices to which the respondents referred could be regarded as prudent or 'enlightened' business practice. For example, financial stewardship principles or the development and utilisation of their employees' gifts and talents will certainly benefit the business. But some responsibilities that the respondents mentioned went beyond that and may have made more of a 'difference'. For instance, D10 was interested in developing his employees' gifts not only so that they can be more effective in their work. He also felt that they should gain a sense of accomplishment in their work, which will contribute to their own personal development. Other examples in the sample were UK11's desire to treat each of her customers equally well, D7's and D4's concern about keeping their staff in employment, or UK7's strong concern about environmental sustainability.

To sum up, even though stewardship as a business-related concept is not a uniquely Christian concept and might be shared with secular business people, the belief that God has entrusted the business and business-related resources may create quite a strong motivation for Christian owner-managers to run the business in a responsible manner. However, they may interpret the stewardship concept in ways that it makes sense to them, and thus may differ in the way they relate the stewardship concept to specific business practices.

4.3 Being a witness

In general terms 'witness' refers to a person who has first-hand knowledge of an event or certain facts and gives an attestation of it – often in a court of justice. In Christian usage, by contrast, witnessing refers specifically to the testimony given by Christian witnesses about Christ and his saving power (Fisher 1960). The first Christian witnesses were the Apostles, who had personal, 'first-hand' knowledge of the ministry of Christ, but witnessing is also thought to be the universal obligation of all believers (ibid.). Christian believers may interpret 'being a witness' in various different ways, either emphasising that their actions should bear witness of their faith or, on the other end of the scale, that they should seek out opportunities to share their faith by word with others, or their interpretation might have elements of both. What 'witnessing' exactly entails might also depend on the believer's interpretation of the ministry of Christ.[67]

In this section we look at the different connotations that 'being a witness' had for the respondents in relation to their business life.

4.3.1 Not bringing Christianity into disrepute

One group of respondents that engaged with the witness discourse rationalised their behaviour in terms of not wanting to bring their faith into disrepute. UK3 was one of them.

> *I try not, I try to make sure that nobody sees me putting a foot wrong.* ...You must remember that this is a very legalistic profession. And um I know that Jesus is not a legalistic um kind of God, is not a legalistic God. Um, and on the contrary, um, he hated religion, legalisation of faith. *But if I'm not to be a bad example, um, and then to be judged as a Christian as well as an estate agent, then I've got to be, if not squeaky clean then at least um reasonably respectable.*
> (UK3a, estate agent)

Those respondents believed that things they did wrong may not just fall back on them but on the reputation of the Christian faith as such. UK5, for example, said that misbehaving or not doing one's job well can make Christianity lose its credibility.

> So sometimes if you've got a Christian not doing his job well, he can be the exact opposite of a good (witness). He can be, it's it's like you've got a vicar misbehaving at different churches. *I mean, people forget they are ambassadors.* And when people hear that it's so bad. *Gives a, I, you lo-, we lose credib-, we've lost so much credibility because of that kind of behaviour.* And yet we need to remember we are ambassadors.
> (UK5a, heating engineer)

We also saw in section 4.2.3 how D5 emphasised the need to be a good steward in order to claim to run the company as a Christian. Referring to the various stewardship responsibilities that he perceived having, he said

> So if I wanna say that my firm belongs to God, then I need to make sure *that it is in a condition that doesn't bring shame upon God*, if it is to be His company.[68]
> (D5b, printing)

[67] 'The saving power of Christ', for instance, might be interpreted as the salvation from sin which enables believers to go to heaven when they have died. Itt may also be interpreted as having meaning for the believers' life on earth, for example, that it enables them to live a 'new', 'different' life.

[68] Es muss also, wenn ich davon rede, dass meine Firma Gott gehört, muss die Firma auch einen einen einen Zustand haben, dass der Gott keine Schande macht, wenn sie Ihm dann schon gehören soll.

4.3.2 Making one's Christianity known as part of one's witness – an external control mechanism

Most people who engaged with the witness discourse had made known to others, in one way or another, that they were Christians. They were either upfront about their Christian faith or they described their business to others as a Christian company. UK3, for example, reported that most of the time he wore a fish on his jacket, which made people recognise that he was a Christian.

Making known that one is a Christian may in those cases have acted as a control mechanism, because from the respondents' accounts followed that they believed that other people had certain expectations of how Christians should behave and that they may be judged accordingly.

D4, for example, believed that the people he deals with in his business were watching him and expected of him to conduct himself in a certain way.

> And uh, one thing is very important, the people who deal with me watch me three times as much. And apply different standards to Christians. But OK, I'd rather they apply those standards than not apply any standards at all.[69]
> (D4a, heating and plumbing)

Similarly, D10 stated that he felt that his conduct was being watched in his community, which kept him under control, particularly as he also believed that this may have an impact on people's decision whether to go to church or not.

> *D10:* Uh, that's first of all how we run the business, how we behave, how customers, suppliers, whether uh, the local people, how they see us. That's how we make our mark, in any event. So. And since I live in the community people know uh that I'm a Christian and they keep an eye on me. You're kind of being checked upon. That's not a bad thing.
> *Interviewer:* What are people looking for?
> *D10:* Well, I guess they're asking 'What are they doing?' They watch us. Um, I mean, if something goes wrong with Christians, it's just the excuse people need to stay away from church.[70]
> (D10a, manufacture of measuring instruments)

4.3.3 Raising people's attention

> Um, *I think it's nice for people to have a Christian company to compare with. And by doing our work well that's a witness in itself.*
> (UK5a, heating engineer)

For some respondents, however, the awareness of 'being a witness' was not perceived in terms of 'not bringing the Christian faith into disrepute' (only), but they also stated that through some of their actions their faith may get noticed in a positive way.

D2, for example, hoped that some of his behaviour might trigger "a light-bulb moment" in others. He particularly referred to his willingness to help tenants who were disadvantaged.

---

[69] Und äh eins ist ganz wichtig, die Menschen, mit denen man zu tun hat, ähm beobachten einen dreimal so toll. Und setzen ganz andere Maßstäbe bei Christen an. Aber ok, es ist mir lieber, die setzen diese Maßstäbe an, als wenn sie überhaupt keine Maßstäbe ansetzen, nicht.

[70] *D10:* Äh, erst einmal ist so wie wir das Unternehmen führen, wie wir nach außen auftreten, wie Kunden, Lieferanten, ob äh, die Bewohner am Ort, wie sie uns sehen. Damit prägen wir erstmal auf jeden Fall. So. Und wenn man hier am Ort wohnt, dann ist erstmal bekannt, äh, dass ich Christ bin und da wird schon Obacht gegeben. Das ist man schon richtig unter der Kontrolle. Ist gut so.
Interviewer: Wonach wird da geguckt?
D10: Ich denke allgemein, da wird schon 'Was machen die?' Das wird schon geschaut. Also ähm, dass, was bei Christen schief läuft, brauchen viele Leute, um eine Begründung zu haben, nicht in die Kirche gehen zu müssen.

D2: Of course, people that we deal with will certainly notice that. Uh, what we've tried to do is to give people who are disadvantaged a chance when they're looking for housing. *And that may trigger a light-bulb moment for others.*
Interviewer: What does it look like when you give those disadvantaged people a chance?
D2: Well, um, people who have been treated for drug addiction and so; that we don't refuse their applications from the outset, but try and do them a favour. ... That we don't use a cookie cutter approach, but try to help them if possible.[71]
(D2b, property management)

And UK5 stated that it gave him a chance to talk to customers about his faith when he insisted on invoicing people properly.

The times for instance, when a customer says 'Oh I'll pay you cash.' It is so easy to take that cash, put in your pocket. Um, it becomes very easy. And that's where your Christian faith has to step in ... and (you) say 'I don't do that.' *And people say, not, would then say 'Why not?' You then got a situation where you've got chance where you can tell them a bit about your faith.* So there's a positive side as well as a negative side 'cause sometimes the government takes the mick of how much they take out of what we earn.
(UK5b, heating engineer)

D7, on the other hand, referred to the belief that Christ works through believers and explained that this was his way of giving witness: making people notice that something was 'different' rather than talking about his faith.

Um, I have so many encounters with customers and employees, I mean, I've got the chance to, witnessing doesn't always mean to evangelise everyone, it's rather important to me, that um 'Christ in you' in Romans, that it is Him, who meets with people, or that they *feel that something is different here or something is happening here.* I want it to be homogeneous, and not contrived.[72]
(D7b, optician)

When D7 was asked how his witnessing to his customers worked out in practice, he gave one example of how he hoped that his Christian faith produced some 'fruit'[73] that others might notice.

D7: In the final analysis, it is the fruit from my dealings with people. In fact, I'd almost say the encounters themselves are what is most important, and what might come out of them.
Interviewer: What exactly do you mean?
D7: Um [pause] that people get a taste of it, um, that they might [pause] think about things more deeply. Because, I notice, that when something or the other happens and they

[71] *D2:* Klar, die Leute, mit denen wir zu tun haben, die ähm kriegen das schon mit. Äh, was wir auch äh versucht haben, dass wir Leute, die manchmal bei der Wohnungssuche, sage ich mal, benachteiligt sind, dass wir denen einfach eine Chance geben auch. *Dadurch auch ja so einen positiven Aha-Effekt manchmal haben, ähm auslösen.*
Interviewer: Wie sieht das aus, dass Sie die benachteiligten Leute, dass Sie ihnen eine Chance geben?
D2: Naja, ähm, Leute, die zum Beispiel aus aus 'ner Entzugsmaßnahme und so dass wir ähm da die nicht von vornherein ablehnen, sondern es mit denen ähm durchaus auch ihnen einen Gefallen tun. ... Dass wir also nicht nicht versuchen, einfach so ähm Schema F das zu machen, sondern so ein bisschen zu helfen, wo es geht.
[72] Mh, ich hab' ja auch viele viel Begegnungen so mit Kunden und Mitarbeitern also Möglichkeit für, es muss ja nicht immer das Zeugnis sein, dass man hier jetzt jeden evangelisieren möchte, also da ist es mir einfach auch wichtig, dass mh dass, Römerbrief, ‚Christus in euch', dass Er es letztendlich ist, der die Menschen äh, oder der den Menschen begegnet oder das gespürt wird, da ist was anders oder dass da was passiert auf der Ebene. Also dass es, dass es was Homogenes hat und nichts Gestelztes.
[73] Which comes from Matthew 7:20 'By their fruit you will recognise them'.

say 'Yeah, what about my insurance, couldn't I, and couldn't we fiddle the invoice a bit, no one would know.' And 'Everybody is doing it.' And uh, if you make your position clear, it's not so bad for them – and they accept it. They come back, even if they had to pay 20 Euros more, or I'll say 'Well, then I'll give you a discount' or something else. *Um, but to reflect something that may make an impression on them.*[74]
(D7b, optician)

The Christian concept of the 'fruit of faith' also came up in D1's account. He said that he was not very upfront about being a Christian in his day-to-day business life but thought that it was important that people recognised the 'fruit' of his Christian faith.

> I never advertise (my faith) openly or anything. ... But uh, well I think, that because I'm a Christian and see things differently from others that, well, how can I put it, that I automatically do things differently. *I'd rather have 'You'll be known by your fruit' as my motto. And then I think it will also mean something to a non-Christian.*[75]
> (D1a, pharmacy)

One example for him was the 'different' atmosphere in his shop, which he attributed to his faith.

> Yeah, finally I think, well, a lot of people, not only staff but also customers who have been in the shop, have told me so, *that there's a different, a special atmosphere here. And uh, I trace that back to (my faith), you know. ... I believe that something of it shines through.* And that people then like coming here because they know that I'll take them seriously no matter how much business I have with them. So I think that people who come in here feel this.[76]
> (D1b, pharmacy)

4.3.4 Observations

The concept of witness is different from the stewardship concept in two ways. First, it is more general than the stewardship concept, as it concerns any sphere in a believer's life, not just the management or responsible treatment of (business-related) 'resources'. Christians should/might be witnesses of their faith wherever they are and whatever they do, and business is just one context among others. At the

---

[74] *D7:* Ich denke, letztendlich ist es einfach die Frucht aus den Begegnungen heraus. Aber so am wertvollsten würde ich fast sagen, dass die Begegnungen sind, und was möglicher Weise daraus äh entsteht.
Interviewer: Was würde das konkret jetzt heißen?
D7: Mh, [Pause] dass die Leute ein Stück weit was schmecken, mh, dass sie [Pause] vielleicht auch ein Stück weit nachdenken. Weil man das merkt man ja, dass äh wenn mal wieder dann mal so 'ne so 'ne Phase kommt, ‚Ja, aber die Versicherung, ich könnte doch dann und können wir denn die Rechnung so, äh, es merkt doch keiner.' Und ‚Ja, das machen doch alle.' Und mh, da einfach klar Position zu beziehen, das ist für die, das ist gar nicht so schlimm, also... das das akzeptieren die auch. Die kommen auch wieder, selbst wenn sie jetzt 20 Euro mehr zahlen müssen oder ich sage ‚Na, dann gebe ich Ihnen eben einen Rabatt' oder irgendwie was. *Mh, aber [Pause] irgendwie was widerzuspiegeln, was was sie ein Stück weit beeindrucken kann.*

[75] Was ich auf jeden Fall nicht mache, ich ich häng' (meinen Glauben) also nicht nicht aktiv nach draußen oder so. ... Sondern äh, also ich denke, dass dass ich dadurch dass ich Christ bin und viele Sachen eben anders sehe als andere, ja, wie soll ich mich ausdrücken, dass dadurch automatisch viele Dinge anders laufen. Ja und, das ist mir dann lieber. *Ja, so nach dem Motto 'An den Früchten sollt ihr sie erkennen.' Und ich glaube, dass dann auch ein ein Nichtchrist was damit anfangen kann.*

[76] Ja, und letztlich ist es, denke ich, ist es auch 'ne, was weiß ich, also haben schon viele gesagt, nicht nur Mitarbeiter, sondern auch äh Kunden, die hier im Laden waren, dass es irgendwie 'ne andere, *'ne besondere Atmosphäre ist oder so. Und äh ich führ' das eben schon auch darauf zurück, nicht. ... Ich glaube schon, dass ein bisschen was davon auch abstrahlt auch nach außen.* Und dass Leute dann auch gerne kommen, weil sie einfach wissen, dass sie ernst genommen werden, äh, unabhängig davon, wie wie groß das Geschäft jetzt ist, was ich mit denen mache oder so. Also ich glaub' das spürt auch jemand, der der hier reinkommt.

same time, it is a more specific Christian concept as believers regard it as a pointer to their faith. Thus no non-religious people would invoke a 'witness' discourse in this sense to rationalise their actions.[77] Yet the respondents engaged with the witness concept in rather different ways.

A number of respondents talked about not wanting to bring their Christian faith into disrepute or about bringing credibility to their faith as part of their witness. Here the motivation to adhere to certain moral values or standards was not because they primarily considered them moral injunctions that one was required to observe as a Christian but because the respondents did not want to reflect something that might discredit the Christian faith. UK3 illustrated this very well in his account, saying that even though he believed that "Jesus is not a legalistic God" he would not want to bring Christianity into disrepute by being "unrespectable" in his business dealings. This kind of reasoning might be called the 'negative' version of being a witness. Here the respondents usually 'judged' themselves against what they imagined to be the opinions of other (non-Christian) people. Going back to Allport's argument that "the thought, feeling and behaviour of individuals are influenced by the actual, imagined or implied presence of others" (1985, 3), the 'others' here did particularly refer to the imagined presence of other people. In other words, the respondents took into account the role expectations that they believed others had towards Christian believers (Weaver and Agle 2002, 83). Especially those respondents who stated that they were very upfront about being Christian - and in some cases also sought specifically to share their faith with others (see section 5.3.2) - said that they believed that they were being watched by others and that this kept them alert not to do anything that might reflect ill on their faith.

Other respondents framed being a witness in terms of raising other people's attention to their faith. They often may have engaged in the actions that they mentioned for other reasons, for instance, because they felt it was right to hold these values as part of a Christian lifestyle (see section 4.4 on 'holiness'). But they still stated that it was important that other people should take notice of their faith in one way or another, and indeed the actions or attitudes to which they referred might have formed an important part of the witness itself. With this kind of witnessing, it was more about other people noticing something 'positive' rather than about others not noticing anything 'negative'. Thus the external motivation of witnessing had a different emphasis here than with those people who did not want others to think ill of their faith. It might have provided more of an additional aspiration to live up to certain values, rather than (merely) exerted a kind of external 'discipline'. At the same time, elements of internal motivation such as wanting to live out a Christian 'lifestyle', or developing a Christ-like character may have been more strongly involved here as well (see section 4.4). But there were differences among the respondents in terms of how they sought to accompany their 'practical' witness with witnessing by word. Whereas people like UK5 regarded their practical witness as opportunities to talk about their faith, D1 and D7 stated that it was more important that others recognised the 'fruit' of their faith. However, this might not have made a lot of difference on their practices as such, although the less upfront the respondents were about their faith, the less strong the external motivation might have been.

The respondents linked the witness discourse to different kind of practices. As the 'negative' version of witnessing was about 'not doing anything wrong' practices tended to relate here to matters of moral conduct, although D5, for example, linked it to stewardship responsibilities. In the 'positive' version the respondents related witnessing to a wider range of practices: matters of moral conduct (UK5), 'acts of kindness' (D2), or they mentioned how they sought to interact with others in a 'different' way (D7). UK5, on the other hand, applied witnessing specifically to the way he sought to provide his service, which he phrased both ways. He said he did not want to be a Christian that was "not doing his job well" as this would damage the credibility of Christians as well as argued that "doing one's work well" was something that people might notice in a positive way.

[77] One can argue here that non-religious people who hold certain moral ideals and are up-front about them might similarly feel the need to be 'role-models' to communicate effectively to others the moral ideals they hold. However, they would not use religious language relating to the 'witness' discourse and their display of a role model would not point to a religious faith. Moreover, there was sometimes a more *indirect* link between adherence to moral standards and values and 'being a witness', which would not happen in a 'secular' version of the concept (see the following arguments).

In summary, considering oneself a witness of God involved an awareness of how other people might judge or take notice of the respondents' actions in the light of their faith. In the 'negative' version of witness this exerted a strong external discipline on the respondents as they 'did not want to do anything wrong', i.e. they did not want to do anything that discredited the Christian faith. In the 'positive' version, however, being a witness seemed to be more about wanting to communicate something positive about the Christian faith and its values that others should notice.

4.4 Holiness

The concept of holiness in the Christian tradition usually refers to the moral qualities of believers such as purity, integrity, moral perfection, sanctity (Mikolaski 1992). It is deeply bound up with the notion of the holiness of God and the belief that He cannot have communion with the unholy (Bockmuehl 1988). Thus believers are asked to respond to God's holiness, which means that they should reflect God's holiness in their lives. This moral imperative is already present in the Old Testament, where God says to the people of Israel "Be holy because I am holy" (e.g. Leviticus 11:44), but is also taken up in the New Testament, where the Apostle Peter repeats this demand (1 Peter 1:15-16). However, the believers' 'road' to holiness or their 'sanctification', as it is also called, is in (Protestant) Christian doctrine linked with the mediating and redemptive work of Christ (Mikolaski 1992). It is held that the death of Christ on the cross, which signifies death to sin, makes holiness possible for sinful human beings (2 Corinthians 7:1). Believers are asked to respond to this sacrifice made by Christ by seeking to live a holy life, as this is held to be God's purpose for them (2 Timothy 1:9).[78] At the same time, they are also thought to receive an indwelling "sanctifying Spirit" (or the 'Holy Spirit'), which enables them to live a life of holiness (Bockmuehl 1988). The person of Jesus Christ also plays a role in that the life of the incarnate Christ is regarded as a role model or pattern of holiness (Mikolaski 1992). Thus living a life of holiness should lead believers to imitate Christ (e.g. Ephesians 5:1-2, 1 John 2:6, Philippians 2:5) and so to display Christ-like qualities in their lives (Hicks 1996).

Some people in the study specifically referred to notions of 'holiness' in their accounts, and we will explore in this section how they engaged with the concept.

4.4.1 Wanting to be "right before God"

Some respondents alluded to the notion of wanting to be 'right before God' that served as a guide for their actions.

UK4, for example, conceptualised his practices in this way when he was asked how his faith related to his business.

> Um, we we won't intentionally ever um rip anybody off or or do anything that was dishonest. Um, I mean, in our kind of business there are plenty of opportunities. OK, um as there are in other areas of business um to to defraud customers and the taxman and anything else. *Um, we do our best to make sure that um we live and operate our business in a way which um um would be approved of by God. At at the end of the day, um, um to do these things would be sin. ... I mean, if we're cleansed by His blood, OK, um, why sin on small items? OK. Um, and spoil your salvation. OK, OK, so we can go and ask for forgiveness OK, and all that sort of stuff. But why why do it? ... Um, if you want to be right before God um then then why um, why go down that line?*
> (UK4a, car rental)

This was echoed by D3, who said that he had to give up certain practices after he had given his life to Christ because he felt he "could not cheat Jesus". But he specifically referred to the concept of the 'Holy Spirit' to explain a change in his conduct.

> Um, when I first started the business, in '91, at that time I wasn't a Christian yet. Well, I, the Holy Spirit later showed me that I shouldn't do certain things anymore. You know, not making out receipts for some things. Things that are open quotes 'normal' close

[78] Christian doctrine usually distinguishes between 'justification' and 'sanctification'. The former signifies the 'once-for-all' substitute sacrifice of Christ, through which believers are 'justified' before God and which is received by grace, whereas the latter refers to the ongoing moral development of believers. They are neither contradictory, nor should one be considered without the other, but rather as linked concepts (Mikolaski 1992).

quotes in the world - and I thought 'No, that's not OK.' And uh, *you can cheat the taxman but not Jesus.* And uh, I cleared up some matters and uh I think the business hasn't suffered as a result.[79]
(D3a, mobile home rental)

4.4.2 Reflecting Christ

Another group of respondents referred more specifically to the moral example and qualities of Christ that should be reflected in their actions.

UK9, for example, emphasised how strongly he felt that Christ was a model that was to shape his character and guide his actions.

> Um, and, you know, in one sense um, I am who I am because of my my faith in the Lord Jesus. That's my character, you know. And, you know, our aim is always, any Christian should try to be more like Jesus every day.
> (UK9b, building services)

For example, he framed the decision to take on a young ex-offender for an apprentice in that way.

> *Um, you know, I guess it's, you know, you know, as a Christian you you've got to look at the uh, you know, Jesus' first ministry was was often to the outcast in society.* You know, the taxmen, the prostitutes and. And I guess, you know, youngsters that's had a brush with the law and has decided to go straight um, you know, ... So I just, I started a new lad last week.
> (UK9a, building services)

D7, on the other hand, referred to the belief that Christ or His Spirit was working through the lives of Christians, which was to shape his interactions with others in the business and was to bring forth 'fruit' (see section 4.3.3).

> Um, I have so many encounters with customers and employees, I mean, I've got the chance to, witnessing doesn't always mean to evangelise everyone, it's rather important to me, that um *'Christ in you' in Romans, that it is Him, who meets with people, or that they feel that something is different here or something is happening here.*[80]
> (D7b optician)

4.4.3 "What would Jesus do?"

Other people in the study engaged specifically with the question "What would Jesus do" as a guide for their actions, thus regarding Christ as a moral example.

UK3, for example, said that he used the question "What would Jesus do" to check whether the actions in his business were correct.

---

[79] Mh, in der ersten Zeit, wo ich also die Geschäfte angefangen habe, '91, wo ich noch kein Christ war. Also da hab' ich, hat mir das ähm ja, mir der Heilige Geist gezeigt, dass hier, diese oder jene Sache, die kannst du eben nicht mehr machen. Also irgendwelche, ich weiß, naja, eben für irgendwelche Sachen keine Quittung ausgestellt halt oder so. Also was jetzt in der Welt sozusagen ganz normal ist in Anführungszeichen, äh habe ich gesagt 'Nee, das ist nicht ok.' *Und äh, das Finanzamt kannst du beschummeln, aber Jesus nicht.* . Und äh, sind dann, ja, sind halt viele Sachen da bereinigt worden und äh ich denke, dass das Geschäft dadurch nicht schlechter läuft.

[80] Mh, ich hab' ja auch viele viel Begegnungen so mit Kunden und Mitarbeitern also Möglichkeit für, es muss ja nicht immer das Zeugnis sein, dass man hier jetzt jeden evangelisieren möchte, also da ist es mir einfach auch wichtig, dass mh dass, Römerbrief, ‚Christus in euch', dass Er es letztendlich ist, der die Menschen äh, oder der den Menschen begegnet oder das gespürt wird, da ist was anders oder dass da was passiert auf der Ebene.

I often find myself asking whether what I am about to do is correct, would um, would this, *I check myself against um what Jesus would do in similar circumstances.* Sometimes. Um I used the word 'often' a minute ago, if I'm honest, it's not often, it's sometimes. But I think it's enough to stop me getting into bad habits, I hope.
(UK3a, estate agent)

When asked to give an example he talked about the things he sought to avoid when interacting with his customers.

Well, um [pause] pushing people to make decisions, um [pause] winding people up um on offers, um you know, the sort of thing that estate agents are renowned for. You know, winding up one purchaser against another. I don't do that.
(UK3a, estate agent)

D2, on the other hand, said that the question "What would Jesus do" helped him whenever he found himself in potential conflict situations in his business. The example he gave in this context referred to his being considerate of his customers' circumstances.

D2: Uh [long pause] not so much, because I set priorities and say to myself *'I want to do things like I see in the Bible, and what Jesus would have done.'* ... And uh, well, I'm trying to remember if I've ever put my business before my faith – but no, I can't remember doing so. So when I'm not sure I put my faith first – and I've done quite well by that.
Interviewer: Can you give me an example of how you've let the Bible guide you, of what Jesus would have done?
D2: Well, particularly in our line of business uh, there is often a kind of tightrope walk when people are behind with their rent. Um, how persistent you are and how long you'll try and chase those debts up. And um, well, I'll look at these people and try to categorise them. And if I believe that someone has problems but they're not of their own making then we'll say 'OK, we'll leave it at that' and we give him another chance. You can decide either way there.
Interviewer: How does that work out when you give someone another chance?
D2: Well, that we cancel their debt. And um, you know, if they owe 5000 Euros, and we sort of make a deal, depending on someone's situation, to maybe ask them for half of it or some other percentage.[81]
(D2a, property management)

---

[81] *D2:* Äh [lange Pause], so stark eigentlich nicht, weil ich Prioritäten setze und äh sage *‚Gut, ich will es so machen ähm [Pause], wie ich's auch aus der Bibel entnehmen kann und wie Jesus das gemacht hätte.'* ... Und ähm, also ich hab, muss gerade mal überlegen, aber ich kann mich jetzt nicht erinnern, dass ich mich äh, sagen wir, gegen den Glauben und für's Geschäft entschieden hätte. Also im Zweifel entscheide ich mich dann für den Glauben. Und ich, ähm ja, im Ergebnis fahr' ich gut damit.
Interviewer: Was ist denn jetzt zum Beispiel konkret, was Sie aus der Bibel entnehmen, und was, wie Sie sagen, was Jesus getan hätte? Fällt Ihnen da was ein?
D2: Ja, gerade in in unserem Bereich äh, ist es ja häufig so 'ne Gratwanderung, wenn man, ähm, Mietschuldner hat. Ähm, wie hartnäckig und wie lange und ähm, wie intensiv äh äh versucht man, die Forderungen einzutreiben. Und ähm, gut, da guck' ich mir die Leute an und versuche dann halt auch zu differenzieren, und wenn ich nachvollziehen kann, dass einer wirklich ähm Probleme hat, die er äh aus eigener Kraft nicht lösen kann, und wenn er hier vielleicht auch unverschuldet reingeraten ist, ähm, das wir dann halt äh sagen ‚Ok, jetzt lassen wir's mal gut sein' und äh geben ihm nochmal 'ne Chance. Also, da kann man so und so entscheiden.
Interviewer: Und wie wirkt sich das aus, wenn so Sie sagen ‚Jetzt geben wir Ihm noch 'ne Chance?'
D2: Ja, das wir halt auch mal auf Forderungen verzichten. Und dann, na gut, ähm, was weiß ich, wir haben 5000 Euro zu kriegen und dann einigt man sich halt, je nach dem, äh, wie derjenige kann, auf die Hälfte, oder irgend einen Betrag.

4.4.4 Observations

Like the witness concept, the concept of holiness is a more general concept that Christian believers may apply in any sphere of their lives. It is also a rather specific religious concept, i.e. it is not shared with non-religious people, as the reference points for the display of certain behaviours have very explicit religious connotations, such as the moral example of Christ or the sanctifying work of the Holy Spirit.

As a religious concept, the notion of 'holiness' is shared with the Jewish tradition, as already in the (Old Testament) book of Leviticus God commands the people of Israel to "Be holy because I am holy" (e.g. Leviticus 19:2). The difference of the Christian understanding of 'holiness' to the Jewish one is the theological context of the saving work of Christ as well as the focus on the moral example that Christ set through his life and ministry on earth.

Yet, unlike the witness concept, the motivation to display holiness is not so much an external but an internal motivation, as it relates to the relationship of the respondents with God/Christ and not to other people observing their behaviour.

In UK4's and D3's account, this internal motivation expressed itself in wanting to be "right before God" or the belief that one "couldn't cheat Jesus". Thus, similarly to the way respondents rationalised their actions through the stewardship frame, the 'imagined' presence of God/Jesus seemed to have had quite a significant impact on the way they structured their practices as it implied that He might hold them to account for their actions. But, similar to the 'negative' version of witness, the actions they described referred to things that they 'did not want to do wrong'.

UK9 and D7 referred to wanting to display Christ's character, which may be regarded as an aspiration to emulate a moral and spiritual ideal – again a more 'internal' motivation. However, it was pointed out in section 4.3.3 that elements of a 'Christ-like' lifestyle formed part of some people's witness to others, and indeed for some respondents the internal motivation to emulate Christ and the external motivation of wanting to bear witness about one's faith might overlap.

Finally, the question "What would Jesus do?" appeared to be a kind of 'control mechanism' that made the respondents stop and consider their actions in the light of Christ's moral example. Although, again, this control mechanism was an internal one, it may have been quite strong as it referred to the presence of Christ in the respondents' lives.

The application of the holiness concept to business practices, again, differed widely, ranging from matters of moral conduct (UK4, D3, UK3), to 'acts of kindness' (UK9, D2), to general attitudes in dealing with people (D7).

In summary, the concept of holiness refers to the motivation of believers to pursue a lifestyle or actions that seek to live up to God's holiness or are reflective of Christ's character. Even though this is an 'internal' motivation, it might still have quite some considerable strength as it strongly refers to the presence of Christ (or God) in the lives of the believers.

4.5 Drawing on general Christian moral tenets

The Bible may be regarded by theologians and believers as a book that speaks primarily of the relationship of God to humans and to His creation as a whole, a book that reveals "God's purpose to redeem and restore mankind and ... all creation" (Stott 1997, 12). Despite this rather 'grand' purpose, a lot of teaching contained in the Bible is practical ethical instruction (ibid., 13). Even though the biblical narrative provides a specific spiritual context for those instructions, they may also be understood and followed independent of the immediate theological context. In the Old Testament, for example, the Ten Commandments lay out basic rules and principles for living together.[82] In the New Testament, the teachings of Jesus Christ, but also various passages in the Epistles (letters written by the Apostle Paul and other Apostles), offer a rich source to draw on for moral guidance. Examples include the Golden Rule "Do to others as you would have done them to you" (Luke 6:31), "Let your yes be yes and your no, no" (Matthew 5:37), "Look not only to your own interests, but also to the interests of others" (Philippians 2:4), but also the more demanding commandments of Christ such as "Love your enemies" (Matthew 5:44) or "If someone strikes you on the right cheek, turn to him the other also" (Matthew 5:39).

In the study, the frame of 'general Christian moral tenets' was ascribed to the respondents' accounts when they explained or rationalised their actions by saying that they feel they should act in a certain way because they were Christian. But here they did not explicitly link their behaviours with wider spiritual frameworks such as calling, witness, holiness or stewardship.

4.5.1 How was it framed?

This is a more encompassing frame, and the people in the study referred to Christian moral tenets in various different ways. They sometimes talked in terms of following 'Christian' principles, duties and responsibilities that they found in or derived from the Bible. But some also framed their accounts in more emotive terms by also referring to their feelings, their conscience or their character.

Unlike with the other concepts, some respondents that drew on this more general frame also tended to reflect more about additional influences that might impact on their behaviour. UK8, for example, said he was not sure whether it was his Christian faith or other influences that had an impact on some of his business practices, and that he did not reflect that much on the influence his faith may perhaps have on his business.

> I hope I have an influence. Um, [pause] but it probably isn't very overt. Um, [pause] we had uh, we occasionally get clashes of culture [laughs], where, you know, I have to, I I will make a stance on on something. And I get told (by my colleagues) 'It's just because (of) your Christian views.' And very often, very often it isn't just that. There is other reasons as well. And [pause] so it's hard to know. I I don't I don't actively think about that a lot. I kind of just get on with the job.
> (UK8a, industrial design)

As a result, he framed a number of his practices as "Christian behaviour and ethics", such as his integrity in his dealings with clients and his responsibility to treat his staff "fairly and not treat them as they're just simply employees", although he was not sure whether they came from an explicit religious motivation.

Other respondents referred to specific influences such as their upbringing – Christian (D8, D6) or otherwise (UK3) – or their wider life experience that might have also had an impact on their behaviour. When D8, for example, was asked whether his motivations to display certain behaviours and attitudes came from his Christian faith, he said that there had been three influences: his upbringing

[82] Originally referring to the community life of the people of Israel, but in the Christian context widened out as general rules for living together.

(which was in a Christian home), his apprenticeship, as well as specific Bible teaching in his church's youth group.

> [Pause] Do I do it because I'm a Christian? I've been thinking about that as well. A large part comes from the way I was brought up. I think a very very large part. Another ... part comes from [pause] when I was an apprentice, yeah, a little bit from my days as an apprentice. [Pause] Another part comes from the days when I was in my church's youth group, the things I learned there. They had a formative influence in my youth and have taken root.[83]
> (D8b, building services)

In the following we will look at some examples from the respondents' accounts that illustrate the different ways of how people engaged with the frame.

4.5.2 Christian principles

A number of respondents referred to what they regarded as Christian principles when they conceptualised their business practices.

D3, for example, referred to the Golden Rule when he talked about his interaction with his customers.

> Well, *that I treat my customers how I want to be treated*, and this is also a Christian principle. And that I do not take advantage of them, and serve them and help them where I can. And I want to give them good value for their money.[84]
> (D3a, mobile home rental)

UK1 talked about reliability as one of his Christian principles, based on the Quaker principle "your word is your bond". He said the following about a verbal agreement that he had had with a business partner.

> I used to ring him up from time to time and say '(NAME), I really think we should have something in writing. What if, what if there is a misunderstanding?' And he said 'I'm sure' he says 'if there is a misunderstanding, we can sort it out.' *So that was on on the basis of Christian ways of doing things, uh, you are reliable. And uh, and your word is your bond.*
> (UK1a, ceramics industry projects and manufacture of birthpool liners)

He later explained that he had been inspired by the principles in the Quaker tradition, and that "your word is your bond" would go directly back to the Gospel where it says "Let your yes be a plain yes".

D9 derived the principle of honesty from his Christian faith. When he was asked how he brings his faith to his business he said

> And from an ethics point of view, we try and live up to certain standards, honesty above all things.[85] (D9a, security analysis)

[83] [Pause] Mache ich, weil ich Christ bin? Habe ich auch schon paarmal drüber nachgedacht. Einen Großteil kommt aus meiner Erziehung. Ich denke mal, ein ganz ganz großer Teil. Ein ... Teil kommt auch aus meiner [Pause] ja aus meinem aus meiner Lehre, ja, ein bisschen aus meiner Lehrzeit. [Pause] Ein anderer Teil kommt so aus der Jungen Gemeinde, was man da so gelernt hat. Was einem ja dann in in jungen Jahren irgendwie geprägt hat und und was sich dann so festsetzt.

[84] Also *dass ich äh die Kunden so behandle, wie ich auch behandelt werden will* und das ist auch ein christlicher Grundsatz. Und ja, dass ich sie nicht übervorteile und ihnen diene und ihnen helfe, wo ich helfen kann. Und da will ich ihnen gute Leistung äh für ihren Gegenwert gebe.

UK2, on the other hand, talked about a whole Christian "code of conduct" that he sought to follow in his business.

> My my code of conduct basically is a Christian code of conduct.
> (UK2a, manufacture of metal parts)

His "Christian code of conduct" addressed a wide range of business practices. For instance, he kept mentioning that he considered acting "unselfishly" in his business relationships a more appropriate practice than seeking his own interests first. UK2 also mentioned how his Christian code of conduct sought to address the problem of target setting and the conduct of his sales representatives (see Appendix II).

4.5.3 'Duties' and 'responsibilities'

Other respondents framed their responsibilities in terms of duties and responsibilities to underline their commitment to certain behaviour.

UK1 stated that it was a Christian duty to speak up when people were unjustly treated. He specifically referred to an incident, where an employee was badly treated by a customer, and he felt he needed to correct this situation.

> So, also *I have a duty in this way. So this is a Christian duty as well because people are unjustly treated or there are systems of treating people unjustly.* That's a system that is wrong. They should not have a system to ring my um, my person and ask her to speak directly to a customer.
> (UK1a, manufacture of birthpool liners)

UK3, on the other hand, said that it was his responsibility to help others.

> I think it's our, it is generally speaking our (Christian) *responsibility* ... *to help* when asked.
> (UK3c, estate agent)

Helping meant for him, for example, providing financial support to local community causes as well as Christian charities. He also mentioned that he tried to help his employees when they had personal difficulties.

Other respondents framed their actions by saying that they would "not think it was right" or "it was wrong" if they acted otherwise. D5, for example, framed his approach to tax paying like this:

> *I don't mind paying taxes, do I, I'm kind of Christian when it comes to taxes, I don't think it's right if you try to evade tax..* I tell my tax adviser ... 'You can do all the calculations for me, but it has to be within the law. I don't want to pay more than I have to, but I don't want to stretch things either. ... The taxes I'm required to pay, I will pay.' I wouldn't have it otherwise, I'd feel terrible if I knew I've knowingly defrauded the government.[86]
> (D5a, printing)

---

[85] Nicht, und äh in der Ethik versuchen wir, äh gewisse Maßstäbe zu leben, das heißt also der Ehrlichkeit vor allen Dingen.

[86] Ich geb' ja gerne Steuern, nee, *ich bin ja auch mit Steuern bin ich ja auch gewissermaßen christlich*, find' das nicht in Ordnung, wenn man versucht, Steuern zu hinterziehen. Ich sag's meinem Steuerberater ... 'Mein Lieber, kannst du mir gerne jetzt alles ausrechnen, aber es bleibt im Rahmen der Gesetze. Ich will nicht mehr zahlen, als ich muss, aber wir machen keine Tricksereien.' ... 'Was an Steuern gezahlt werden muss, das muss gezahlt werden.' Das kenn' ich dann nicht, also das wär' mir wär' mir schrecklich, wenn ich wüsste, ich hab den Staat wissentlich beschissen.

4.5.4 "I don't feel I can do that" – reflecting on conscience

Some respondents framed their 'Christian' commitment to certain behaviour in a more emotive manner by, for example, referring to their conscience.

Going back to D5's quote in section 4.5.3, he stated that he would pay taxes not only because he did not think it was right to evade tax, but he also explained his stance by using more emotive language, i.e. that he would "feel terrible" if he defrauded the government.

UK11, on the other hand, said that she "felt" she could not do certain things, because she was a Christian. When she was asked about potential conflicts between her faith and her business, she related an incident where she felt she could not behave in a dishonest way.

> Yeah, it's probably silly things. And I can think of a silly thing that's happened this week. Um, I got a new piece of equipment and I dropped it. From a height as high as myself down onto the floor. 'Oh no.' And the staff just said 'But it's alright, parcel it up and say it's been damaged in transit.' *And I just don't feel I can do that. Because it's not honest.* ... But you're probably talking 300, 400 pounds. Stupid me. Um, it's that sort of conflict.
> (UK11a, optician)

Others reported that Christian moral tenets played a role in their conscience, even though they may fail to live up them, like D8 reported.

> With many decisions, *if had to make decisions only according to the law, that is Christian law, our law, I would make different decisions.* Uh [pause] the Jews have 613 or -73 commandments. We've got only ten. You could certainly include the majority of the 600 in those 10 commandments. It's just that the 10 aren't so specific. [pause] *Well, and also in my conscience, I'd make different decisions.* But because of the pressures, there are those pressures and one can't simply ignore them.[87]
> (D8b, building)

The "pressures" he mentioned referred to his being forced to work with backhanders. He said that he had refused to engage in bribery on a bigger scale, but that he would sometimes do it on a smaller scale as he feared that otherwise his employees would lose their jobs.

> There are 20 families or 20 people [i.e. the employees], who depend on you making the right decision, and I'd have liked to make decisions based on my Christian beliefs. But because I know that 20 people are relying on me I've made decisions against myself. Or against my convictions or my faith. ... Then I get a guilty conscience and feel pretty bad about it. But then I'd think about my people and the fact that they've got their jobs, and that we're making money there.[88]
> (D8b, building)

---

[87] In vielen Entscheidungen, *wenn ich nach nach dem Gesetz, nach dem christlichen Gesetz, nach unserem Gesetz entscheiden müsste, würde ich anders entscheiden.* Äh [Pause] die Juden haben haben sechshundertdreizehn oder –dreiundsiebzig Gebote. Wir haben ja bloß zehn. Nach denen kann man dann vielleicht, mit Sicherheit also einen Großteil der 600 da einschließen. Aber nicht so genau beschrieben sind, nicht. [Pause] Ja, und vom Gewissen her würde ich auch gewisse Dinge anders entscheiden, aber weil die Zwänge, die Zwänge sind eben eben da und und denen kann man sich nicht so ohne weiteres entziehen.

[88] Da sind ja sind ja 20 Familien oder 20 Leute, die da an deiner Entscheidung hängen und und von meinem christlichen, von meiner christlichen Einstellung hätte ich oft in den letzten Jahren anders entschieden. Aber bei der Überlegung, dass die 20 Mann hinter mir stehen, ... habe ich dann eben mich gegen mich entschieden. Oder gegen meinen, meinen [Pause] ja, gegen meine Überzeugung oder meinen Glauben oder. Hab' dann immer ein schlechtes Gewissen und fühl' mich dabei auch nicht wohl und. Aber dann habe ich immer an die Leute gedacht, dass doch die Arbeit haben, dass wir da Geld verdienen.

4.5.5 Showing love, consideration and forgiveness

Lastly, although all kinds of different practices may be framed using the Christian moral framework, it was noticeable that a number of respondents used their Christian faith specifically to explain their 'soft' side. They referred to the Christian tenets of love, forgiveness and the consideration of others. At the same time, some respondents also felt that acting according to these tenets this may also have to do with their character, as we shall see in the following examples.

D9 referred to the Christian tenets of "love and forgiveness" that he felt should guide his relationship to his staff. He told how holding on to these tenets helped him to solve a conflict with one of employees.

> Love and forgiveness are also some important standards when dealing with staff. This one employee that I sometimes clash with, uh, I was once on a business trip and on a train in Switzerland and thought long and hard about what to do about him or how we could move forward. Because, I mean, I don't want to sack anyone, or something. ... Uh and then at some point a young lady sat opposite me and read a book ... 'The power of forgiveness'. ... This title alone spoke to me and I knew that I had to forgive him. And I did that inwardly, that freed up my relationship with him.[89]
> (D9b, security analysis)

The interviewer later asked whether people noticed that he applied those values and he replied that his employees might consider him to be softer than others because of that, and that this might cause him some problems.

> *Interviewer:* And with love and forgiveness, do people notice that or is that something you do more inwardly?
> *D9:* That is mostly something more inwardly, uh although, they've noticed that I'm a bit softer than average. It's possible that this is the cause of the problems I have with displaying authority.[90]
> (D9b, security analysis)

For D8, the tenets to forgive others and to consider others had a particularly strong meaning. He said that being more forgiving and more willing to give in was how his faith primarily impacted on his business life.

> *Interviewer:* How does your faith influence what you do in your business? [paraphrased]
> *D8:* Well. [pause] can you separate them? You can't look at them as separate issues. Maybe my employees say at times that I'm too ready to give in, too soft [pause], but I simply can't, perhaps, it's certainly to do with one's character, too. But I believe you can, you can't treat them separately. You can't be a Christian in your private life and think

---

[89] Nicht, also, im Umgang mit den Mitarbeitern ist natürlich Liebe und Vergebung auch teilweise äh ein wichtiger Maßstab. Nicht, diesen bei diesem einen Mitarbeiter, mit dem ich manchmal im Clinch liege, äh da, ich war da mal auf 'ner Dienstreise und saß in der Schweiz in irgend 'nem Zug und äh war so richtig am Nachdenken, was mache ich mit dem und wie kann das weitergehen. Denn ich mein, ich will auch keinen rausschmeißen oder so was. ... Äh und dann äh setzte sich irgendwann mal 'ne junge Frau mir gegenüber und äh, die las ein Buch ... 'Von der Macht der Vergebung'. ... Allein der Titel, der hat mir das Stichwort gegeben und hat das, äh hat mir gezeigt, also dem musst du jetzt erstmal vergeben. Nicht, und ich hab' äh das dann innerlich gemacht und äh konnte ihm dadurch ein bisschen äh freier gegenübertreten.

[90] *Interviewer:* Und mit der Liebe und Vergebung, kriegen das die Leute mit, dass Sie das tun oder ist das mehr so was innerliches oder?
D9: Das ist meistens mehr was innerliches, äh allerdings äh, dass ich an der Stelle vielleicht ein bisschen weicher bin als der Durchschnitt, das haben sie mitgekriegt. Das kann sein, dass das die Ursache von meinem Autoritätsproblem auch ist.

differently in business, I believe. Perhaps others can. *Of course, you are then, well, perhaps more forgiving. More willing to give in, more willing to compromise.*[91]
(D8a, building)

In his account he explained that this, among other things, meant that he sought to forgive those business partners who had done him wrong. Note that even in his account he excused the behaviour of those people.

Interviewer: To what extent does your faith influence your business decisions?
D8: [pause] That's a good question – to what extent does it play a role? [pause] I forgive them. Most of the time [laughs]. Then I do business with them again or give them some advice or tips, or help people who have perhaps knowingly or unknowingly cheated me. But if someone asks me I can't say 'no'. [pause] He must have really disappointed me in business and personally if I refuse to help him. ... One does this these days, and in this economically very difficult time. It's very often the case that someone goes bankrupt, and can't pay or won't pay, because their 'charity begins at home' or because he simply can't do it or or he's got even worse obligations elsewhere. And so we lost a lot of money to business partners or people we thought we knew well. And yet, after a certain period of contemplation, waiting or mourning or whatever you want to call it, they phone you and ask 'Can you help me, can I have a word with you' and.[92] (D8a, building)

He also considered this approach to dealing with people a Christian duty, even though he was aware that others might exploit this.

They know um that I think as a Christian, and then this, it gets exploited more or less, or they try to exploit it. My good-naturedness or my willingness to forgive others. And then they, I think, say to themselves 'Well, he's one of that sort, he'll surely overlook this.' *Um, but that is what you should do, shouldn't you.*[93]
(D8b, building)

Finally, D5 stated that he felt that being a Christian made him more considerate and 'softer' towards his employees.

---

[91] *Interviewer:* Wie bringen Sie Ihren Glauben in Ihren Geschäftsalltag ein? [paraphrased]
D8: Tja. [Pause] Kann man das trennen? Man kann das an sich nicht trennen. Vielleicht in vielerlei Hinsicht sagen unsere Angestellten, dass ich zu nachgiebig bin, zu weich bin [Pause], aber ich kann das einfach, wahrscheinlich, es ist mit Sicherheit auch 'ne Charaktersache. Aber ich glaube man kann, man kann das schlecht trennen. Man kann nicht privat Christ sein und äh geschäftlich anders denken. Das glaub' ich nicht. Vielleicht können das manche Leute auch. *Natürlich ist man dann, ja, vielleicht verzeihender. Nachgiebiger, kompromissbereiter.*

[92] *Interviewer:* Inwieweit spielt Ihr Glaube eine Rolle in Entscheidungen, die Sie im Geschäftsleben treffen?
D8: [Pause] Tja, inwieweit spielt der 'ne Rolle? [Pause] Ich vergebe denen. Meistens. [lacht] Ich mach' dann auch wieder Geschäfte oder gebe Ratschläge oder Tipps oder helfe Leuten, die mich vielleicht wissentlich oder unwissentlich mal betrogen haben. Aber wenn mich dann jemand bittet, kann ich nicht ‚nein' sagen. [Pause] Also der muss mich dann schon wirklich schwer enttäuscht haben, auch menschlich enttäuscht haben, dass ich dem nicht weiterhelfe. ... Man macht das eben, in der heutigen Zeit, in dieser wirtschaftlich schwierigen Zeit, ist es schon noch so, dass das jemand in Konkurs geht, nicht bezahlen kann, nicht bezahlen will, weil ihm das Hemd näher ist als der Rock und.weil es einfach nicht geht oder oder weil andere Verpflichtungen viel schlimmer sind, weil dann, ja, und dann, haben wir also schon an Geschäftspartnern oder oder an Leuten, die man an sich auch gut kennt, viel Geld verloren. Und trotzdem rufen die wieder an nach 'ner gewissen Bedenkzeit, Karenzzeit oder Trauerzeit oder wie man das nennen soll, und fragen dann ‚Kannst du mir mal helfen, kann ich mal kommen und'

[93] Die wissen äh, ja, dass ich vielleicht christlich denke und dann wird das, wird das mehr oder weniger dann so ausgenutzt oder versuchen das auszunutzen. Diese Gutmütigkeit oder dieses Verzeihen oder da wird das, denke ich mal, schon ‚Naja, der ist ja einer von der Sorte, der wird da schon drüber hinwegsehen.' *Äh, aber soll man ja auch, nicht.*

> How else does my being a Christian affect the company? [pause] Well, OK, the difficulties of not being able to have a callous attitude towards my employees, well, whether that's my Christianity or just being being decent. That you don't dare to' hire and fire'. That you try anyway to get along well with your people.[94]
> (D5a, printing)

It was difficult for him, however, to determine whether it was his character or his faith that led him to treat his staff in that way.

> Mh, well, this is, I'm perhaps, yes, sometimes my production managers criticise me and tell me that I'm too soft on the staff, that I should be stricter and more demanding. But, that isn't so much to do with my Christianity, but I'm simply a harmony-craving person. It's, I think, less to do with my Christianity. Well, perhaps a bit, because I'm convinced that these things are temporary, and that perpetually striving for success is not the most important thing in life. And that is, but it's perhaps also more down to character that I like to have peace around me, if possible.[95]
> (D5a, printing)

4.5.6 Observations

As a more encompassing frame, respondents engaged with general Christian moral tenets in various different ways. Some referred to them as principles, duties or responsibilities that they felt they had as Christians, others engaged with them in a more emotive manner and also referred to their feelings or their conscience.

When respondents drew on Christian moral tenets without a wider spiritual reference it was difficult for the researcher (and indeed sometimes for the respondents themselves) to determine whether it was the respondents' faith that influenced their actions or whether their actions were influenced by other factors. For instance, respondents sometimes referred to their conscience or their character as a possible influence on their actions, and it is debatable whether their faith had an impact on their conscience and character, or whether they just happen to be Christians and just happen to have a stronger conscience or a softer character.

Even in the latter case, however, the framing of practices as Christian behaviour could still have a different impact on Christian owner-managers compared to people who construct their moral framework without any recourse to religious beliefs. Although the framing did not explicitly refer to overarching theological concepts that were mentioned in sections 4.1 to 4.4, the belief that one is accountable to God for one's actions or that Christians should seek to emulate Christ in their lives could still have been underlying motivations. Those motivations, although they were not verbalised, could have added extra force to their conceptualisation of their practices. They could, for example, have impacted on their moral awareness (Weaver and Agle 2002, 83), even though they might not have always been able to live up to it. D8, for example, did not dismiss the practice in his trade to pay backhanders as something that one just had to do, but it caused him a guilty conscience because he felt that he did something that also went against Christian moral principles.

---

[94] Was wirkt sich noch aus, wenn ich Christ bin auf die Firma? [Pause] Na ja, gut, die Schwierigkeiten, nicht so kaltschnäuzig mit den Mitarbeitern umgehen zu können, also (ob) das das Christentum oder normaler Anstand. Dass man eben sich nicht traut, zu heuern und zu feuern. Man überhaupt versucht natürlich mit den Leuten im im im Guten klar zu kommen.

[95] Mh, na ja, gut. Das ist, ich bin vielleicht, ja, die Kritik krieg' ich auch manchmal sogar von meinen äh Produktionsleitern, dass ich etwas zu zu mild bin mit den Leuten, dass ich manchmal mehr auf den Tisch hauen sollte. Aber, das hat auch mit Christentum weniger zu tun, sondern ich bin einfach ein relativ harmoniesüchtiger Mensch. Das ist, glaube ich, weniger mit dem Christentum. Ja, vielleicht doch ein bisschen, weil ich sehr stark weiß, dass es vorläufige Dinge sind, und dass es dass der unbedingte Erfolgswille auch nicht ist, das wichtigste im Leben ist. Und das, aber ist vielleicht auch mehr Charakter, dass ich eben gerne, gerne Frieden um mich rum hab', wenn's irgendwie geht.

Even though the tenets or principles that the respondents mentioned were of more general nature, i.e. they could be applied in any sphere of life, their application in a business context may take on a greater significance. For example, the obligation to pay tax has wider implications for a Christian who runs a business than for a Christian who does not. Similarly, whereas the display of love and forgiveness may already present a challenge for a Christian in their personal life, it might be more challenging for a Christian owner-manager to reconcile these Christian values with business life, where they might seemingly or actually be in the way of achieving results. At the same time, some values that the respondents mentioned, such as honesty and reliability, might also help them to build up a good reputation, and thus be in their 'enlightened' self-interest.

The values or principles to which the respondents referred were often not unique to the Christian faith. For example, the Golden Rule is shared with a number of other religious belief systems and is also part of the secular moral framework that people in Western societies often draw on. At the same time, some use of religious language such as the reference to "loving and forgiving others" might be more peculiar to Christianity and may thus more likely mark the respondents out as Christians.

In summary, when believers draw on Christian moral tenets without explicit recourse to overarching theological concepts it is more difficult to determine to what extent they are actually influenced by Christianity or whether other influences play a role as well. The framing of practices as Christian behaviour, however, might make the motivation to display such behaviour stronger.

5. The Christian faith providing contexts for action

Not all statements that the people in the study made regarding the influence of Christianity on their business practices could be captured within the framework of the Christian concepts that were outlined in chapter 4. The respondents sometimes referred to some wider contexts that the Christian faith provides, and those contexts will be explored in this chapter. Such a contextual perspective helps to provide a more complete picture of how Christianity might influence Christian SME owner-managers' conceptualisation of practice.

A rather obvious context was the Christian community of faith, which constituted for most people in the study an important influence on the conceptualisation of their practices. Section 5.1 explores how faith community membership structured the practices of the respondents, and will regard here both the more sociological aspects of community membership as well as some theological aspects, i.e. how the respondents engaged with Christian beliefs and concepts concerning the community of believers. This section will also look at how the respondents related to the Christian community as a potential provider of spiritual and moral support for their business life.

Section 5.2 takes up the point that was made in chapter 4 about the presence of God that was implied in the Christian concepts that the respondents used, and how this had a potential impact on their behaviour. This section looks at some of the respondents' statements in which the presence of God played some role in the way they explained and rationalised their practices, but which were more independent of the use of specific concepts or frames. As this context refers to the respondents' 'inward' spiritual beliefs, this context is less obvious than faith community membership, but might still have some impact on their behaviour.

Finally, a number of the respondents' statements indicated that they regarded their business as an environment that carried spiritual significance. Section 5.3 explores how differently the people in the study made sense of the spiritual meaning of their place of work, and how those spiritual meanings impacted on the conceptualisation of specific practices. This contextual perspective seeks to complement the perspective provided in chapter 4, as those spiritual meanings might also cut across some of the Christian concepts and frames that were outlined there.

5.1 Working as member of the Community of Faith

Being a Christian also means to be a member of the Christian community of faith, and this faith community membership might have, in turn, an impact on the way Christian SME owner-managers conceptualise a range of different practices. Their conceptualisations might be influenced by both, general sociological aspects relating to community membership but also by certain spiritual beliefs concerning the community of faith.

This section looks at some aspects of the community of faith that, according to the respondents' accounts, had quite a significant impact on their conceptualisations of practice. First, we will look at the faith community as a social network and how this influenced their business practices. Secondly, we will consider the significance of the faith community in terms of their business-related civic and charitable engagement. Lastly, we will look at how the respondents related to the notion of the faith community as a provider of spiritual and emotional support for their business life.

5.1.1 The faith community as a social network

The Christian community played quite a central role in UK5's (heating engineer) conceptualisation of business practices. We will therefore focus first specifically on his account and later discuss the points he raised in his account by bringing in the views of other respondents.

For UK5 the Christian community constituted a very important network with regards to his business. Firstly, the community presented quite a large market for him. He said that although he initially treated advertisements in Christian magazines more as a means to give donations than to gain business, joining a nation-wide Christian business directory proved to be a very prudent business decision.

> And the first one that actually ever paid off absolutely hugely was Christian Pages. And again, there was another one, came round, yes, 80 pounds, off you go. Within a week I had probably twenty times that. It it was huge. And the nice thing about it, they rung up and expected us to be Christians. Which we found excellent. 'Cause then you're going and actually talking to Christians. And that's been, that's been very good.
> (UK5a, heating engineer)

He stated that as a result he did a lot of business with Christian individuals as well as with churches. But he said that he would also like to see more networking with Christians who work in other building trades, as he recognised that there were many opportunities to pass work on to them.

> It'd probably be helpful to know other Christian companies that are in the same or um similar um trades. You know, if I knew Christian builders, for instance, uh Christian electricians, Christian carpenters, um, I'd be without any shadow of doubt be able to give them considerable amount of work. At the moment, ... there is no there is no Christian tradesman that I know. That would be that, seriously lacking. Seriously lacking. ... I can't say it works, I don't know how it works for others, but as I say, *I would love to see more community*, so to speak. In in the trades. 'Cause there must be some good Christian builders out there.
> (UK5a, heating engineer)

Secondly, he recounted how he recruited nearly all of his staff from churches of which he had been a member or from a wider circle of Christian friends. The reasons for this varied. First, he believed that Christian employees would have the morals that were required in his line of business.

> But I would love, I must admit I do, the thing is, you're going in people's homes. And we are regularly given the keys. So, we're going to an empty house. Um, they often leave

blank cheques on tables, and that's also a common occurrence. *So anybody that works for me has to be absolutely trustworthy.* And you've only got to go, you know, if something gets stolen, I mean, that'd be ..., you know, bad word travels much faster than a good one, unfortunately.
(UK5a, heating engineer)

He also referred to the aspect of wanting to be a witness through his business, for which he needed his employees to be trustworthy Christians.

That was one of my prime incentives to have Christians that were trustworthy. They're going into people's homes, they would do their job right, do their work right. And and leave that essence behind. Because then it's a witness as well as a job as well a means of earning money.
(UK5b, heating engineer)

Secondly, he said that he preferred to employ Christians for his own protection, as he expected them not to cheat him.

If you take on somebody that that is not honest with you, as in not a Christian, it quite likely starts taking as much private work off the back of your customers and then go and build their own business.
(UK5a, heating engineer)

At the same time, he was aware that being a Christian "doesn't always guarantee", which he said he had experienced a couple of times. He mentioned that once he had to make one of his Christian employees redundant as that person did not work well. In his second interview he reported that he had recently found out that another of his Christian employees had defrauded him and secretly started a business by taking away his customers – doing exactly the things he had sought to avoid. These occurrences, however, did not seem to have changed his overall attitude.

A third reason for taking on Christian staff was to help people of his community to get into employment. He gave the following explanation as to why he took one of his employees on.

(NAME) was also taken on by myself. Um, because he was (working for) a printing company ... And he knew it was a dead-end job *and, ... because he is a Christian, took him on, put him through college.*
(UK5b, heating engineer)

Business through the faith community

A number of other respondents recognised like D5 the value of having a market in the community of faith, either through their local congregation or through the wider Christian community. UK9 was one such respondent.

I get I get a lot of work from the congregation. Um, and uh, you know, the reputation is spread through them, I suppose.
(UK9a, building services)

D6, on the other hand, was excited about the possibilities of a business directory that his church had recently issued and that listed all business people that were members of the congregation.

It was interesting in that more and more people from the congregation turned to us, uh and we got a lot of work through it. And uh this will continue to happen. And uh I told an

old friend of mine about it ..., he runs a larger company. And he, very dryly, remarked ... 'Remember, that's how the Jews have survived for 5000 years.'[96]
(D6b, decorating and special surface coatings)

Others had signed up like UK5 with various regional or even nation-wide Christian business directories, hoping to get business through it.

We also have (here), a Christian business directory. ... Christian, there are several things. If anything gives that impression, I'm in it.[97]
(D10b, manufacture of measuring instruments)

Some respondents, however, did not feel very comfortable with overly advertising their faith in order to gain business. One example was UK3.

On the other hand I don't flaunt my Christianity as I feel, sometimes I feel I should flaunt my Christianity. Um I should, um I should make it clearer. And then I think to myself, well, then it looks as though I'm **using** it to get instructions, you know. So it, it's very difficult to strike a balance if you, if you're serious.
(UK3a, estate agent)

Shared values

UK5's account implied that dealing with other Christians - customers and employees - in his business was also underpinned for him by a sense of shared values that arise from the Christian belief system.

UK3, by contrast, gave the sense of 'shared values' a slightly different emphasis, when he reported on his dealings with Christian clients. He expressed his belief that the basis for them doing business with him was more an extension of their trust in God, probably referring to the accountability to God that being a Christian implies.

Um people that I know are Christians that I do business with um are happy to do business with me and they know that if, as I'm a Christian I take it seriously. I'm not just sort of a ... Sunday Christian. Then they're usually quite happy just to say 'That's fine, (NAME), whatever it takes, that's that's fine.' Just. And leave it all up to me. Um, and to trust me implicitly because they know they're not trusting me, they're praying about it and they're trusting God.
(UK3a, estate agent)

As in the case of UK5, the accounts of some respondents also reflected the tension of their belief that Christians make better employees and of their experience that Christians do not necessarily work better than others.

D8, for example, expected employees to behave more ethically if they had an affiliation to a church. He reported that religious affiliation would be a crucial criterion in selecting a new secretary (as the previous one had to be made redundant due to some irregularities in her work).

And when we recruit our new secretary, I'd like to apply different criteria. ... I'd love to give her a questionnaire that she needs to fill in. *I'd like to know, I'd really like to know*

---

[96] Es war interessant, dass sich immer mehr aus der Gemeinde an uns gewandt haben, dass äh dort also doch 'ne ganze Menge Aufträge reingekommen sind. Und immer noch äh äh reinkommen werden. Und äh ich hab' das also einem langjährigen Freund ... der ist ähm Industrieunternehmer ... erzählt. Da sagte der so ganz trocken, ... 'Denk' mal dran, so haben die Juden 5000 Jahre überlebt.'

[97] Gibt's auch (hier), ein christliches Branchenbuch. ... Christliche, es gibt mehrere Sachen. Also was da irgendwo den Touch hat, da bin ich mit drin.

whether she is member of a church, whether it says Protestant or Catholic[98] *on her tax card.*[99]
(D8b, building)

But other respondents were clear that although they had taken on Christians, it did not mean that they worked better than others. D4, for example, said how disappointed he had been by the behaviour of one of his Christian employees.

> And with another (employee), he is also a Christian, and we'll need to talk to him again, he's a young Christian. I'm really hurt by this. But I think, as long as he hasn't grasped it and continues to say 'I don't give my best for the company in the first place, but in the first place to God', uh then something isn't quite right.[100]
> (D4b, heating and plumbing)

Helping each other out

Whether shared values played a role or not, employing or trading with other Christians often had a sense of 'helping each other out' for the respondents, rather than a (mere) personal benefit from the trade relationship. As we have seen, UK5 took fellow Christians on "because they needed work". UK4 took the same approach by providing part-time employment for the pastor of a small church.

> Um not all the staff are Christian. Um, but quite a quite a few of them are. *Um, I mean, we have a pastor who comes and works for us um from another small church. To help his income a little.* Just, again, part-time.
> (UK4a, car rental)

And UK10 said that he chose to trade with an independent Christian supplier and employed a Christian as his stock-taker.

> Um, but I'm I'm sure there are other independent pharmacists who who do support independent traders in the same way, partly because they're independent as well. So so it it's probably not just something I do but it's only, I mean, (NAME) I I specifically deal, like to deal with him because, you know, he is a Christian as well. ... My uh stock-taker that I employ once a year um major part of the reason for keeping him on is because he is a Christian. Um, so it probably does affect, I haven't really thought about it before, but actually it does affect who you trade with.
> (UK10b, pharmacy)

Sometimes respondents even regarded their trading with other Christians as a specific obligation, rather than something from which they could personally benefit. UK3, for example, said this about his decision to advertise in a nation-wide Christian business directory.

---

[98] In Germany members of mainstream churches pay church tax as part of their income tax and church affiliation is noted on their tax card

[99] Und äh werden bei der Auswahl unserer neuen Sekretärin ja doch vielleicht andere Kriterien ansetzen. ...Am liebsten würde ich einen Fragebogen hinlegen, der dann auszufüllen ist. Ich würde schon wissen, mich würde schon interessieren, ob sie kirchlich, auf ihrer Steuerkarte EV oder KATH steht.

[100] Und mit 'nem anderen [Mitarbeiter], ist jetzt auch ähm ein Christ, mit dem wir nochmal ein Gespräch haben werden, das ist ein junger Christ. Das tut mir richtig weh. Aber ich denke, äh sobald das im, solange nicht jemand das in den Griff bekommt und sagt, Ich geb' nicht mein Bestes an erster Stelle für die Firma, sondern an erster Stelle für Gott', äh dann stimmt irgendwas nicht.

Interviewer: Do you get any business through the Christian business directory?
UK3: No. [laughs] No, I get problems from it. 'I'm over here in (PLACE NAME IN SOUTHERN ENGLAND) and I've got a property in (PLACE NAME IN NORTHERN ENGLAND) that I've been left by Auntie Maude. Can you help?' No. I only, I only subscribe to it because I know the bloke who runs it. ... He's a nice bloke. And it's a nice idea. It doesn't help me, but it helps everybody else. And if he didn't have an estate agent, you know, he's got an estate agent in at the moment, and that's me. [laughs] One in the country.
(UK3c, estate agent)

5.1.2 The community of faith as a context for business-related civic engagement and charitable giving

The community of faith also had an impact on the way the respondents conceptualised practices that were to benefit others beyond their day-to-day business activities. This section will explore how the respondents considered the community of faith a place for offering practical help and financial support to other Christian individuals and to the Christian community as a whole in their capacity as business people.

Some people in the study reported how they specifically offered help to members of the Christian community that was in one way or another related to their business activities. D6, who runs a decorating business, for example, stated that he liked to offer practical help through his business to fellow church members who were in need.

> Um, I would, for example, we've done this before, if there was someone in our church, whoever, be it man, woman, young, old, uh family, on benefits. Uh, and someone would tell me 'Listen, their flat looks quite shabby, no one has done anything there in 20 years. Would you like to help?' Or 'Can you help?' Uh, I would, of course say yes.[101]
> (D6b, decorating and special surface coatings)

D7, on the other hand, stated that he used part of his company profits to support a Christian family that lived on benefits.

> There is a family that we support. At the moment they have no income apart from unemployment benefits. They are friends of ours. We've known them for a while, *they are spiritual people* and we provide them with a certain amount of money every month.[102]
> (D7a, optician)

The reason to help specifically fellow Christians – rather than other individuals - may have varied, and proximity to those people may probably have played some role there, too. Some respondents, however, gave more specific reasons as to why they particularly support Christian people. D7, for example, rationalised his support of that Christian family (see above) as a way to show his gratefulness, as the person he supports had been important for his own spiritual development.

---

[101] Ähm, also ich würde zum Beispiel, haben wir auch schon gemacht, ... wenn die wenn jetzt, wenn wenn ich jetzt erfahre, innerhalb unserer Gemeinde ist jemand, der also, was weiß ich, Frau, Mann, egal wie, jung, alt, äh Familie, Sozialhilfeempfänger. Äh und mir würde jemand erzählen ‚Du hör' mal, in der Wohnung sieht's aus, also seit 20 Jahren ist da nichts gemacht worden. Äh würdest du da mithelfen?' Oder ‚Kannst du da helfen?' Äh, würd' ich sofort ja sagen.

[102] Wir haben eine Familie, die wir unterstützen. ... Die hat im Augenblick außer Arbeitslosenhilfe, ähm, kein Einkommen. Sind Freunde von uns. Wir äh kennen uns schon 'ne Weile, *sind [Pause] geistliche Leute*, und die versorgen wir also mit einem gewissen Betrag im Monat.

Interviewer: What made you support this family?
D7: [pause] Mh, firstly he is like a spiritual father to me. Um, he's been mentoring me a lot in my walk as a Christian, ... mh yeah, and plain and simply because we see that they can hardly make ends meet. Uh, and if there is no other source of income, it became clear to us that they're really struggling.[103]
(D7a, optician)

UK5 had also reported on helping fellow church members in need through his business. For instance, he said that he sometimes fitted heating systems for free or at very cheap prices for them. He, however, rationalised his prioritisation of the faith community like this:

> The only hard thing about that is that there are a lot of people out there who would take advantage. And I've seen that as well.
> (UK5b, heating engineer)

Other people in the study mentioned that they also supported the community as a whole through their business. The following quotations are some examples of how respondents reported on their benefiting the church community through offering their business skills for free or at highly discounted prices.

D8 reported on the practical and free help that he offered when a home for a vicar was being built.

> When one or the other vicar is having a new home built, then we level off the garden and drill a few holes et cetera.[104]
> (D8a, building)

D6 also referred to building work, and specifically the high discount that he had offered when he refurbished his local church's chapel.

> As a company we refurbished the chapel, and we only charged for the materials.[105]
> (D6a, decorating and special surface coatings)

UK2, finally, reported on his willingness to use his more generic business skill of being a good project leader in church committee work.

UK2: And I much prefer, I'm a bad committee person. ... [laughs] But I'm a very good project person. So if there is a project to do, which somebody wants to get off the ground. Um then I'm I'm the person to do it. ...
Interviewer: What sort of projects?
UK2: Well, it can be um 'Should we do this or should we do that?' sort of project. Um don't give it to a committee 'cause they will never decide. Um ,What do you think about this, (NAME)? Could you give us some thought and talk to one or two people and let me know?' ... Um the work of that finance committee that I was chair of was project was project-based, really.
(UK2a, manufacture of metal parts)

---

[103] *Interviewer:* Was hat Sie denn bewogen, die Familie zu unterstützen?
D7: [Pause] Mh, erstmal ist das für mich 'n geistlicher Vater. Ähm, er hat mir also auch sehr viel auf dem so meinem Weg, hat er mich begleitet. .... mh, ja und letztendlich auch einfach, wir sehen, dass [Pause], dass es mit der Grundversorgung äußerst knapp ist, ja. Äh, wenn da nichts mehr reinkommt, dann, das das war für uns deutlich, das hat sich abgezeichnet, dass dass die sehr knapp sein müssen, dass es da sehr eng wird.

[104] Wenn einer oder der andere Pfarrer ein Haus baut, dann müssen wir den Garten machen und paar Löcher bohren und.

[105] Die Kapelle zum Beispiel haben wir als Firma gemacht wo also nur die Kosten des Materials bezahlt werden mussten.

A large number of people in the study specifically mentioned that they had committed themselves to financially supporting their church or other Christian community activities. Whereas any Christian that receives some kind of income could make such a commitment, the respondents usually referred to the income that their business generates for them. Only few respondents made a clear distinction between what they supported as a business and what they supported personally.

Some respondents referred, like UK9, specifically to 'tithing'[106], which implied that their charitable giving was to be used within the faith community context.

> Yeah, I I guess, I mean, with um um [pause] uh as I, as a believer um I I my my giving, I, my, I tithe my income. So I give the 10 percent of my income. Um, I give 5, half of it I give to my local church. I think as Scripture says, yes, that you give, that you give money to the elders and then they distribute as they think fit. Um, so I I, there is other bits of Scripture that, you know, allows to to give to what you believe in yourself. So, half of it I give to the church directly. The other half I give to ... other areas of need. But all my giving is Gospel-based.
> (UK9a, building)

For a number of respondents, their commitment to pay tithe to his church was something that surpassed any other commitment to other charities, like D1 reported.

> My tithe goes mainly to my church, because I have, you know, I've committed myself to it or so. That's therefore important to me.[107] (D1b, pharmacy)

UK3 also said that although he supported 'secular' causes as well, the larger part of his financial contributions went to Christian charities.

> Financially, it's Christian charities. ... *Um because I think that's an appropriate thing to do. Um, it it comes out of my tithe. And therefore it's not my money.*
> (UK3b, estate agent)

A few respondents drew a connection between financial giving to the faith community and the well-being of their business and so referred implicitly to the biblical promises that giving one's tithe entails (see footnote 106). Such reasoning provided them with an additional motivation to direct their charitable giving towards faith community activities. D3 was one such respondent.

> I've also had the feeling with giving my tithe that when I had particularly good business and then I gave some of it away, and then again something good came along. Well, that's a kind of affirmation for me.[108] (D3a, mobile home rental)

---

[106] Tithing is a Christian practice that has its roots in the Old Testament. The key passage for understanding what tithing is about is Deuteronomy 14:22-29. From the passage two meanings of tithing can be derived. The first one is that God commands the people of Israel to eat a tenth of all that their fields produce in the presence of God in order to revere and be grateful to Him. The second purpose of tithing refers to the provision of food for the Levites (those who performed religious duties and did not have allotments to support themselves) as well as for the strangers, orphans and widows who lived among the people of Israel and who had no means to support themselves. Another passage that is often referred to in Christian teaching is Malachi 3:4, where God promises that if the whole tithe is brought into the storehouse, God will bless the people.
In the less legalistic New Testament the emphasis is not on setting exactly ten percent aside, but on giving what the believer "has decided to in his heart to give ... for God loves a cheerful giver." (2 Corinthians 9:7). The Apostle Paul often addressed in his letters the subject of giving in terms of supporting fellow Christians and churches that were in need. In the contemporary context, believers often consciously set one tenth of their income aside to give them to the church or church-related purposes.

[107] Mein Zehnter geht hauptsächlich äh in unsere Gemeinde, weil ich mich da auch, ich sag' mal, äh für die Sache irgendwo verpflichtet habe oder so. Ist mir dann auch wichtig.

Yet even though the respondents reported that a large part of their charitable giving and engagement was strongly linked with the community of faith, the faith community activities that were supported included activities that sought to 'reach out' to people outside the faith community. This 'reaching out to others' that the respondents talked of had either a strong spiritual dimension or was of more 'practical' nature. Examples of 'spiritual' outreach related to the support of missionaries and missionary organisations (e.g. D2, D5) or of organisations that sought to reach other business people with the Gospel (e.g. D3, D10).[109] Examples of 'practical' outreach related to the sponsoring of children in Third World countries through Christian charities (D5, UK5, UK11) or the support of other kinds of Christian social projects (e.g. D3, D4, D8, UK2, UK8, UK9). However, some respondents who supported Christian social projects stated explicitly that it was important for them that those projects had a spiritual context. The respondents' support of these kinds of faith-community related activities will be explored a little further in section 6.3, when we will look at the respondents' relationships to wider society.

5.1.3 The Christian community offering spiritual and emotional support

Some scholars (e.g. Verstraeten 1998, Rossouw 1994, Childs 1995) stress particularly the importance of the communal aspect of the Christian faith (see section 2.2.1). They argue that if the faith community offers spiritual and emotional support to Christian business people, they are more likely to think about their business activities from a spiritual point of view and to integrate their faith into their business lives. This section reports how differently the people in the study related to the community of faith in terms of the support and help that they received or expected from it.

UK3, for example, said that he did not expect his church to provide specific support with regards to his capacity as a business person. For him it was sufficient that his church provided a space for communal worship, from which he gained general encouragement.

> I get support from my church because I go there on Sunday and they give me an opportunity of worshipping God with other people. And that in itself is support. Um it encourages my faith and my faith is really the important thing when it comes down to it. Um, it's important in my business, although it's not to the front. It's it's in the background what I rely on in the end. No, I don't need (any other) support from the church.
> (UK3a, estate agent)

For others, it was important that the community of faith provided some kind of space, in which they could discuss business-related issues and problems.

D5 and UK11 took a rather personal approach. Both reported that they had prayer partners with whom they discussed their business problems and prayed over them. D5 specifically emphasised the opportunity to pray for guidance together but also on the opportunity of receiving pastoral care.

> Once a week we do something very pietistic[110], once a week my brother and I meet up and pray for the company. We do that on a regular basis. ... That is extremely important for me, because I run the company as a Christian and because when I have to deal with difficult problems, whenever possible, I really want a little bit of guidance and wisdom

---

[108] Also auch so mit dem mit dem Geben des Zehnten habe ich dann auch immer irgendwie so die, das Gefühl gehabt, also, ja wenn man eben besonders gute Geschäfte gemacht hat und hat dann irgendwie was abgegeben, dass danach kam dann wieder was Gutes. Ja, also, so diese Bestätigung habe ich dann schon.

[109] 'Spiritual' denotes here efforts to 'spread the Gospel'. Interestingly, when the researcher asked some respondents why they supported missionaries they did not give a spiritual reason but rather said simply that they wanted to help those people or that they helped them because they were friends of theirs.

[110] 'Pietistic' refers to Pietism, a Protestant Christian renewal movement in Germany that started in the 17th century

from God. And it's also a way, it's also a kind of pastoral care thing with my brother.[111]
(D5a, printing)

UK11, on the other hand, felt that her prayer partner was a person to whom she was specifically accountable for her actions.

> Um, I would, um what's the word, oh there is a word, um, I have a close friend who I would um, who I talk with and pray with a lot. And um I can't remember that word when you're with someone and they keep an eye on you sort of thing. ... Um, but she is almost, I would feel responsible, if I did something silly in the business or something way off line (NAME) would pull me back on it.
> (UK11a, optician)

Other respondents talked about their church home groups, in which they received some support and help for their business life.

D2, for example, said that he was involved in a home group that was also attended by other business people. He said that although it was not the focus of the group to specifically talk about work, a lot of the biblical stories they looked at there related to issues in the workplace. This, so he said, was often the trigger to discuss work-related problems, such as honesty and dealing with difficult customers.

UK7 on the other hand reported that he had started a home group in which they specifically focused on how the Christian faith relates to the world of work, thereby promoting his integrative view of business and faith.

> We we we, my wife and I run a a Monday night home group (which) is related to our church there. Um but ... it's a very unusual group, it's for it's for, specifically for business people. Um, and we look at issues that affect people in the, in business or in the workplace. And and we we pray a lot for each other's businesses. We enjoy that. It's good.
> (UK7a, engineering)

However, especially in the context of the wider church, some people in the study reported on a more uneasy relationship with the faith community in their capacity as business people.

D5 specifically complained about ministers who have left-wing attitudes and are critical of capitalism and, as a result, business people's activities. He specifically referred to the fact that the profits that business owners generate could be put to good use in church and here reflected his own understanding of how business and faith should interrelate (see sections 4.1.1 and 5.3.1).

> I once discussed this with a minister and said to him 'If only you looked after your business people better. And if you managed to attract business people to church and then preach at them so that they part with their tithe, then you would be better off.' That's really true. ... And uh I'm sure there are quite a few bad business people out there. But what the church is lacking at the moment, are really not poor people who need help.[112]
> (D5a, printing)

[111] [E]in Mal die Woche machen wir was ganz pietistisches, ein Mal in der Woche treffe ich mich mit meinem Bruder zu einer Gebetsstunde für die Firma. Das machen wir halt regelmäßig. ... Das ist mir extrem wichtig, weil ich den den, die Firma als Christ führe und weil ich auch wirklich möchte, dass ich da in in in schwierigen Problemen, a, sagen wir mal, wo wo immer es möglich ist, doch ein bisschen Leitung und Weisung von Gott haben will und auch 'ne Art, das ist auch ein bisschen was seelsorgerliches mit meinem Bruder.

[112] Ich hab' mal zu 'nem Pfarrer in der Diskussion gesagt ‚Wenn ihr bloß eure Unternehmer pflegen. Und wenn ihr euch die Unternehmer unter die Kanzel holen, und dann den Zehnten abpredigen, dann tät's euch wohl besser gehen', ja. Ja, das ist so. ... Und und äh, es gibt bestimmt viele Bösewichter an Unternehmern. Aber was momentan der Kirche fehlt, sind wirklich nicht die Armen, an denen man Gutes tun kann.

UK2 did not feel, either, that churches understand the benefits of business activities. But he, by contrast, referred more to his understanding that businesses were also 'caring' professions.

> I mean I I used to do the intercessions. And um, in church, and I used to I used to pray for business people and I used to pray for businesses. But I instead of, and I didn't want people to think that I was me praying for me. So the way that I used to do it was, um I used to talk about the health businesses. Um, that they, you know, that they may do better and they'd be more healthier and bring happiness and wealth to our community for instance. Or when firms were in trouble you know, hope that they will get better soon. And if there were redundancies, you know, that they were in difficulty and there was clearly a lot of unhappiness .... So trying, I try and pray for it in that sense. And try and and get people to try and think but actually business is part of the caring professions. You know, you get in church, they pray for the caring professions. And I think 'Oh good, that's business.' Well, most people's concept is that it is not a caring profession, being in business. But it should be, and I think in a lot of cases it is.
> (UK2a, manufacture of metal parts)

UK11, on the other hand, said that she did not think that the work she does deserved the same attention in church as activities that she considered to be more worthwhile causes within the Christian context.

> I don't think it needs to be a church-wide thing, because it's not as if I'm doing any sort of ground-breaking evangelistic work or anything totally worthwhile. You know what I mean. I mean, it is a business in the end, it's not a charity or something like that or.
> (UK11a, optician)

5.1.4 Observations

A number of respondents regarded the community of faith as an important social network for their business. We see here the typical constituents of what scholars call 'bonding' social capital (Putnam 2000, 22, Adler and Kwon 2002). Members of the community of faith recognise their common bond in terms of their religious identity, and, in most cases, also in terms of shared moral values ('Christian' values or 'biblical' values). As a result, community members may prefer to give business to Christian business people or Christian business people prefer to trade with each other or recruit Christian employees. As mentioned by some respondents, this sense of community is fostered through church-wide or even nation-wide Christian business directories. In both countries, Germany and the U.K., the researcher came across a number of web-based business directories, which Christian business people could subscribe to. This phenomenon may appear to be a little odd in cultures that are largely based on Christian values. It may, however, indicate that committed Christians now constitute a minority in Western secularised societies and that they therefore see more of a need to show mutual solidarity. D6's comparison of the Christian community to the history of the Jewish community underlines this. This behaviour also shows some similarities to that within ethnic minority communities, where the strong bond of ethnic identity may shape the practices of an SME owner-manager who is member of this ethnic group (Portes 1998, Janjuha-Jivraj 2003). At the same time, the Christian moral heritage may no longer be taken for granted in a secularised society, so that practising Christians may see the need to stand out by openly affirming their commitment to 'Christian' values and by trading with people who have the same basis for their values.

Although the respondents often reported that they benefited personally from the social network that was constituted through the community of faith, some of the respondents' actions were more characterised by 'giving' rather than 'receiving'. Examples were UK3's willingness to advertise in a Christian business directory even though it did not get him any business or UK10's decision to trade specifically with a Christian supplier. At the same time, some respondents reported that despite shared identity, Christian employees or business partners did not always live up to the respondents' expectations (UK5, D4). Moreover, even though they recognised the benefits of being able to trade with the faith community, a few respondents said they were cautious about instrumentalising their faith just to gain more business (UK3).

More generally, the business seemed to be a context for some respondents in which they could offer help to fellow Christians. Some respondents reported that they had offered employment opportunities to fellow Christians who were in need (UK4, UK5), whereas others talked about providing Christian individuals who were in need with financial (D7) or business-related practical (D6, UK5) support. They may thus have regarded the community of faith, rather than the geographical or any other community, as their primary community within which they help others. On the one hand, proximity to fellow Christians rather than to people outside the community of faith may play a role here. At the same time, one could argue that in those cases the Christian commandment "Love one another" (1 John 3:11), which refers to fellow believers only, takes precedence over the more inclusive "Love your neighbour" (Luke 10:27), which refers to everybody.

A number of respondents also reported on being engaged in the community of faith in their capacity as business people. For instance, they either stated that they provided substantial financial support to their church and church-related activities from their business income or that they provided business-related practical support (e.g. through offering free services or advice), all of which was to benefit the community as a whole. This engagement may have been regarded by some respondents as a natural element of being an active faith community member. However, other respondents might have considered their engagement in and for the community of faith as having particular spiritual importance and/or something that was more in line with their Christian identity, rather than engagement in 'secular' communities. For example, some respondents referred to the Christian concept of 'tithing' when they talked about their charitable giving. As 'tithing' has strong spiritual connotations, the financial giving of those respondents was naturally geared towards the community of faith and specific Christian causes, although a number of these had a 'social' dimension, i.e. they also benefited the wider community.

Lastly, the section also investigated to what extent the community of faith was considered to be a source of spiritual and moral support for the respondents' business life. Not all respondents said that they expected their faith community to provide such support. UK3, for example, felt that the general spiritual input that he received was sufficient to give him encouragement for his day-to-day life and that he did not need any extra support for his business. And UK11 said that she did not feel that her business was spiritually important enough to deserve church support. Other respondents stated that their church did not appreciate business activity as an important activity from a spiritual point of view and thus they did not expect helpful guidance or support from the church for their business. Particularly UK2's frustration over the failure of his church to recognise business as "a caring profession" gives an indication that business people might indeed be confronted in their churches with what the theologian Childs (1995) calls a 'shareability gap'. In other words, they are confronted with the failure of the church to understand that business activity is also an important activity from a spiritual point of view.

Yet some people in the study said that they appreciated the ability to have fellowship with other Christians and considered this as helpful and beneficial for their business life. Some respondents reported that they had prayer partners, with whom they could talk through and pray over issues regarding their business. UK11 particularly mentioned that she also felt accountable to her prayer partner for the way she runs her business. Her prayer partnership might thus have quite a significant impact on her business practices as it might exert some kind of discipline on her. Other respondents said that they felt that their home group or Bible study group provided space to discuss or pray over situations and problems that they faced in their business life. Again, this kind of support might lead Christian owner-managers to consider business practices from a spiritual point of view and thus might have an impact on their behaviour.

To sum up, the community of faith may play a role for Christian owner-managers in a number of different ways, all of which are related to their identity as a faith community member. From a social capital perspective, the community of faith may offer business opportunities based on the recognition of a shared identity (and shared values), but might also create 'obligations'. For example, some Christian owner-managers might feel that they have to do other Christian business people a favour and might not always seek their own benefit in such business relationship. The community of faith may also be an important - and for some Christian owner-managers the only – context in which they benefit others by, for example, offering employment opportunities to fellow Christians or by offering practical and financial help to individual fellow believers. This also applies to Christian owner-managers' business-related civic engagement, which might in a number of cases be particularly focused on the faith community and faith-community related causes. Finally, whether the community of faith is a source of moral and spiritual support for a Christian owner-manager might depend a) on whether the owner-manager is looking for such support there and b) on the availability of smaller groups – prayer partnerships, homegroups etc. – which provide a 'space' for them to discuss and pray over business issues.

5.2 Working in the presence of God

Most of the Christian concepts to which the respondents referred in chapter 4 implied the presence of God in one way or another. It was pointed out that this implied or imagined presence might have quite a considerable impact on the respondents' conceptualisation of practice and subsequently on their actual practices. This section explores this aspect further by looking at some statements where respondents invoked certain spiritual beliefs that referred to the presence of God, but this time as a more general context and not tied to specific concepts. Those beliefs referred to 1) God's provision for believers 2) the Christian faith protecting believers from 'unrighteous' behaviour 3) God providing guidance for the business.

5.2.1 God providing and sustaining

Some people in the study drew a specific connection between their belief that God sustains and helps them and their business practices. They often brought this up when they talked about their refusal to engage in illegal behaviour.

UK9, for instance, mentioned his strong belief that God will provide for him, which he said kept him from engaging in illegal business practices.

> Scripture tells me quite clearly that God provides all my needs. So I don't have to go chasing business. That's illegal. Because God provides all my needs. So I have that assurance that I don't, you know, don't need to act illegally. ... I don't have to worry. He doesn't provide my wants. Just my needs.
> (UK9a, building services)

D2 similarly said that he believed that unrighteous behaviour does not pay off and that putting one's trust in God will help one through situations in which unrighteous behaviour seems to be the easy way out. In his account he referred to a specific situation in his business life, when he was about to go bankrupt.

> No, I don't think it would pay off. I uh believe that I can't fall deeper than into the hands of God. Uh, this is sometimes difficult but I trust in this and uh, I'd rather follow the more difficult path, also in this respect. ... In my past ... I had a ... very difficult business situation and I had the choice to stick it out or to act illegally. And uh I decided to stick it out. It was very difficult for 10 years, but I think, it paid off in the end, because I put my trust in the Lord and I now feel blessed by Him.[113]
> (D2b, property management)

Both UK1 and D10 referred to the passage in the Bible "Seek first his Kingdom and his righteousness and these things will be added" (Matthew 6:33) as a promise of God's provision for the business.

[113] Nee, ich glaube das äh würde sich nicht auszahlen. Ich äh glaub' schon dran, dass ich nicht tiefer fallen kann als äh in Gottes Hand. Äh, ja, das ist manchmal schwer, aber ich vertraue darauf und äh ich, lieber ähm gehe ich einen schwierigen Weg also, das auch in der Richtung. ... (I)ch habe in meiner Vergangenheit ... eine schwierige geschäftliche Situation und ähm da stand ich quasi auch vor der Wahl, jetzt alles durchzustehen äh oder einen illegalen Weg zu gehen. Und äh ich hab' mich dazu entschieden, das durchzustehen. Das war sehr schwierig 10 Jahre lang, aber es hat sich dann, denke ich, auch äh ausgezahlt, weil ich eben mein Vertrauen auf den Herrn gesetzt habe und ähm ich mich nun wieder reich beschenkt fühle.

> But I would actually go further and say 'Seek first the Kingdom of God and these things will be added.' And if if you are doing the right right things I found that you survive. You're doing the best.
> (UK1a, ceramics industry projects and manufacture of birthpool liners)

> The things that I'm passionate about could be something that God put into my heart. … And if He has put something into my heart, he will make sure that you accomplish it as well. *And, of course, 'Seek first the Kingdom of God and his righteousness.' To seek those principles, and then you will be provided for.*[114]
> (D10a, manufacture of measuring instruments)

What 'seeking the Kingdom of God first' meant for them was shaped, however, by their particular interpretations of the Kingdom of God. UK1 referred in his account to things such as having a passion for the product, and the practices that he associated with a Christian ethic in business. D10, on the other hand, might have primarily referred to his vision of being a witness in his business to other people and of transforming his employees through working in an environment that is shaped by Christian values (see section 5.3.2).

Lastly, D7 stated that his belief that God provides for his business kept him from engaging in business practices that he did not feel comfortable with, although they might be considered legitimate by others. He specifically referred to the aggressive use of advertising (see also section 6.1.6).

> But I have my problems uh with, even if my staff sometimes suggest getting a move on. 'Business is slacking at the moment, now we need to boost our advertising. We now need to go one step further. We need to do another promotion. Uh, we need to change this and that.' Um, I always need to find some balance there, to tell myself 'Lord, I know that you'll provide for me, I know this, even if I don't pull out all the stops of advertising.' This is a balancing act, sometimes.[115]
> (D7a, optician)

5.2.2 Protection from temptation

Other respondents reported on how they felt that their Christian faith protected them from personal temptations to become greedy, to engage in unrighteous behaviour etc.; although, unlike the respondents in section 5.2.1, they did not rationalise it in terms of God rewarding this kind of behaviour but rather as a kind of inner control mechanism.

UK2, for example, said that his Christian faith helped him to run his business in an "unselfish" manner rather than giving in to the temptations that business life presented.

> *I don't know how people are owner-manager without faith* [laughs]. I feel really, I feel really sorry for some, for some people, I wish they, I wish they'd open their minds and their hearts to the faith. Because I see, you know, what what being in business without a faith does to them. If they haven't got a code of conduct um for one thing I think that's ex- becomes exceptionally difficult. In many cases. Um because um being in business is

---

[114] Dass das, wofür mein Herz schlägt, was vielleicht in mir drin steckt, schlummert, könnte etwas sein, was Gott in mich hineingelegt hat. … Und wenn es das ist, was Er hineingelegt hat, gibt Er auch das Vollbringen dazu. *Und natürlich ‚Trachtet zuerst nach dem Reich Gottes, nach Seiner Gerechtigkeit.' Das nach dem, was dort die Maßstäbe sind, und dann geht auch die Versorgung auf.*

[115] (A)ber ich hab' meine Probleme, ähm, selbst wenn meine Mitarbeiter mir das teilweise vorschlagen, so jetzt auf die Tube zu drücken. ‚Jetzt ist das Geschäft ein bisschen flauer, jetzt muss die Werbung angekurbelt werden. Jetzt müssen, jetzt muss noch was draufgesetzt werden. Jetzt muss noch 'ne Aktion herhalten. Ähm, jetzt muss das und das noch verändert werden.' Ähm, dabei muss ich immer wieder'n Balanceakt finden, für mich zu sagen ‚Herr, ich weiß, dass du mich gut versorgst, ich weiß es auch, wenn ich nicht (alle) Register, die ich jetzt habe, aus dem (Werbe-) Bereich jetzt ziehe'. Das ist 'n Spagat mitunter.

is a real invitation to the world of temptation. Um, and indeed a a lot of business people enjoy business for that reason. Um, you know, they love the fast cars, they love the expense account, um they love not paying all their taxes. Um, they love being sly on a deal. And, you know, doing better without anyone knowing, getting. They love paying themselves big money. And like, you know, four hundred times more than the person on the shopfloor. Um without a thought, of any of those equality or fairness ratios. *Um, so there's a lot of [pause] there're a lot of issues, where where business um from a self-regulatory point of view um really doesn't work. It feeds the selfish.*
(UK2a, manufacture of metal parts)

He continued to say that he felt that God had protected him from "falling off a precipice" by keeping him from making unwise business decisions that would have been based on seemingly lucrative opportunities or his own ambition, but which could have been harmful to the business and his employees.

UK2: There's, I'm very conscious about, um, you know, the the path, the journey um was was one which um certainly I had the hands in in decisions of mine, if you like, how I went down a particular journey. But I know full well that um I was encouraged and protected. So if you look at the Pilgrim's Progress um, you know, *I wasn't I wasn't allowed to fall off a precipice. You know, other people have done, lots of people have done. But I wasn't allowed to, I was uh prevented from doing that....*
Interviewer: What does this mean? [paraphrased]
UK2: Um, [pause] well I think I think there are so many, ... if we if we follow our own selfish, if we follow our own selfish desires, um without restraint, then we fall off a precipice. That's my definition of a precipice. If we follow our desires in an unrestrained way, um then I think we're lost. That's my personal view. And I think that even if, let's say you don't have raging desires but you have moderate desires. But you can still take very selfish business decisions. Um, without, which take your your um viewpoints, 90 percent or 95 percent is what you listen to, and you pay only 5 percent of attention to um external issues, like, what would the consequences be and so on and so forth. ...It's it's, the adrenalin of the of the um, it's the adrenalin of the physical rather than looking at a holistic sense of what's the intellectual viewpoint, um what's the other side of the argument, um, what would be um, you know, the argument of the devil, um, the devil's advocate for instance. Um, what if it went wrong, et cetera, et cetera, et cetera. And, you know, what are the constituents of making a good decision? Um, what would other, you know, what would the other interests, stakeholders have got to say about this? Employees, shareholders and so on. Or is it just me, me, me, me, me. And 'This is **my** idea and what **I** am going to do'. And I think that, OK, sometimes people can just get it right. But there are an awful lot of stories that you never ever hear, where people have got it awfully wrong.
(UK2b/c, manufacture of metal parts)

D3 talked about his faith as a specific inner control mechanism that kept him from exploiting situations that present opportunities to make money in an unethical or illegal manner.

D3: Uh, well there are, if you if you don't have a control mechanism there, which we have as Christians, uh, you can exploit a lot more situations.
Interviewer: Control mechanism meaning ...?
D3: Well, if someone does not have this conscience, this control mechanism inside you, then there are, starting with what you choose what you account for in your books and what you don't. There are, these are things that cannot really be checked or, so, if you have no inner restrictions there, you can really exploit this.[116] (D3b, mobile home rental)

[116] *D3:* Äh, so, also da gibt's, wenn man wenn man da äh keine Kontrollinstanz dazwischen hat, die wir als Christen ja haben, äh ist da sicherlich eine ganze Menge noch möglich, ja.

And UK3 even went as far as to say that he would not give anyone else who is not a Christian a say in his business. He stated that he believed that the Apostle Paul's warning not to "yoke oneself together with the unbeliever" (2 Corinthians 6:14) referred to business and would protect him from doing something unrighteous.

> Well, the only the only ones that are going to make any decisions in the in the business me or or God. I'm not gonna sort of stand in the way of Him, if He needs me to do something. But I'm not gonna have someone uh else who either doesn't know about the business or doesn't know about God telling me what to do with the business. It's me, it's me and Him. Um, and I mean, He doesn't get much of a say I've got, you know, but um I don't think anybody else having an opinion. 'Oh well, of course, it's all very well you doing this, (NAME). But really, if you do that, you know, it may be a bit dodgy but it's gonna make lots of money.' Um, that might be a persuasive argument. And if someone else were a partner or if someone else had a stake in the business, they might feel that I should do that. ... 'Don't yoke yourself together with the unbeliever' is what I'm talking about. And I **think** that that's actually talking about business.
> (UK3b, estate agent)

5.2.3 Asking for God's guidance

Finally, a number of respondents stated how important it was for them to ask God for guidance in decisions related to their business. They referred to seeking guidance for the larger decisions regarding the direction the business should be taking or the day-to-day decisions and conflicts that they were confronted with. They also mentioned different meditative practices, such as prayer and reading in the Bible, through which they sought God's help and direction.

UK7, for example, stated that prayer was important for him in terms of gaining direction for the business. This resulted from his understanding that God is the 'Lord of the business'.

> Yy, yes, I I think, prayer meetings are very important in business, because um, you know, if you believe, um, if you believe that um 'The earth is the Lord's, and (the fullness) thereof', that we believe that *He is the Lord of of your business*, then I would say the the prayer meeting in that business is every bit as important as the board meeting in that business. You know, because you're seeking direction [pause] from the Lord of the business. Um, so it's not, we, you know, we we in those prayer meetings, of course, we pray for for people and the good of people. We specifically pray for for people who are who are ill or are in trouble or whatever. *But primary purpose of that prayer meeting is to gain direction for the business.*
> (UK7a, engineering)

For a number of respondents it is important to ask for guidance with regards to specific business-related decisions and situations. UK11, for example, mentioned some specific things that she prayed for.

> Can I give an example? .... Certainly taking on new staff. I'm thinking now about needing somebody else, I need another optician, whatever. I certainly pray a lot about that. ... Um, probably maybe in the big decisions. Perhaps perhaps not in the little decisions, you know, 'Should I give this person bifocals or varifocals' wouldn't be anything that would,

---

Interviewer: So mit Kontrollinstanz meinen Sie jetzt ...?
D3: Ja, also wenn wenn einer nicht direkt dieses Gewissen hat, diese Kontrollinstanz dann noch in sich, dann dann sind da ganz, allein schon von, was man in die Bücher nimmt und was man nicht in die Bücher nimmt, nicht. Also das sind jetzt, sind ja Dinge, die sind eigentlich äh kaum kontrollbar oder also wer wer da keine Beschränkung hat in sich, kann man viel machen.

you know, that I would sort of think very much about. And I pray every day that I'll I'll see the things that I need to see. That I pick up eye-diseases and things that I need to see. So I ask for God's guidance in that way.
(UK11a, optician)

For D10 it was particularly important to seek God's wisdom regarding management decisions that concerned his employees. The context for the following quotation was his account of the difficult situation that he was in when he realised that an employee was 'not up to the job'. He said that he turned to various spiritual practices that would help him to deal with such situations.

And for me it means that 'In Christ are hidden all wisdom, all the treasures of wisdom and knowledge' We can gain direction from the Bible in all things. That means, it's important to study the Bible, to have a quiet time, to pray, and to be still in prayer. This is a very important thing for me, simply to have a time of prayer and be still. ... And I've had some good experiences with that. To get given wisdom for concrete situations. Very important. Very important.[117]
(D10a, manufacture of measuring instruments)

Others referred to specific moral conflict situations in which they sought God's wisdom and guidance. D9 felt it was particularly important to turn to God in dilemma situations. As an example, he referred to situations where he felt he had to compromise his value of honesty in order to balance out his responsibilities to his employees with his responsibilities to his clients.

I have a responsibility to the Lord, to lift these things up to Him. And that I try and listen to him in those conflict situations.[118]
(D9a, security analysis)

5.2.4 Observations

This section looked at the different ways the respondents engaged with certain spiritual beliefs that related to the presence of God in their working life, and how they were linked to their business behaviour. This is a less obvious context than the community of faith as it relates to the respondents' 'inner' relationship to God, but nevertheless may have some kind of psychological impact on the respondents' behaviour.

The first set of respondents referred to the belief that God would sustain them and their business if they acted in a certain way. Some respondents invoked this when they talked about their refusal to engage in illegal business activities (UK9, D2), their unwillingness to engage in practices that they perceived to be unethical (D7), or their aspiration to act according to the principles of the Kingdom of God, whatever that entailed for them (UK1, D10). UK1 and D10 specifically referred to the passage in Scripture that says "Seek first the Kingdom of God and his righteousness and these things will be added" (Matthew 6:33), which may have been the underlying rationale of all of the respondents' accounts. Such a belief can be a powerful motivator for a Christian owner-manager, even though it would be difficult to prove that this belief is actually true. Weick (1995, 56) argues that sensemaking does not rely on accuracy but is rather driven by plausibility. Likewise, the belief that God provides if one acts in a certain way is not dependent on accuracy to be effective. If it is plausible to the owner-

[117] Das heißt für mich, erst einmal ‚In Christus liegen alle Weisheit, alle Schätze der Weisheit und der Erkenntnis.' In (der Bibel) können wir alles erfahren. Das heißt, entscheidend, Bibellese, Stille Zeit, ins Gebet gehen, und im Gebet äh zu schweigen. Das ist für mich also eine ganz ganz wichtige Sache, ... einfach ins Gebet hineingehen und schweigen. ... Und dort äh habe ich also sehr sehr gute Erfahrungen gemacht. Von dort also Weisheit in in konkreten Situationen sich geben zu lassen. Ganz wichtig. Ganz wichtig.

[118] Die Verantwortung gegenüber dem Herrn ist eigentlich darin, dass ich diese Dinge vor Ihn bringe. Und dass ich in solchen Konfliktfällen versuche, auf Ihn zu hören.

managers that God might act that way, this may create a strong enough motivation not to act illegally/unethically or a positive motivation to engage in certain practices.

One could argue here, first, that this is a rather 'instrumentalist' view of faith – "I behave in such and such way and God will sustain me in return" - and secondly, that it is easy to make such a claim when business is going well. However, some respondents particularly mentioned it when they talked about difficult business situations, in which 'unethical' or illegal business behaviour would have seemingly ensured the well-being and continuity of the business – something that became particularly apparent in D2's and D7's account. At the same time, the belief that God will sustain the business if the owner-manager acts in a righteous way may have been not only something that the respondents claimed for themselves, but they may have also had their responsibility to their employees in mind here. This indicates that often there might be a dilemma for Christian owner-managers between 'righteous', morally correct behaviour and their responsibility to their employees – and referring to the belief that God will sustain the business might be one way of coping with such a dilemma.[119] Hence the power and credibility of statements regarding God's provision for the business may depend on the context in which they are said.

Other people in the study did not refer to the promise of God's provision for them if they acted in a certain way but referred to their faith as an internal control mechanism that keeps them from giving in to temptations that their business life presents, and whose consequences might be harming others or even themselves. Although they were not specifically asked why that might be so, they may have sensed somehow that God might be judging them and their behaviour or they might have thought that not to give in to temptation was just a more appropriate and Christian way to live. UK2 stated that having a faith had kept him from making 'selfish' business decisions, for example, from making decisions that were driven by his own ambition and that did not regard possible harmful consequences for others. D3 and UK3, on the other hand, referred to the fact that God might keep them from doing something illegal or unethical. D3 stated that he believed that his Christian faith acted as a control mechanism through his conscience. UK3, on the other hand, referred to a specific passage in the Bible, where the Apostle Paul warned "not to yoke oneself together with the unbeliever", which made him cautious not to be persuaded by others to engage in unethical business behaviour. Again, the respondents' beliefs created a 'plausible' rationale for not engaging in certain practices, even though they did not state that they expected any 'extrinsic' reward from God for their behaviour. The absence of such 'extrinsic' motivation in their reasoning might make the statements they made here about the influence of their faith more credible.

The final set of respondents referred to some spiritual practices that they engaged in, such as prayer or reading scriptures, which they said they used to get spiritual guidance for their business lives. Not all of the issues that they said they committed to God in prayer or they meditated on may have had a clear moral dimension. "Asking for guidance" encompassed issues such as "gaining direction for the business" (UK7) or recruitment decisions (UK11), which may be more matters of prudence, but some issues clearly did have a moral dimension. Examples were D10's search for guidance on how to deal with an employee that was not 'up to the job', UK11's prayer for wisdom that she would not fail her customers or D9 committing a specific moral conflict situation to God in prayer. It is uncertain whether the respondents actually do receive guidance from God or biblical texts or whether the decisions that the respondents subsequently make are merely the product of their own thinking. But again, the belief that God might provide guidance creates sufficient motivation for the respondents to stop and consider things within a spiritual context, which may lead them to make better or more ethical decisions.

Interestingly, asking God for guidance was often mentioned by respondents who drew very heavily on the stewardship discourse. Thus the obligation or aspiration to commit business decisions to God may form part of their accountability to God as the "Lord of the business".

To sum up, the context that was described here as 'working in the presence of God' is a rather uncertain context, as the effectiveness of the spiritual beliefs that the respondents mentioned cannot be

---

[119] Not all respondents invoked this belief when they addressed this specific dilemma. D9, for example, felt that this was a conflict situation that he needed to bring before God to ask His advice (see section 5.2.3) and D8 stated that he sometimes needed to make a decision in favour of his employees and against his Christian moral convictions (see section 4.5.4)

proven. Yet those beliefs seem to be strong enough to create a plausible motivation for the owner-managers to act in a certain way. This motivation was linked with refraining from illegal or unethical practices, with acting in a way that considered the interest of others, or with considering business decisions that have a moral dimension in the light of the Christian faith.

5.3 Working in an environment carrying spiritual significance

Some of the respondents' accounts implied that the environment in which they worked carried some kind of spiritual significance and that this had quite a significant impact on how they structured their business practices. This context is rather difficult to grasp as the respondents framed and interpreted it in many different ways. Trying to categorise the respondents' accounts regarding the spiritual significance of their working environment, the section will first look at statements that respondents made relating to their business activities as such and then at some statements that related more to the people the respondents interacted with through their business. The observation section (section 5.3.3) will look a bit more closely at the theological context and show in more detail how different theological understandings might have influenced the respondents' conceptualisation of practice.

5.3.1 "Working for the Lord"

In this section we look at statements that some people in the study made regarding the spiritual significance of their business activities.

Doing one's work well

Some respondents stated that what they did in their business they did "for God" or "for the Lord" and that this gave them a strong motivation to carry out their work in a way that "pleased the Lord".

D8, for example, explained how the belief that one worked "for the Lord" was embedded in the traditions of his trade and how this influenced the way he carried out his work.

> *Interviewer:* To whom do you feel you have a responsibility as a Christian in your business?
> *D8:* [pause] When I was apprentice my old foreman always told me 'You don't work for our boss, you don't work for me, either, you only work for yourself. You have to like what you do with your hands. **You** have to be happy with it. When you've finished your day's work, you should go home saying 'I've done this well.'' ... And later I learned what this 'You work for yourself' means. It means, builders don't like saying this, of course, and it may have been a bit distorted over time *'We always work for the Lord'. That is what is important.*
> *Interviewer:* And what does this mean precisely?
> *D8:* That means that when I work for our Lord, I always have to do my work well. Always do it right. Always to please the Lord. And that means, if I please Him, I will be pleased as well. And then I go home happy. And then you don't mind if it takes a bit longer, you're not watching the clock. But you want to do it well and only then you are happy as well.[120] (D8a, building)

[120] *Interviewer:* Wem gegenüber sehen Sie denn 'ne Verantwortung als Christ in Verbindung mit Ihrem Geschäft?
D8: Ja ist [Pause], ich habe während meiner Lehrzeit von meinem alten Polier immer gehört ‚Du arbeitest nicht für unseren Chef, du arbeitest auch nicht für mich, du arbeitest nur für dich alleine. Das, was du mit deinen Händen herstellst, muss dir gefallen. **Du** musst zufrieden sein. Wenn du dein Tagwerk verrichtet hast, musst du nach Hause gehen und sagen „Das hab ich gut gemacht." ...Und später hab' ich dann gelernt, was dieses bedeutet ‚Du arbeitest nur für dich.' Es ist im übertragenen Sinne, Bauleute sagen das natürlich nicht so gerne und und es ist dann auch wahrscheinlich im Sprachgebrauch so'n bisschen verfälscht worden ‚Wir arbeiten immer für unseren Herrn.' Das ist das, was wichtig ist.
Interviewer: Und was bedeutet das konkret?
D8: Das bedeutet, dass ich das, wenn ich für unseren Herrn arbeite, muss ich meine Arbeit immer gut machen. Immer richtig machen. Immer zur Freude des Herrn. Und das bedeutet eben, wenn ich es Ihm zur Freude mache,

UK9, who also works in the building trade, took a similar stance about doing things well. But as someone who frequently stated how he sought spiritual guidance by directly engaging with Scripture, he referred to a specific passage in the New Testament[121] that shaped his understanding of what he does in his business he does "for the Lord".

> Um, [pause] but I'm but I'm very conscious now of of what the Bible says, about, you know, *what what we do, we do for the Lord not for men.* And and to me that's an encouragement, you know, if I, you know, I I'll do a job and I'll look at it if I'm not happy with it, I'll redo it. You know, if I'm, you know, and I set myself fairly high standards. *Because what I do I do for the Lord.* .... Uh, yeah, so I set my standard by um, you know, I may be, I might go over the top sometimes to make sure it's absolutely spot on. I get I do get very critical of my own work. But at the same time, you know, it has to, you know, the speed with which I work has to be commercially viable. 'Cause there is no point being in business otherwise. ... So um at the end of the day maybe things aren't perfect because to make them perfect would not be commercially viable. But it's got to be to a standard that that the customer is gonna be happy with. It's got to be to a standard I'm happy with. Which may be higher than the customer's standard.
> (UK9b, building services)

UK1 shared the belief that it was a spiritual duty to do one's work well because it was done for the Lord, but he also introduced a further notion that underlined this commitment: the belief that Christ was "Lord of all creation" and that Christ was therefore involved in all forms of human creation.

> And uh I tried to work out a theology of work and so on. Uh, so it begins with the product, actually. ... And um the things we make actually belong to Christ because He is the Lord of all creation. So any, any, any form of creation Christ is involved in it. And if I do something badly, he suffers. And if you make we make something well, he rejoices in that. ... (T)he object in itself is something that God rejoices in. It's not simply whether it helps human beings or not. So it's complicated by the fact, it's the object itself but it's also the fact that it's a a joy to humans. ... And it's because I'm doing it for God, because my customer, I don't see them, I I don't know who they are um, then I can make a product better to my best ability. Do everything in the name of the Lord Jesus. So the actual product itself, yes.
> (UK1a, ceramics industry projects and manufacture of birthpool liners)

All three accounts implied that "working for the Lord" provided a rather strong if not the primary motivation for the respondents to do their work well, but particularly UK9 and UK1 acknowledged that their efforts to work well would also benefit their customers. This aspect was also specifically important important to UK5, who explained that his belief that his work was actually done for God helped him to deliver his work at a high quality standard even when he found some customers difficult to deal with.

> Um, and teachingwise it says 'Do your work as unto God.' So if you're working for someone, even if they're rude, obnoxious, horrible, smelly, all those things, you're asked to work as if you were working for God. In which case you're gonna do the best job you possibly can.
> (UK5b, heating engineer)

---

dann freut's mich ja auch. Und dann geh' ich auch zufrieden nach Hause. Und dann guckt man auch nicht so auf die Minute. Oder auf die Stunde. Sondern man will es dann gut machen und dann, dann ist man erst befriedigt.

[121] Probably Colossians 3:17

Caring for God's creation

UK1 referred in his account to Christ as "the Lord of all creation", which inspired him to do things well as God's 'co-creator'. In UK7's account we found similar references, such as "the earth is the Lord's" and "Jesus is Lord of all". Bu he translated this spiritual notion specifically into stewardship responsibilities, and this, among other things, particularly led him to consider the role of his company "in making this planet more sustainable" and to feel strongly about environmental responsibilities (see sections 4.1.3 and 4.2.4).

Working for 'spiritual' causes

D5, however, understood the spiritual significance of his business in quite a different way. Unlike the respondents above, D5 did not consider his main business activity – offering a printing service – to carry any spiritual significance as such, but only the parts of his business that had an overt connection to 'Christian' causes. First, he particularly referred to his chance to contribute to the "Kingdom of God" through being able to print Christian literature (see section 4.1.1).

> And if I could do something like that, because, it is, it's perhaps not so important, because it has to, there are so many trades, where you say 'If I, I can't contribute anything to the Kingdom of God with what I do' When you when you grow cucumbers or something. But in the printing industry you may have a bit of chance, because it's not a pure manufacturing company. Because it doesn't make sausages, but there are some non-material aspects as well. ... And as a Christian you are itching to do something. That you don't have to say 'We only print forms'. Or with advertising material, most of it will just be thrown into the bin, more or less.[122]
> (D5a, printing)

But he also specifically regarded the chance to fund Christian causes with his company as his contribution to the "Kingdom of God".

> But I can try to earn money here, and with the money that is left over, I can, well, what needn't be put back into the company, I can try to do something worthwhile in the Kingdom of God. That's a very nice feeling. But this is nothing to do with having a printing business; any other company could do that.[123]
> (D5a, printing)

As a result, he considered the majority of his business activities first and foremost as a means to generate profits and to fulfil his obligations to his employees, particularly because he was clear that printing only for Christian causes would not make the company financially viable. His account also

[122] Und wenn man sowas wieder machen könnte, dann, das ist, das ist vielleicht nicht so wichtig, weil das muss auch, es gibt ja so viel Berufe, wo du sagst 'Wenn ich, kannst ja gar nichts zum Reiche Gottes beitragen, beitragen von mit der Arbeit.' Wenn du wenn du Gurken anbaust oder so. Aber 'ne Druckerei hat eben bisschen die Chance noch, weil sie eben so ein, kein richtiger Produktionsbetrieb ist. Weil er weder Mettwurst macht noch, weil da eben was Ideelles dabei ist. Und da tut's einem als Christ immer in den Fingern jucken, dass man nicht auch, dass man da auch etwas tun könnte. ... Und da tut's einem als Christ immer in den Fingern jucken, dass man nicht auch, dass man da auch etwas tun könnte. Dass man nicht sagt 'Wir machen nur Formulare'. Oder gerade in der Werbung machst du ja viel Zeug, was was für den Papierkorb produziert wird, mehr oder weniger.

[123] Aber ich kann versuchen, hier Geld zu verdienen, und mit dem Geld, was übrig ist, kann ich, also was die Firma ab-, nicht unbedingt braucht, um sich zu refinanzieren, kann ich auch schon versuchen, im Reich Gottes was vernünftiges zu tun. Das ist ein sehr schönes Gefühl. Hat aber mit der Druckerei selbst nichts zu tun, könnte jeder andere Betrieb sein.

shows that he used the phrase "working for the Lord" in quite a different way to the respondents above.

> And in such a printing company, with the company, if you consider the 20, 24 people and their relatives, who depend on the company, there's perhaps 80 people for whom you have responsibility in the end. Uh, then you can't really work one hundred percent for the church. Because, you always have to reckon, that when missionary organisations or vicars or, when they want to have something printed. A lot of them basically give you the job and want a donation at the same time. ... And so I think a mix of 60 percent orders from industry that bring in a steady income and 40 percent from the church. *I consider this to be a healthier mix, rather than saying 'I'll reject all orders from industry, I only want to work for the Lord. I will only print for missionary organisations.'*[124]
> (D5a, printing)

5.3.2 The spiritual significance of dealing with people through the business

Whereas some respondents attached spiritual significance to their business activity as such others seemed to specifically regard the interaction with other people in their business as being of spiritual significance.

D10, for example, stated very strongly that he thought the main spiritual focus in his business should be on people and not on the products he made.

> And uh, how I see this as a Christian, *God is not interested in any way in my manometers* [his products]. *Because they will go to the scrap yard eventually. That means they're not of eternal value. Um, God is always interested in people.* [125]
> (D10b, manufacture of measuring instruments)

Other respondents who mentioned the 'people' aspect of their business did not so strongly reject the notion that the products or the services they offered had some kind of spiritual significance. Indeed, they may have regarded the 'people' aspect as yet another dimension of their business that had spiritual significance next to the business activity itself.

Bringing about a change in other people's lives

A number of respondents who talked about the 'people' aspect of their business stated that they regarded their business as a place that might be used to bring about a change in other people through their Christian input; leading people to develop, or to change their behaviour. We will look at some example here where respondents referred to this notion of bringing about a change in others.

D10, for example, emphasised how the Christian faith may "positively change" people, and regarded his company as a suitable vehicle for accomplishing this. We already saw in section 4.2.4

---

[124] Und man muss aber in so 'ner Druckerei, da ich ja nun mit der Druckerei, wenn man die 20, 24 Leute rechnet mit ihren Angehörigen, die von der Druckerei leben, sind das vielleicht 80 Leute, für die man ja letztlich Verantwortung hat. Äh, dann kann man eigentlich nach Lage der Dinge gar nicht 'ne hundertprozentige Druckerei sein, die für kirchliche Aufgaben druckt. Weil, Sie müssen ja immer rechnen, also Missionswerke oder oder Pfarrer oder, die was gedruckt haben wollen. Da gibt's ja viel, die die kommen ja im Prinzip gleich in der rechten Hand den Auftrag, in der linken die Spendenquittung ... Und von daher, denke ich, ist eine Mischung, wo man sagt, ich hab' vielleicht mal 60 Prozent Industrieaufträge die gut laufen, und 40 Prozent Aufträge aus dem kirchlichen Bereich. *Das halte ich eher für eine gesunde Mischung, als wenn man sagt ,Ich lehne jetzt alles Industrie ab, ich will nur für den Herrn dasein. Ich drucke jetzt nur noch für Mission.'*

[125] Und in der, in der Sichtweise, die (ich) hier als Christ verstehe, ist, dass es, *den lieben Gott in keinster Weise, also überhaupt nicht um meine Manometer geht. Denn irgendwann landen die mal alle auf dem Schrott oder was. Das heißt, es hat keinen Ewigkeitswert. Äh, Gott geht es immer um Menschen.*

that he sought to develop his employees' gifts and talents so that they "can develop as persons". When he was asked what contribution he could make to society through his business, he mentioned yet another aspect. He specifically referred to the atmosphere that he sought to create in his company, which should have a positive impact on the behaviour and attitude of employees in their personal lives.

> ... that there is an atmosphere in our companies, and that we live out values that are based on the Word of God. That is for me the most important influence that we have on society. *My, my dream or the vision that I have is basically that people feel happy at work, and that their thoughts, their attitudes, their thinking, that they are changed in the right way, positively changed. Then these men and women will go home changed, positively changed.* And that will have an impact on their marriages. Changed marriages will bring about changed children. And when our children are changed, that's the best investment into the future. *It was a huge encouragement, when people said in the community 'Since so and so has been working for your company, he has changed at home. He doesn't shout anymore and he's changed somehow.' That was, I think, one of the greatest joys in my life as a businessman.*[126]
> (D10a, manufacture of measuring instruments)

UK2, on the other hand, talked about his Christian responsibilities to develop his employees' potential and to encourage them to interact with others in the workplace in a 'positive' way.

> Well, I think yes, I think it is, you know, once once being (in business) um you're having a responsibility of care to individuals. Um, I think your, I think commitment to training. Uh, you don't want them to go off the way, you also want to give them the best chance. Um you want to feel that they are developing their potential, you want them to believe in themselves. Um and yet, you're also wanting them to believe in that colleagues are are good not bad. Um, and I think also it's a Christian duty really, which I wish I'd spent more of my life thinking about, is um Satan is out there prowling around. And for every good deed you do, he is out to try and nullify it cancel it out. Um, and I think there are certain people, certain people are faith people, and I think in the same way certain people are Satan people and being apathetic is a good illustration of being a Satan person, I think. Because they're not doing things positive in in life they're doing things perhaps negative or or selfishly or whatever. And I think we see, I think we see that in business.
> (UK2b, manufacture of metal parts)

In his account he also gave some specific examples of how he translated his concerns into practice. The following example related to his concern of providing a space with his business in which people could develop their potential. He stated that he and his (Christian) personnel manager had decided to take on a young boy who had been given an exclusion order from his school.

> Um, and we've had one notable one last year who was um an excluded child. They wouldn't have him back at school. But (NAME OF PERSONNEL MANAGER) said 'I think there is something in him. I think probably he's not a school boy. He is much more,

---

[126] ... dass in diesen Firmen eine Atmosphäre da ist, und und Werte gelebt werden, die (vom) Wort Gottes sind. Das ist für mich, das ist der der wichtigste Einfluss, den wir in die in die in die Gesellschaft rein haben. *Mein, mein Traum oder meine Vision, die ich habe, ist im Prinzip, dass wenn wenn Menschen sich in 'ner in 'ner Firma wohlfühlen, und auch von von den Gedanken her, von den Ansichten her, vom Denken in eine, in die richtige Weise, ich sag' jetzt mal, verändert werden, positiv verändert werden. Dann gehen diese Männer und Frauen verändert, positiv verändert, auch nach Hause.* Und das wird Einfluss zu Hause in ihre Ehen hinein haben. Veränderte Ehen bringen veränderte Kinder. Und wenn wir Veränderungen, positive Veränderungen in unsere Kinder hineinbringen, sind das die besten Investitionen in die Zukunft. *Also für mich war es ein Riesen-Riesengeschenk, ... als Leute im Dorf gesagt haben ,Seit der und der bei euch in der Firma arbeitet, der ist zu Hause wie verändert.Schreit nicht mehr so 'rum und und und, der ist wie verändert.' Das war für mich, ich denke, eines der größten Freuden in meinem Unternehmerleben.*

> he is much happier here on our shopfloor.' And um he is now, left school and um he works for us. And he is terrific. There is no, he is here before time every day, there is no question of um any disciplinary procedures against him. He is fantastic.
> (UK2b, manufacture of metal parts)

In Appendix II, we will find an example of how UK2 sought to influence the behaviour of his employees, his sales people in particular, so that they would not engage in 'selfish' practices.

The concern about the moral behaviour of others from a spiritual point of view was also voiced by D7. As pointed out in section 4.3.3 he said that he liked to challenge his customers when they sought to defraud their insurance and hoped that his engagement with the customers would bring about some 'fruit'.

> Um [pause] that people get a taste of it, um, that they might [pause] think about things more deeply. Because, I notice, that when something or the other happens and they say 'Yeah, what about my insurance, couldn't I, and couldn't we fiddle the invoice a bit, no one would know.' And 'Everybody is doing it.' And uh, if you make your position clear, it's not so bad for them – and they accept it. They come back, even if they had to pay 20 Euros more, or I'll say 'Well, then I'll give you a discount' or something else. Um, but to reflect something that may make an impression on them.[127]
> (D7b, optician)

D8 in particular placed his Christian concern over the moral behaviour of others in the context of wider societal developments and considered that his business had quite an important part to play there. He stated that he considered it his responsibility to set an example with his company and particularly to encourage his employees to behave in a way that was considerate of others.

> That an attitude of mind is setting in, like everybody only considers their own interests. Not the common good. Then this nihilism. Some churches are growing, but this is not enough. That's far too little to have an impact on society. This moral decline. It's therefore very important. And I see with our small business how important it is to be an example. That is, people tend to, people tend to follow the example of their leaders; uh, you wouldn't know how subliminal that is. When I, when I also tell my employees who are a bit older 'No we don't this, and that is out of the question.' And 'Leave it, go and clear it up with the other company's foreman.' Or 'And when this person comes along, be kind and polite and if he asks you then help him and don't work against each other, always work with each other.'[128]
> (D8a, building)

---

[127] *D7:* Mh, [Pause] dass die Leute ein Stück weit was schmecken, mh, dass sie [Pause] vielleicht auch ein Stück weit nachdenken. Weil man das merkt man ja, dass äh wenn mal wieder dann mal so 'ne so 'ne Phase kommt, ‚Ja, aber die Versicherung, ich könnte doch dann und können wir denn die Rechnung so, äh, es merkt doch keiner.' Und ‚Ja, das machen doch alle.' Und mh, da einfach klar Position zu beziehen, das ist für die, das ist gar nicht so schlimm, also... das das akzeptieren die auch. Die kommen auch wieder, selbst wenn sie jetzt 20 Euro mehr zahlen müssen oder ich sage ‚Na, dann gebe ich Ihnen eben einen Rabatt' oder irgendwie was. Mh, aber [Pause] irgendwie was widerzuspiegeln, was was sie ein Stück weit beeindrucken kann.

[128] (D)ass eine Geisteshaltung eintritt, jeder denkt nur noch an sich. Keiner ans Allgemeinwesen. Dann der Nihilismus. Die Kirchen haben teilweise steigende Besucherzahlen, aber das reicht nicht. Das ist einfach für unsere Gesellschaft absolut zu wenig. Dieser Ethikverfall. Das ist also 'ne ganz, ganz wichtige Sache. Und ich seh' das an unserem kleinen Betrieb, dass Vorbildfunktion ist ist äußerst wichtig. Das ist äh, die Leute orientieren sich, die Leute orientieren sich einfach an an an der Führung, an dem, äh, man soll nicht meinen, wieviel, wie wie unterschwellig das ist. Wenn ich, wenn ich auch zu älteren Mitarbeitern sage ‚Nein, sowas machen wir nicht und bei uns kommt sowas nicht in Frage'. Und 'Lass das und geh hin und klär' das mit dem anderen Polier der Firma'. Oder 'Und wenn der kommt, sei nett und höflich und wenn der fragt, dann dann hilf ihm, und nicht gegeneinander arbeiten, immer miteinander arbeiten.'

Sharing one's faith

Finally, some people in the study regarded their workplace as a context in which they should openly share their faith with other people, thereby seeking to attract others to the Christian faith.

D3, for example, was one of the respondents who regarded evangelising as one expression of his faith in his business.

> Well, I'm also trying to evangelise. ... I've got, when someone looks very closely at my website, he will see the Ichthys symbol, and when he clicks on it he will be on the [NAME OF CHRISTIAN BUSINESS ORGANISATION] website. Uh, in my emails, in my signature there is a link to a kind of Bible verse thing or so. So when, and uh in my mobile homes there are little 'treasure chests'. For, 'for times of quiet and rest'. And there are, there is a New Testament in it, uh taped sermons and all sorts of missionary leaflets ... I also say to the customers 'Well, you don't often find someone who runs a mobile home company and prays for his customers that they will have a safe journey.'[129]
> (D3a/b, mobile home rental)

UK3 also said that he was very upfront about his Christian faith by wearing a fish on his jacket and that he believed that he should share his faith whenever the opportunity arises, also in a business context.

> We should all, if we are Christians, wear a Christian symbol, we should all have a Christian symbol on the collar. And we should all tell people that we are Christians and we should all tell people what Jesus has done for us. In an ideal world we would. And it's not right for everybody. Some people are so shy about it. But I think that that's, what I would say to someone in business is 'Don't hide it. Don't hide your light under a bushel. Let your light shine.' Even if it's very very dull. And even if you don't think people will notice. Let it shine.
> (UK3a, estate agent)

It was, however, difficult to pin down what 'sharing one's faith' entailed for such respondents.[130] Was it primarily about the 'salvation of souls for eternal life', was it about the Christian faith providing spiritual comfort and psychological well-being or did it also entail notions of a faith that had repercussions on people's lifestyle and behaviour? And to what extent did that desire to share one's faith have an impact on the respondents' own behaviour? Section 4.3, which looked at the witness frame, may give some insight here, and we saw that in the case of UK3, he - as a minimum - did not want to behave in a way that brought Christianity into disrepute.

Other respondents provided a clearer account of how their desire to share their faith was linked with their business practices or how sharing one's faith entailed a desire to 'change' other people's outlook on life and behaviour. UK10, for example, said that he hoped that people take notice of the way he runs his business and may recognise that it came from his Christian faith. Being a part-time

[129] Na, ich versuche auch, äh, irgendwie auch missionarisch zu sein. ... Ich hab' also, wenn wenn ein geschultes Auge äh über die Internetseite streift, wird den Ichthys da erkennen, und wenn er darauf klickt, dann ist er auf der IVCG-Seite. Äh auf meinen Mails, auf meinem ähm, sozusagen ja auf meiner Absendererkennung ist auch ein Link zu einer, zu einer Art Losung oder so. So, wenn wenn, und äh in meinen Wohnmobilen ist eine kleine ‚Schatztruhe'. Ist eine Blechschachtel, da steht drauf ‚Schatztruhe'. Da, für ‚für Ruhe- und Mußestunden' und da sind, ist ein Neues Testament drin, äh, Predigtkassetten und alles mögliche an an missionarischen Schriften. ... Ich sag' auch den Leuten ‚Also, Sie werden kaum einen Wohnmobilvermieter finden, der für ihre Kunden betet, dass sie gut wieder zurück kommen.'

[130] The researcher often failed to probe further here, as – at the time the interviews were conducted – she did not consider that people might have different understandings of what 'sharing one's faith' means.

minister as well, he was conscious that his business and the way he runs it was also an opportunity for 'reaching out' to other people.

> Yes, I I think, you know, I'm fairly upfront about it I think. I I don't, you know, I'm not there on the streets selling the church to people. *Um, it's, there is something about um [pause] the way I run the business I suppose, which people will see.* Um, there is something about the way I interact with people. And and hopefully care for people um beyond from what is expected from a pharmacist which I hope people will see as being different. And uh because I'm fairly upfront about being a Christian and being a minister, hopefully people will see that that comes from from who I am. Um, I don't ever push it down people's throats. I'm not a street street corner evangelist from that point of view. But certainly, I will seek opportunities to talk about faith.
> (UK10b, pharmacy)

In D10's account we can recognise a similar connection between seeking to share one's faith and hoping that this will transform others. He considered it a specific responsibility to tell his employees about God.

> I am convinced that when we die we'll stand before Jesus. We'll be asked whether we told our employees about God.[131]
> (D10a, manufacture of metal parts)

But as pointed out in the previous section, he also specifically sought to create an atmosphere in his company that sought to "positively change" people's outlook on life and behaviour and that was openly inspired by his Christian faith and presumably his desire to share his faith with his employees.

But is the workplace the appropriate place for seeking to share one's faith? Although some respondents regarded it a specific Christian responsibility, other respondents consciously rejected 'evangelism' as being relevant for their business.

UK11, for example, stated that she did not feel God had given the business to her to evangelise, but that she rather wanted to consider how God wanted her to run the business.

> Um, so I want to run the business in the way that I think He [God] would want me to. So, that way. Yeah. *I don't particularly feel like that I've been given the business to use it as a tool for evangelism, certainly.*
> (UK11a, optician)

Lastly, some respondents – even though they might have sought to share their faith elsewhere – particularly stated that they would not seek to evangelise their staff, given the specific characteristics of a workplace situation. D5, for example, said that he did not want to exploit the power he has over his staff for evangelising.

> I don't always carry this about. I, I don't deal with my staff in a way that I constantly thrust my faith upon them. That doesn't seem to be fair. Because as owner-manager you always have an influence. You are a person with influence and power, I can make this person redundant and take on that person, I can be nice to this person and not nice to that person. Um, and there, in the business I don't want to espouse my faith in a way so that people get the impression that if they just behave a little like a Christian, they will be better off here. They shouldn't be forced to do this, you know.[132] (D5b, printing)

---

[131] Ich bin davon überzeugt, dass wir in der Ewigkeit vor Jesus mal stehen werden. Wir werden gefragt werden, ob wir unseren Mitarbeitern was äh von Gott gesagt haben.

[132] Also ich trag' das nicht so vor mir her. Ich, ich geh' also nicht mit dem mit den, mit den Leuten so um, dass ich meinen christlichen Glauben ständig vor mir hertragen muss. Das scheint mir nicht fair zu sein. Weil man ja als Unternehmer immer einen Einfluss ausübt. Man ist eben eine Person, die Einfluss und Macht hat, ich kann den entlassen, ich kann den einstellen, ich kann zu dem nett sein und zu dem nicht nett sein. Ähm, und da, ich

5.3.3 Observations

This context revolves around the question: 'To what extent and how can 'mundane', 'worldly' activities such as business activities be of spiritual significance?' This is quite an important theological question that can have a profound impact on the way Christian business people conceptualise their business practices. The statements that the respondents made in this regard were quite diverse - reflective of different theological understandings and beliefs. Those beliefs may not always have been the result of deep spiritual reflection on the part of the respondents, but the respondents might have just adopted them from teaching that they had been exposed to. But regardless of whether the respondents had engaged in spiritual reflection or not, those beliefs had an impact on their conceptualisation of business practice.

The statements of the first set of respondents implied that work itself, 'mundane' business activities, were spiritually significant for them. They stated that what they did in their business was done "for the Lord/for God"- which they derived from passages in Scripture (UK5, UK9) or the spiritual tradition of their trade (D8) - or they used beliefs such "Christ is Lord of all" or "Christ is Lord of creation" (UK1, UK7) which formed the spiritual context for their 'worldly' activities. This had two implications for the respondents. First, the belief that one "worked for the Lord" provided some respondents (D8, UK9, UK1, UK5) with quite a powerful motivation to always seek to deliver their products and services at high-quality standards. The respondents pointed out, moreover, that because one "worked for God" the delivery of high-quality work did not depend on any expectation of social 'rewards'. For example, UK9 stated that his standards may have been higher than the customers' standards and UK5 pointed out that because his work was done for God he would always try to deliver high quality work independent of whether he liked the customer or not. For UK7, on the other hand, the spiritual significance of his business activity had a different implication: he regarded it his spiritual responsibility to contribute to environmental sustainability with his business.

Apart from the respondents' (implied) understanding that 'this-worldly', 'mundane' activities are spiritually significant, the respondents' accounts – particularly UK1's and UK7's - touched on another, but related dimension of spiritual significance: the spiritual significance of the material world. God would be regarded as the creator of this world who takes an interest in the 'material' world, thus He would take an interest in what people do with his created world, and this would also apply to business activities. Interestingly, UK1 and UK7 engaged with this idea somewhat differently: UK1 considered himself a co-creator through engaging in 'creative' activities in his business, and UK7 regarded himself as a steward that had, among others, a specific responsibility to care for creation (Byron 1988).

In D5's account we found quite a different understanding of the spiritual significance of his business. He related it primarily to that part of his business that served the Christian market and to his ability to raise funds for Christian causes through the business, but not to his main business activity – the provision of a printing service. As such, he did not confer spiritual significance to 'mundane' business activities as such – unlike the respondents above – and rather focused on the contributions that he could make to the faith community through his business.

D5 primarily made use of the theological term "the Kingdom of God" to rationalise his actions, a term which can - like the phrase "working for the Lord" - serve as a powerful motivator for believers to engage in certain kinds of actions. What the 'Kingdom of God' denotes and how it relates to 'worldly' activities, however, has been a matter of an ongoing debate among Christian scholars and believers, and can already be found in the teachings of church fathers like Augustine and Martin Luther (Pawlas 2000, 92). On one end of the spectrum the Kingdom of God may be interpreted by Christian believers as something separate from the world: God's Kingdom is the future Kingdom in Heaven, and – until it is brought about - is manifested in this world by the Church and the spread of the Gospel only (Gaffin 1988). If one interprets the Kingdom of God that way, it will not motivate believers to 'make a difference' in the world. By contrast, other believers may have a more integrative understanding of the relation of the Kingdom of God and the 'earthly kingdom', which might inspire

---

möchte also nicht jetzt auf 'ne Art christlichen Glauben in der Firma vorleben, dass Leute den Eindruck haben, wenn sie sich nur ein bisschen christlich benehmen, dann haben sie bei mir ein besseres Leben. Das soll also nicht unter Zwang kommen. Ja?

them to pursue the values of God's Kingdom that Christ described such as goodness, justice, peace etc. in this world as an anticipation of a future with God (Bauckham and Hart 1995, 182-183). Here 'the Kingdom of God' has more of a potential to 'make a difference' in the world and it also follows more closely the spiritual concept of 'Christ the Lord of all' (see above). D5 clearly had a more separatist understanding of the Kingdom of God, which led him to focus particularly on the Christian community and its 'spiritual' causes and not on the wider community (although he recognised that he also had 'mundane' responsibilities, particularly to his employees – see section 4.2.3 and 6.2.2). Yet it is possible that other Christian SME owner-managers might use the concept of the Kingdom of God to engage in a range of business practices that benefit the wider community. UK1's and D10's reference to the Kingdom of God in section 5.2.1 implied, for example, that the Kingdom of God was in one way or another relevant to business practices which were meant to benefit others.

Another interesting aspect relating to D5's account was his regard of the 'material' world in terms of its spiritual significance. He argued that a "pure manufacturing company" would not be able to contribute to the Kingdom of God as such but that his company was able to do so because some "non-material" aspects were involved in a printing business. As a result, he did not consider dealings with the 'material' world, i.e. the 'creative' process that is involved in the manufacturing of products and the related benefits to other human beings, to be spiritually significant – in contrast to the respondents above. This implies that he might have regarded faith as being primarily significant for the 'non-material' aspects of human existence such as the human 'soul'. At the same time, the kind of products and services that the other respondents offered might have enabled them more to recognise their spiritual significance, as they were either of more lasting value or it was more obvious that they 'helped' other human beings. By contrast, D5's account implied that he might have felt a bit more uneasy to ascribe spiritual significance to the service that his printing company provided – as the products often had a rather 'short-lived' existence ("That you don't have to say 'We only print forms'. Or with advertising material, most of it will just be thrown into the bin, more or less").

The next group of statements related to the fact that through running a business owner-managers interact with a number of people and the respondents here regarded those social interactions as an area that had spiritual significance.

D10 rationalised this focus on people by rejecting the view that God was interested in the products he made – again a contrast to the belief that was consciously or unconsciously held by the respondents in section 5.3.1, i.e. that every aspect of human existence, even the making of a product or the delivery of a service, is of spiritual relevance in the context of God's creation. Similar to D5, the perception that manufactured products are of ephemeral nature ("Because they will go to the scrap yard eventually. That means they are not of eternal value.") might have led him to place his spiritual focus specifically on people. His account implied that he considered this focus to be of more lasting value, probably implicitly referring to the belief that people have an 'immortal', 'eternal' soul. He was the only respondent that explicitly expressed such a strong view, even though more respondents might have held the same view implicitly or unconsciously. Other respondents, however, who also regarded interactions with other people as being spiritually significant, may not have regarded this focus as exclusive of the spiritual significance of the 'material' aspects of the business.

A number of respondents specifically talked about their spiritual responsibility or desire to bring about a change in other people's lives – and they often referred to their employees in this context, but also to other people that they interacted with in their business, such as customers etc. They might have hereby alluded to ideas of 'transformation' or 'renewal' of the human person ('metanoia'), which play a central part in Christian teaching (Verstraeten 1998, Mikolaski 1992). The respondents used different language to describe this spiritual responsibility and also placed different emphases on different aspects of this 'transformation'. However, the respondents broadly referred to two aspects a) the development of people's potential as part of their personal development and b) a change in other people's behaviour and attitudes towards themselves and in relationship to others.

In terms of the former aspect, the respondents regarded it as their responsibility to be committed to their employees' training (UK2) and to develop their gifts and talents in the workplace (D10) so that people "had a sense of achievement" (D10) or started to "believe in themselves" (UK2). UK2 gave a specific example of how he had sought to give a young person who had been excluded from school the chance to 'develop' by taking him on as an employee.

With regards to the latter aspect, the respondents regarded it as their (spiritual) responsibility to encourage others – employees, customers etc. - to behave in a different way. For example, it led D7 to challenge his customers when they wanted to exploit insurance schemes and D8 and UK2 talked about how they wanted to encourage their employees not to engage in selfish behaviour in their workplace. D10, on the other hand, said that it was his responsibility to create a 'positive' atmosphere in his company, which may inspire his employees to change their behaviour. Interestingly, D10 seemed to be more concerned about the change that such an atmosphere could bring about in the employees' personal lives, whereas all the other respondents seemed to be primarily concerned about other people's behaviour in business, or more generally in the public sphere. This difference – although this might not be reflected by the respondents – echoes the concern of some scholars that conservative Christians might sometimes focus only on their private, personal morality and not link their faith with moral behaviour in the public sphere (see section 2.2.2; Bellah et al. 1996, 231). But this was not the case with UK2, D7 and D8. Even though their approach might have been rather 'personal' they obviously addressed the 'public' morality of others. D8, moreover, explicitly regarded his active concern about people's behaviour in the public sphere as his responsibility to wider society as he believed that the church alone could not change public morality. This concern about the moral behaviour of others in the workplace might not be unique to Christian SME owner-managers (cf. Spence 2000) and one could argue that concern over the reputation of the business might sometimes play a part as well. However, the Christian faith provided Christian owner-managers with a distinct motivation to be concerned about the moral behaviour of others in the public sphere.

The final group of respondents mentioned in this section regarded their business as a social context in which they should share their faith with other people. At first sight, this kind of spiritual significance may have the least impact on Christian owner-managers behaviours as it does not directly translate into particular business practices. This is even more so the case, if the Christian faith is communicated only in terms of the 'salvation for eternal life' - which implies a more 'forward-looking' perspective on faith[133] with the focus on people's souls - and/or in terms of the spiritual comfort that Christianity can offer. Hence if the Gospel message that people seek to communicate does not contain any reference to a Christ-like lifestyle or (changed) moral behaviour, there might not even be an 'indirect' impact on society. But there was evidence in the sample that a number of people did link their desire to share their faith with their own behaviour, and also with the desire to bring about a changed behaviour in other people. UK10, for instance, sought to share his faith in the context of his approach to running his business – which he stated was reflective of his Christian "mission to care for and love others" (see section 4.1.4). Thus he linked his 'witness by word' with his own conception of a Christian lifestyle of service and care for others. In D10's account, on the other hand, there was some inference that his desire to share his faith with his employees was linked with his concern about bringing about a "positive change" in his employees' behaviour and about contributing to their personal development. There were more examples in section 4.3 of how the respondents' desire to share their faith may have linked with certain behaviours and practices, even if it was only about not bringing the Christian faith into disrepute. At the same time, the idea of sharing one's faith through business was rejected by a number of respondents as, for example, they acknowledged the specific characteristics of a workplace situation, which they did not want to exploit for evangelising.

In conclusion, if a Christian owner-manager regards various aspects of his business activities as being of spiritual significance this might, similar to the concepts mentioned in chapter 4, provide him with a strong motivation to engage in certain practices. Yet owner-managers may have different understandings of what 'spiritual significance' encompasses, and might consequently apply it to different kinds of practices. If the owner-manager, for example, follows the understanding that only souls matter spiritually he might focus specifically on sharing his faith with other people through his business, but this would have no direct impact on concrete business practices. If he regards it of spiritual importance to bring about a change in other people, then this could lead him, for example, to be particularly concerned about the skills development and training of his employees or to seek to influence other people's (employees, customers etc.) moral behaviour in a positive way. Finally if he considers the material world to be spiritually significant, he might be particularly interested in environmentally friendly practices. Using a different categorisation, the desire to bring about a change

---

[133] Which was also implied in the 'separatist' understanding of the Kingdom of God (see above)

in other people and the interest in the material world may be regarded as having a 'this-worldly' spiritual focus. Another example for a practice that has a 'this-worldly' focus is the concern to provide a high-quality service or product if work is regarded as something that is 'done for the Lord'. One can argue here that the practices that owner-managers link with 'this-worldly' dimensions of spiritual significance may benefit wider society as well. By contrast, if the spiritual focus is on dimensions that are more separate to 'worldly' activities, such as the concern of the salvation of souls for eternal life or the community of faith and their spiritual causes, then the spiritual concern has less of a direct impact on wider society.

The findings in this section also offer some explanation for the diversity with which the respondents engaged with some of the Christian concepts that were mentioned in chapter 4. For example, the concept of calling might not have much impact on business practices if the 'other worldly' or 'soul' dimension only is regarded to be of spiritual significance, e.g. if people apply the concept of calling only to their perceived responsibility to share their faith with others in the workplace and not to their workplace activity as such. If, however, Christian owner-managers apply a 'this-worldly' spiritual focus to their business activities, this might lead them to conceptualise a number of different business practices in the context of calling, which may also 'make a difference'. Likewise, the concept of stewardship might include or exclude the 'care for creation' depending on whether the 'material' world dimension is regarded to be spiritually significant or not.

6. Reported Practices

Having looked at the way the respondents framed their actions by drawing on concepts that are available in Christian discourse, and how they related to various contexts that are linked with the Christian faith, the focus of this chapter are the practices that the respondents reported.

Section 6.1 and 6.2 will specifically look at the *business* practices that the respondents linked with their Christian faith. Practices in this context will refer to both attitudes and behaviour. Although sections 4 and 5 already mentioned practices, for instance, as illustrations of the respondents' framing, sections 6.1 and 6.2 will take a different starting point by seeking to categorise the different practices that the respondents described and to discuss questions such as: Which of those practices are specifically Christian? Where are the areas where Christian beliefs and subsequent framing may 'make a difference' in the respondents' behaviour? To what extent does it make a difference? How might other motives influence the respondents' conceptualisation of practice?

In doing so, the space between beliefs, attitudes and behaviour will be investigated. Following the methodological framework that was chosen for this study – as outlined in section 3.1.3 –, we assume that talk and behaviour are not two entirely separate phenomena, but that the reference to certain concepts and beliefs in the respondents' accounts also influence both their actual attitudes and/or (subsequent) behaviour (Alvesson and Karreman 2000b, Watson and Harris 1999, 6). Given the chosen research method (interviews), answers to those questions will have to be rather open-ended, and some suggestions will be made as to how to investigate the issues further.

Section 6.1 will look at general attitudes and behaviours that the respondents reported. In each subsection we look at a specific set of behaviour and/or attitudes and in this context raise and discuss some specific issues such as motivation, the influence of framing etc.

Section 6.2 will focus on practices that specifically refer to employees, as this was the stakeholder group that the respondents mentioned most frequently. The issues that were raised in section 6.1 and particularly the themes of sections 6.1.4 to 6.1.6 will be explored further here.

Both sections will sometimes refer back to the practices that have been mentioned before in chapters 4 and 5 but also use additional examples from the data.

Section 6.3 will go beyond business practices and focus on the respondents' engagement with wider society. Although, compared to their day-to-day business life, this engagement might play a relatively minor role, it is nevertheless interesting to investigate how the respondents related to wider society, and what influence their faith might have had here. The section will focus on charitable giving and civic engagement in the context of local and professional communities and will also consider the presence of other motivations.

6.1 General attitudes and behaviours

This section deals with some general attitudes and behaviours that the respondents reported. Section 6.1.1 will look at some practices that could be regarded as specifically Christian. Sections 6.1.2 and 6.1.3 will look at practices that the respondents reported but that are not specifically Christian, even though they were framed in Christian language. Sections 6.1.4 to 6.1.6 will then look at some areas and practices where Christian beliefs may make more of a 'difference' in the respondents' attitudes and behaviours. Whereas the results are not exclusively Christian, Christian beliefs may impact on attitudes and behaviour in a distinct way so that it may make a difference in the way the owner-managers run their business.

6.1.1 Specific Christian practices

In the sample, a few respondents gave some examples of practices that could be regarded as specifically Christian.

For instance, two respondents referred to practices in which they would not engage, because those practices related to what they perceived to be immoral sexual behaviour. D5, for example, said that it posed a difficulty for him when customers asked him to print material that promoted licentious sexual practices, but that customers increasingly understood that he was not willing to print such material because of his faith.

> Once, a customer asked me to expose some films for him. And when the data came, it was all advertisements for … some sex mail order company. … So I called him … and said 'Listen, you may not know this, but I manage this company as a Christian. And I just wanted to tell you that this is the last time that I'll print this kind of material for you. Next time round I'll take a raincheck on it. If you bring me something like this without asking me beforehand, I'm not gonna do it for you, I'd be willing to bear the damage. … We still work with him, I haven't lost this customer. But he wouldn't dare to ask me to do something like that again. And these are things that come up only once in a while. And over the years we haven't had to point this out much, because people know you and they know that they can't ask you to quote for certain things.[134]
> (D5a, printing)

Similarly, D7 reported that he did not want to use some promotional material that the purchasing organisation of which he was a member offered, because it included sexual connotations.

Another example of specific Christian behaviour was the insistence of a few respondents – all of them British - of not working on Sundays. UK4, for instance, stated that he had made a decision to keep his business shut on Sundays when he bought the business from his predecessor.

> Um, and when we first bought it, we, it was always open seven days, we shut uh we shut Sundays. Because we we wanted to keep the Sunday special. Uh, and uh we shut Sundays, we couldn't afford to shut Sundays, um, because we got income from Sundays.

---

[134] Ich hab mal Anz-, hab mal Filme belichten sollen für einen Kunden. Und als die Daten kamen, waren das lauter Anzeigenfilme für ... irgendein Sex-Versand. ... Da hab' ich ihn angerufen, ... hab' gesagt ‚Passen Sie auf, so und so ist, ich, Sie sehen's vielleicht dem Betrieb nicht an, aber ich führ' den Betrieb als Christ. Und ähm, ich wollte Ihnen nur sagen, dass das das letzte Mal ist, dass ich Ihnen das drucke. Das nächste Mal lass' ich Sie an die Wand laufen. Wenn Sie mir so was bringen, ohne mich, ohne vorneweg anzufragen, dann mache ich Ihnen das nicht, dann bin ich bereit, jeden Schaden zu tragen. ...' (W)ir arbeiten noch mit ihm zusammen, den hab' nicht verloren, den Kunden. Aber solche Sachen traut er sich nicht mehr anzufragen. Und das sind Sachen, die kommen alle Jahre mal ein Mal vor bloß. Und mit der Zeit ist es aber nicht mehr so oft nötig, weil die Leute dich kennen und die wissen das, dass sie nicht mit allem zu uns kommen dürfen.

> Um, but uh, we prayed about it and we shut it didn't make the slightest difference to our income.
> (UK4a, car rental)

Lastly, D1 reported that because of his Christian worldview he refused to overly promote 'esoteric' drugs in his pharmacy, i.e. drugs that did not have a scientific basis but were rather based on 'new age' philosophies.

These practices stand out as specifically Christian in the context of the increasing de-Christianisation of society. In a Christian society, 'public' morality would not condone sexual licentiousness and Sunday trading. D1's Christian concern about 'esoteric' drugs also stands out in a society in which an increasing number of people do not think anything of turning to different 'spiritual' philosophies for help.

This does not mean that non-Christians cannot be concerned about some of those issues, but it is more likely that Christians are specifically concerned here. Moreover, Christians may specifically invoke 'spiritual' reasons to rationalise such practices. In the case of Sunday trading, for instance, Christian might talk about observing a 'day of worship', whereas non-Christians would perhaps more argue in terms of observing a 'public day of rest'. The example of Sunday trading also shows that the extent of de-Christianisation may vary in different national contexts. It was not surprising that only British respondents mentioned this as one of their Christian values, as in the German context Sunday trading is not yet so much of an issue because regulations in Germany currently only allow a limited number of businesses to trade on Sundays (even though this is likely to change). In the U.K., however, owner-managers may stand out more if they decide not to do business on Sundays, particularly when most of their competitors do.

6.1.2 Morally correct behaviour

Most people in the study, however, reported mainly on practices that are not considered specific Christian behaviour but that may be regarded simply as morally correct behaviour or 'normal' moral behaviour. They talked about paying taxes, being honest, open and fair in their business dealings, being reliable and standing by one's commitments, paying bills and wages on time, paying correct wages, not taking advantage of others or ripping others off, adhering to health and safety standards, not engaging in illegal practices etc.

So if these practices could be regarded as commonplace behaviour, where is the specific influence of Christianity? An obvious difference lies in the framing of those practices. The respondents often very explicitly drew on Christian concepts such as witness, which, for instance, implies that Christian should not display any behaviour that might bring Christianity into disrepute (section 4.3); holiness, which, among others, refers to the Christian aspiration of moral blamelessness (section 4.4); they framed it as a specifically Christian principle or Christian duty (section 4.5) or even invoked the stewardship discourse, by regarding morally correct conduct as part of their stewardship responsibilities to God (section 4.2).

Moreover, some respondents drew on specific passages in Scripture to rationalise their moral behaviour. D2, for example, referred to the passage "Render to Caesar what is Caesar's" (Matthew 21:22) to explain that he would not do anything illegal in his business.

> Well, one thing that comes up again and again is the black market, for example. And uh, first of all, that we should have certain repair work carried out without proper contracts. Or when I do a property deal and customers come and say 'Come on, I'll pay your commission cash in hand, forget about VAT' et cetera. And um, I say no and uh, this is a thing that often comes up. I try to *'Render to Caesar what is Caesar's'*. And uh, even though it's often rather tempting and it really hurts, but um, yeah, I'd rather have a clear

conscience, I feel better that way. And I think it also does a Christian good, if he takes this to heart.[135]
(D2a, property management)

Apart from this difference in the way the respondents describe their behaviour, it is difficult to determine to what extent those practices that fall under the category 'morally correct behaviour' compare with the type and extent of moral behaviour that SME owner-managers who do not explicitly draw on Christian discourse might display. It would require a different kind of study, one which considers this comparative element and is perhaps also more based on observation than solely reliant on self-reported behaviour.

For one thing, it is possible that the explicit Christian framing may create a stronger motivation to display moral integrity as it is considered not only important within a given social context but also relates to additional religious dimensions (Hicks 1996). Thus it provides additional distinct reasons as to why a Christian owner-manager should adhere to those values (see chapter 4). At the same time, if such a comparative study was to be carried out, one might want to investigate the following aspects, which were highlighted by the respondents.

Firstly, a number of respondents pointed out that they had been presented with opportunities to be dishonest or to be able to take advantage of others in the context of their business but said that they chose not to exploit this because of their Christian moral standards.

D1, for example, said that due to the way his sector is regulated there would be numerous opportunities to be dishonest.

> Well it means eventually that how I behave as a businessman and, you know, this conflict between ethics and money-making, that I'm completely upright there. ... (W)ell, there are enough opportunities to, say, to submit prescriptions that you have only partly supplied or not supplied at all. *Because this is only regulated indirectly in Germany, uh it's so easy to do.* And uh, we keep, you know, we stay out of this game.[136]
> (D1b, pharmacy)

Whether there is an actual difference in behaviour with respect to the 'exploitation of opportunities', however, may be difficult to draw out, particularly when those situations that encourage exploitation may only be visible to the owner-managers themselves.

Secondly, some respondents particularly mentioned the illegal or unethical practices that they perceived to be happening in their trades, and that they disassociated themselves from by explicitly making a stand about their (Christian) moral values.

UK9, for example, referred to what he perceived to be the employment practices of a number of his competitors in the building trade.

> You know, so um [pause] um there is also the area of um uh taxation. You know, the building industry is is notoriously um um bent. Um, so from that point of view, um um I I stick rigidly to the letter of the law in absolutely everything. So I don't employ people um unless they have the right, you know, well, I I either have to employ people on PAYE

[135] Naja, 'ne Thematik bei uns ist ja immer zum Beispiel Schwarzarbeit auch. Und äh, erstens mal, dass dass gewisse Reparaturen ähm in Schwarzarbeit gemacht werden sollen. Oder jetzt in äh einem Maklergeschäft, dass Kunden kommen und sagen ‚Komm', die die Provision schieb' ich so über den Tisch, vergessen wir mal die Steuer' und so weiter. Und ähm, da sag' ich halt nein und äh das ist so ein das ist so ein Punkt, der ähm häufiger wiederkehrt. Also eben auch das zu beachten *'Dem Kaiser, was des Kaisers ist.'* Und äh ja, wenn's auch oft äh verlockend ist und eher weh tut, aber ähm, ja ich hab' dann lieber ein reines Gewissen, da fühl' ich mich wohler. Und ich denke, dass es einem Christen auch gut zu Gesicht steht, wenn er ähm, das auch beherzigt.

[136] Na ja, das das heißt heißt natürlich letztlich, dass ich mit dem, wie ich mich verhalte als Geschäftsmann und äh, ich sag' mal auch dieses Spannungsfeld Ethik-Monetik, äh, das so zu gestalten, dass äh, dass es eben astrein ist. ... (A)lso es gibt genügend Möglichkeiten, was weiß ich, Leistungen abzurechnen und nur halb zu erbringen oder nicht zu erbringen oder so. *Dadurch, dass es dass es hier in Deutschland ja eben alles recht indirekt geregelt ist, äh, ist ist das eigentlich kein Problem.* Und das äh, halten wir schon, ich sag' mal, da halten wir schon den Ball flach.

these days or they have a um a current certificate, subcontractor certificate. So, I mean, so many builders employ um Eastern Europeans and um just take short-cuts, you know, they're paying cash.
(UK9a, building services)

UK3, similarly, said that he did not want to get involved in practices that he felt his trade was renowned for (see section 4.4.3).

> Well, um [pause] pushing people to make decisions, um [pause] winding people up um on offers, um you know, the sort of thing that estate agents are renowned for. You know, winding up one purchaser against another. I don't do that.
> (UK3a, estate agent)

Yet in some cases morally correct behaviour did not seem to be so 'normal' in the context of certain sectors. Some respondents pointed out that they found it increasingly difficult to follow their (Christian) moral values in their sectors, as it seriously affected the profitability of their business.

D6, who works in the building trade, said that his Christian value of paying correct taxes posed a particular challenge for him. He reported that he encountered more and more customers who were not prepared to pay VAT, which he had to accommodate somehow if he did not want to turn contracts away.

> We've got, there are always people who come, uh for example just recently, we'd been working for two people for a week, ... And both of them told me very clearly 'We're not going to pay VAT.' Both customers. ... And that is where the Christian thing comes in. What do you do? Normally you shouldn't do it. Normally you should say 'As a Christian, I don't cheat.' So. At the end of the day we cheat ourselves, because we do pay tax. That means, we get 16 percent less[137], and still do the job and say 'OK'.[138]
> (D6b, decorating and special surface coatings)

Again, it might be difficult to draw out here to what extent the Christian beliefs of the respondents may make a difference in their behaviour. In some cases, however, a specific religious motivation might be necessary to sustain both law-abiding and moral behaviour (or at least some kind of moral awareness), particularly when such behaviour is punished rather than rewarded. Studies that specifically focus on certain industry sectors may be helpful here, as they might illuminate, among other things, as to why Christian respondents feel driven to make an explicit stand about their moral values and behaviour.

In summary, the display of morally correct behaviour is nothing specifically Christian, and the only difference between Christian owner-managers and their non-Christian counterparts might be the way those practices are described. However, Christianity might make more of a difference when owner-managers are presented with opportunities to exploit situations for monetary gain that no one else would find out about, when they operate in sectors that do not enjoy a high reputation or when morally correct behaviour threatens the survival of the business. Those possible differences, however, would have to be explored in comparative studies that do not solely rely on self-reported behaviour.

---

[137] This is a reference to the then current VAT rate in Germany.

[138] Wir haben, immer wieder kommen Leute, äh äh wo also zum Beispiel jetzt, wir waren jetzt 'ne Woche (bei) zwei arbeiten, ... Da haben beide mir klipp und klar erklärt 'Wir zahlen ohne Mehrwertsteuer'. Beide Kunden. ... Und da kommt jetzt das Christliche, was machen Sie? Eigentlich dürften sie es nicht machen. Eigentlich müssten Sie sagen als Christ betrüge ich nicht. So. Letztendlich unter'm Strich betrügen wir uns selber, weil wir nämlich versteuern. Das heißt, wir kriegen 16 Prozent weniger und äh gehen das trotzdem ein und sagen ‚Ok.'

6.1.3 Providing a good service

The people in the study also frequently mentioned the importance of providing a good, high quality service, which, again, would be nothing specifically Christian. The respondents used different Christian frames to explain their practices but they also frequently referred to various other motivations that might influence their aspiration to provide a good service. Thus this section presents a good opportunity to demonstrate that there might be influences on the owner-managers' conceptualisation of practice beyond Christianity. The following examples illustrate the existence of the different motives among the owner-managers but also show that those motives can easily mix.

Section 5.3.1 showed how some people in the study believed that they worked primarily "for the Lord", which led them to seek to provide a high-quality service. UK9 was one such respondent.

> Um, [pause] but I'm but I'm very conscious now of of what the Bible says, about, you know, *what what we do, we do for the Lord not for men.* And and to me that's an encouragement, you know, if I, you know, I I'll do a job and I'll look at it if I'm not happy with it, I'll redo it. You know, if I'm, you know, and I set myself fairly high standards. *Because what I do I do for the Lord.*
> (UK9b, building services)

UK5, on the other hand, stated that his aim to provide a good, high quality service was influenced by a character trait of his, i.e. his perfectionism.

> I'm a perfectionist. In fact, it's one of my, some people would say, it's a flaw in that um if I'm not happy with something, I'd take it out and do it again. ... And um, well people forget when you're in a trade you've got to fi-, get something out of that trade other than money. And if all you get out of it is money, I think, you've got a problem. It's not gonna be something that you can do for the rest of your life. So you've got to get some some fulfilment out of what you're doing. And I I like to be able to walk away from a job when it's a really well done job.
> (UK5a, heating engineer)

In another part of the interview, however, he maintained that doing a "well done job" was also part of his Christian witness to his customers (section 4.3.3).

> Um, I think it's nice for people to have a Christian company to compare with. And by doing our work well that's a witness in itself.
> (UK5a heating engineer)

D7 made a specific reference to yet another influence. He regarded the provision of a quality, expert service as part of his Christian responsibility. When he was asked to summarise what was important to him in his role as Christian business owner, he mentioned, among other things, the provision of a good quality service.

> *Interviewer:* What is important to you in your role as Christian business owner? [paraphrased]
> *D7:* There is this lovely word authenticity. So, to be authentic. And um [pause] what else is important? [pause] Um, that people have a good feeling when they come to us or when they leave the shop, the customers. That employees have the opportunity to contribute to the business and feel happy. Um [long pause] well, and to *provide good quality* and have a good reputation.[139] (D7a, optician)

---

[139] *Interviewer:* Was ist Ihnen wichtig als christlicher Unternehmer? [paraphrased]
D7: Gibt ja, gibt dieses schöne Wort Authenzität. Also dieses authentisch sein. Und ähm [Pause] mh (Pause), was ist mir noch wichtig? [Pause] Ähm, dass Leute ein gutes Gefühl haben, wenn sie herkommen, oder wenn sie

However, in another part of the interview he specifically stated that he also wanted reflect the professional standards of his trade and explicitly considered this his responsibility to society.

> Expertise is very important, of course. I can't sell someone varifocals for 1000 Euros and just tell him that the glasses are better for him, but I need to provide more information about them as well. Um, or at least display the technical know-how, to signal 'Well, we are competent. You are in good hands here.' *So it's ... about reflecting a professional image. And about expertise.* But um you can say that there is definitely some sort of societal responsibility.[140]
> (D7a, optician)

Other respondents emphasised that it was important for them to offer a service that was truly reflective of their customers' needs. UK7, for instance, said that he took customer care very seriously and that he would sit down with the customer and jointly find out about the customer's needs, which would then lead to delivering work that the customer was satisfied with. In the interview, he illustrated his approach to customer service by talking of a project that his company had recently been involved in – the building of a nursery. But his account also made clear that he was aware that the provision of a good service was at the same time very much in the interest of his company.

> Because we want uh, yes, the best the best investment for this business is is to satisfy our customer, who will say to people; we can send people to that place and he will say 'Yeah, (COMPANY NAME) did a great job for us.'
> (UK7a, engineering)

In sum, the respondents' accounts of their concern to provide a good service illustrate very nicely that their practices might have various different motives, which may mix with a more specific Christian motivations. The influences that the respondents mentioned in this particular context were certain character traits as well as the adherence to professional standards; and some respondents were also openly conscious of the fact that providing a good service may be in their and their business' self-interest.[141]

6.1.4 'Spirit' in which service is provided

Several respondents, however, referred to certain fundamental attitudes that guided the provision of their service and that went beyond wanting to provide a good service, and this was identified as one important area where Christianity might make more of a 'difference'. Those attitudes were highly marked by Christian beliefs and the framing suggested that their faith had quite a strong impact on the attitudes and subsequent behaviour that they described.

Some people in the study, for instance, placed a particular emphasis on treating others equally, independent of what they themselves got out of that business relationship, thereby alluding to the

---

rausgehen, (die) Kunden. Dass die Mitarbeiter die Möglichkeit haben, sich hier auch einzubringen und sich wohlzufühlen. Ähm, [lange Pause] ja, *gute Qualität auch zu liefern* und 'n guten Ruf zu haben.

[140] Kompetenz ist auch 'ne wichtige Sache, klar. Klar, also ich kann nicht jemand 'ne Gleitsichtbrille für 1000 Euro verkaufen, und ihm erzählen, dass die Gläser einfach nur besser sind für ihn, sondern er möchte schon dann auch schon ein bisschen was wissen. Mh, oder zumindest das technische Know-How auch zu haben, um zu signalisieren ‚Also, damit können wir umgehen. Hier seid ihr gut aufgehoben.' *Also das, ... das ist einfach das, das Berufsbild widerzuspiegeln. Und hab' 'ne Kompetenz, klar.* Aber, ähm, dass man schon sagen, dass 'n gew-gewisse gesellschaftliche Verantwortung durchaus auch da ist.

[141] The respondents who talked about *morally correct behaviour* may have also been influenced by other factors that led them to display such behaviour, such as concerns about their reputation, 'enlightened' self-interest or their upbringing.

Christian belief that everyone is equal before the eyes of God and that therefore everyone should be treated with equal dignity and respect.[142]

As one example, UK11 stated that God would disapprove of her if she did not try to treat her customers equally and fairly – independent of how much business she was going to do with them or how 'pleasant' they were (see section 4.2.4).[143]

> *One thing I've been thinking about is treating everybody equally.* So it's easy in our job, you know, somebody comes in who looks well, … like they got plenty of money it would be very easy to treat them differently to somebody who comes in, who obviously isn't going to spend very much money. So I just thought about it yesterday, about making sure to give everybody the same care no matter what they're gonna spend on their glasses. *And I think that would be something that God would disapprove of, to discriminate between people.* And in other ways as well, you know, when somebody comes in and you think 'Oh no, not them again' 'Oh no, not them again. It's that smelly lot.' [laughs] And um, yeah, treating everybody (equally) and fairly.
> (UK11b, optician)

The intention to treat all customers equally was also implied in UK5's account, who said that because he did his work "as unto God" he sought to do a good job even for those customers that he perceived as being unpleasant (see section 5.3.1).

> Um, and teachingwise it says 'Do your work as unto God.' *So if you're working for someone, even if they're rude, obnoxious, horrible, smelly, all those things, you're asked to work as if you were working for God. In which case you're gonna do the best job you possibly can.*
> (UK5b, heating engineer)

Other respondents stated that they wanted to regard their customers in a way that went beyond a pure transactional relationship because of their faith. We can recognise a link here to the Christian belief that every human being is created in the image of God (Genesis 1:27) and that therefore others should be treated as persons and not – in this context – in terms of an economic relationship only.

For D7, for example, it was important from his faith perspective to treat his customers in a way that went beyond a purely transactional relationship and that made them feel appreciated or, in his Christian terms, "feel blessed" (see section 4.2.2).

> Well I guess it's that when people who come here feel at home, um that they realise that they're important to us. Um, let's say, that many of them will feel blessed. Well it's not particularly to do with starting intense conversations, also about other things, but simply through the way I deal with them. That they notice that things are a bit different here.[144]
> (D7a, optician)

Later on in the interview he gave a specific example of how he tried to bring a personal element to his relationship to his customers.

> We have quite a few Turkish customers. And I connect well with them. There are also a lot of young men, 17, 18, who want to take their driving licence and need an eye-test for

[142] This belief is, for instance, spelt out in Proverbs 22:2: "Rich and poor have this in common: The Lord is the Maker of all" (NIV). Other passages in the Bible also allude to the equality of all people.

[143] D1 talked about treating customers equally in a similar way (see section 4.3.3).

[144] Schwerpunkte sind, dass mh Leute tatsächlich auch, die hier 'reinkommen, mh, dass sie sich wohlfühlen, dass sie wissen, dass dass sie uns wichtig sind. Ähm, ich sage auch einfach mal so, dass dass viele einfach auch gesegnet werden. Also, das das hat nicht unbedingt jetzt damit zu tun, dass man äh jetzt so intensiv das Gespräch sucht, auch über andere Themen, sondern einfach durch die Begegnung. Dass sie merken, dass da ein bisschen was anders ist als sonst.

that. And they sometimes turn up in a crowd, which can be sometimes quite a challenge. And dealing with them, I notice, that sometimes giving them some sort of recognition or simply saying 'Well done. Super. Excellent.' is sufficient to break the ice.[145]
(D7a, optician)

For UK10, on the other hand, his belief that "everyone is special to God" strongly impacted on the way he sought to run his business in that the service to his customers - including the 'difficult' ones such as drug addicts - came before the well-being of his business.

> I mean that that I perhaps value the person, um, if you like, recognising that each one, each one is special not just to to God, but it has to be special to me as well. *And and therefore trying to value each person and rather than just seeing them as a a source of cash.* Um and that does mean that ... especially when it comes to the more difficult patients I mean I may I may make decisions sometimes, which are [pause] not beneficial to the business or sometimes even risky for me. Um, particularly with the addicts.
> (UK10a, pharmacy)

To sum up, the accounts of the respondents cited here indicate that their faith might make a fundamental difference in terms of how they seek to interact with others in their business. In particular, the respondents stated that they sought to treat people equally or to treat others in a way that recognised that every human being is made in the image of God. In other words, their faith might lead them to provide their service in a way that goes beyond pure business or other utilitarian considerations.

6.1.5 Other-regarding behaviour

Another area in which the Christian faith may make some difference is so-called 'other-regarding behaviour'. Respondents either described how they sought to respond to certain situations or mentioned some specific behaviour in which they showed themselves considerate of others. In all of those the influence of Christian beliefs might have played a role, to varying degrees.

Considering the circumstances and interests of others

Some respondents referred to certain situations that they encountered in their business life where they felt that they should be considerate of the circumstances or interests of others.

D2, for example, said that "not reacting in a merciless manner" in certain situations should be something that marks out a Christian business person.

> Well, I'm always concerned that Christian business people are an example in terms of their behaviour, in how they do things, you know. And uh, I think, uh, it shows in how you do your work. And uh [pause], how can I put this, well it's often very very difficult to see, is that person a Christian or not. I mean, every business man will try to do his work properly. *Um, it depends on what happens in specific situations, I think, how you react to problems and so. Um, [pause], perhaps looking under the surface in one or the*

---

[145] Also, wir haben sehr viel, mh türkische Kunden auch. Und ich hab' 'n guten Draht. Da sind auch sehr viel junge Männer, 17, 18, die ihren Führerschein machen wollen, dazu 'n Sehtest benötigen. Und sie tauchen manchmal auch sehr pulkartig auf. Und das ist manchmal auch 'ne echte Herausforderung. Ähm, und ihnen zu begegnen, mh, ich merke, dass da manchmal so'n bisschen manchmal ausreicht, bisschen Anerkennung zu signalisieren oder sage 'Mensch, das haben Sie aber toll gemacht. Klasse, toll.' Wie das reicht, um das Eis schmelzen zu lassen.

other situation and not, you know, reacting in a merciless manner. Or ... whatever problem needs to be solved.[146]
(D2a, property management)

We saw in section 4.4.3 that he sought to apply this by seeking to understand his debtors' situations and to find a solution when they were not able to pay their full debts.

D3, similarly, referred to certain incidents in which he tried to be considerate of his customers' interests. This happened, for example, customers damaged the vehicles that they had rented from him.

> Well, in the car rental business you have a lot of scope, and uh a customer just returned from Spain ... (and) the bumper was broken. And, of course, I could say 'Well, that's your 1000 Euro deposit. The damage is that much – if not more.' But I can also say 'Well, OK' and put something else to them or I do the repairs myself and charge for the materials, and perhaps one or two working hours at 70 Euros. Uh, and will not have it done by a garage, which would certainly charge a lot more.[147]
> (D3b, mobile home rental)

Later in the interview he also framed this as "showing mercy" to his customers.

> Well, this is a kind of mercy when I forego opportunities to make profit for the benefit of the customer. If I look at this, I think that's showing mercy.[148]
> (D3b, mobile home rental)

Helping others

Other respondents referred to some specific practices with which they sought to help others through their business. They referred particularly to how they sought to help some disadvantaged people.

UK9, for example, reported that it was his aspiration to "be like Jesus" that led him to employ a young man that had breached the law (see section 4.4.2).

> *Um, you know, I guess it's, you know, you know, as a Christian you you've got to look at the uh, you know, Jesus' first ministry was was often to the outcast in society.* You know, the taxmen, the prostitutes and, and I guess, you know, youngsters that's had a brush with the law and has decided to go straight um, you know, ... So I just, I started a new lad last week.
> (UK9a, building services)

---

[146] Also mein Anliegen ist immer, dass möglichst christliche Unternehmer eben auch in ihrem Verhalten, in ihrem ihrem ganzen Tun Vorbild sind, sage ich mal. Und ja, ich denke, jja, zeigt sich auch darin, wie man seine Arbeit tut. Und äh (Pause) ja, wie soll ich das formulieren, also das ist oft sehr, sehr schwierig zu erkennen, ist das ein Christ, oder ist das kein Christ. Ich mein', jeder Unternehmer wird sich bemühen, seine Arbeit ähm ordentlich zu machen. *Ähm, das muss sich aus der Situation heraus ergeben, denke ich mal, wie man bei bestimmten Problemen reagiert, und so. Äh [Pause], vielleicht im einen oder anderen Punkt doch ähm mehr hinterfragt und nicht, sag' ich mal, gnadenlos reagiert Oder ... was für'n Problem äh gerade zu lösen ist.*

[147] Also da hat man natürlich auch äh als als Vermieter viel Spielraum und äh ist jetzt gerade ein Kunde zurück, Spanien zurückgekommen ... (und hatte) die Stoßstange kaputt gemacht. Ja, und da kann ich natürlich gleich sagen 'Naja gut, die 1000 Euro, die sind weg von der Kaution. Der Schaden ist mindestens so.' Aber ich kann jetzt auch sagen 'Naja gut, ok.' Erstmal ein Angebot machen oder ich mach's selbst und und und rechne den Materialpreis, und von mir vielleicht ein bis zwei Stunden mit 70 Euro. Äh, und lasse das nicht von der Werkstatt machen, wo dann sicherlich ein ganz anderer Rahmen ist, ja.

[148] Also das ist ja eine Form von Barmherzigkeit, dass ich also zu Gunsten des Kunden äh auf Profit für mich verzichte. Also wenn ich das halt so sehe, das ist Barmherzigkeit.

We further saw in section 5.3.2 that it was UK2's (and his Christian personnel manager's) desire to 'develop people's potential', which, among other things, led him to take on a boy that had been expelled from school.

> Um, and we've had one notable one last year who was um an excluded child. They wouldn't have him back at school. But (NAME OF PERSONNEL MANAGER) said 'I think there is something in him. I think probably he's not a school boy. He is much more, he is much happier here on our shopfloor.' And um he is now, left school and um he works for us. And he is terrific. There is no, he is here before time every day, there is no question of um any disciplinary procedures against him. He is fantastic.
> (UK2b, manufacture of metal parts)

Finally, D2 (property management) reported that – as part of his Christian witness - he did not refuse from the outset applications for accommodation from people with a difficult background but that he tried to help them through his business whenever that was possible (see section 4.3.3)

> Uh, what we've tried to do is to give people who are disadvantaged a chance when they're looking for housing. ... Well, um, people who have been treated for drug addiction and so; that we don't refuse their applications from the outset, but try and do them a favour. ... That we don't use a cookie cutter approach, but try to help them if possible.[149]
> (D2b, property management)

Environmental responsibilities

A few respondents also mentioned that they engaged in environmental practices because they felt it was important from a Christian perspective. UK9, for example, stated that he felt that as a Christian he should have a conscience about the environment. He reported that had joined an environmental group and that he sought to be environmentally friendly in his business.

> *UK9:* (A)bout a year ago I I joined um, it's it's actually on my web-site, if you look to my web-site, there there's a link to um an environmental group... I think, we've, you know, we've got to we've got to handle things right. ... So for instance, asbestos is ... gonna be dealt with in a proper manner. ... But in terms of conservation um, you know, if any materials can be reused then I will reuse them. Um, in terms of um waste uh recycling. Recycling is is a major issue, both both my work and my home. Um, I think as Christians we we do we should have a conscience on the about the environment, the way we treat it.
> *Interviewer:* So what was your motivation to join the environmental group?
> *UK9:* Um [pause] I think just just just the, just the need to um [pause] uh I think, we, you know, we we live in a world in a world that man is slowly destroying. And I think if Christians don't don't take a stand in in in looking after the environment, then, you know, who is going to?
> (UK9a, building)

Even though those other-regarding practices they were not exclusively 'Christian' practices the Christian faith provided a distinct rationale or explanation for the respondents' behaviour. Whether they felt they should consider the interests of others in certain situations (D2, D3), whether they felt

[149] Äh, was wir auch äh versucht haben, dass wir Leute, die manchmal bei der Wohnungssuche, sage ich mal, benachteiligt sind, dass wir denen einfach eine Chance geben auch. ... Naja, ähm, Leute, die zum Beispiel aus aus 'ner Entzugsmaßnahme und so dass wir ähm da die nicht von vornherein ablehnen, sondern es mit denen ähm durchaus auch ihnen einen Gefallen tun. ... Dass wir also nicht nicht versuchen, einfach so ähm Schema F das zu machen, sondern so ein bisschen zu helfen, wo es geht.

they should help some disadvantaged people through their business (UK2, UK9, D2), or whether they felt had a responsibility as Christians to engage in some environmentally friendly business practices (UK9), all of those were behaviours that were in one way or another motivated by Christian beliefs. In contrast to section 6.1.4, where Christian beliefs guided the respondents' approach to running the business in a rather fundamental way, the examples in this section referred to specific situations or some specific practices. As such, the Christian impact was somewhat less 'forceful', as the behaviours described could be regarded as being more selective or more limited in scope and intensity, yet the respondents' faith made some difference here.

6.1.6 'Far-reaching' application of Christian concepts and beliefs to business

The final area, in which Christianity may make a difference, was when respondents reported about practices which indicated that they sought to apply their Christian beliefs and values to their business in a rather far-reaching manner.

Christian concepts affecting a whole range of business practices

A few people in the study reported that they sought to apply Christian concepts across a whole range of their business practices. Particularly those respondents who said they felt a calling by God for their business (see section 4.1) framed their practices by referring to Christian concepts which had the potential to shape a whole range of practices.

It was pointed out in section 4.2, for example, that UK7's strong beliefs about Christian stewardship ran through a range of his business practices.

> *If you if if you are a good steward of your, of your business then you will be looking at the well-being of the environment, the well-being of your of of the people in the business.* As well as looking after, um, amounts of money on a on a profit and loss statement or your balance sheet.
> (UK7a, engineering)

Particularly his passion for "looking after the well-being of the environment" seemed to be particularly strong, and he framed it as stewardship over creation (see section 4.2). In terms of actual practices he specifically referred to the part of the business that offered renewable energy related services and products. Although his engineering business operated in a wide range of different fields, and not all were to do with renewable energy, he sought to ensure that across all their operations environmental policies were in place, even though that might sometimes prove difficult.

> Well, I I think where we can um I think, particularly in the in the field of renewable energy um I think um we we have quite a large role to play in in making this planet more sustainable. Um, and and that that has a number of of different aspects. It's not only the the products that we produce, but it's also um utilisation of materials, for instance. Uh, to try, where we can, to use um to use materials that are of, that have, that are not um damaging to the environment. It's very difficult to do it. I mean, one of the, one of the metals that we work with is aluminium. Um, which is probably the um, you know, the extraction of (bauxite) ore um is quite damaging to the environment. But there is a limited amount of influence we can have on that. Because um um because, you know, if something needs to be in aluminium, it needs to be in aluminium. And it's certainly better to make it from aluminium than from plastic. Um, but we have to make sure, everything we work with is recyclable. Recyclability is a very important aspect of sustainability. And that we we build into design.
> (UK7a, engineering)

Another area of concern for UK7 was to "look after the well-being of people" and led him to consider his employees in his business in quite a noticeable way (see section 6.2.2).

We also saw in section 4.1 that UK10 (pharmacy) and UK11 (optician) talked about providing a service to the community. Like UK7, they applied this frame to quite a range of business practices - as described in section 4.1.4 – and by doing so, they often put the service-motive before the profit-motive.

Although the concepts of stewardship and service for the community are concepts that are not exclusively Christian, the religious slant may lie here in the fact that the respondents talked about these things in the context of God's calling (see section 4.1) and so the motivation to engage in those practices might be stronger. It is perhaps also showing in the way UK10 and UK11 were willing to forego their self-interest or opportunities to make profit.

Christian beliefs deeply affecting specific aspects of business behaviour

Whereas a few respondents applied specific Christian concepts to a wide range of their business activities, others seemed to be driven to extensively consider 'other-regarding' values in terms of some specific practices – even though it was likely that they and their business might be placed at a disadvantage because of that.

The Christian commandment to "Consider the interests of others", for example, might have played quite a significant role in UK3's stance towards his competitors. He said that he had realised that he should refrain from "bad-mouthing" his competitors in his advertisements, even though he might make truthful statements and it might help him to gain business.

> *UK3:* I've recently I've done a couple of advertisements saying um 'Fed up with empty promises? We won't give you any empty promises, we'll tell you the um, you know, tell you the facts and give you the honest answers.' But I had been a little bit concerned that saying that is effectively um bad-mouthing the opposition. Well, it **did** get me an instruction, and it **did** get me a property, which we sold. But I have decided, for example, not to run that advertisement again, because I don't think it does, I don't think it's I don't think it's right that you should be rubbishing the opposition. I know we **say** things, but I think to actually advertise that as well that that's going too far. Yeah.
> *Interviewer:* And that is what you think is Christian about you?
> *UK3:* Yes, because there is no other reason why I want them not to do it I don't think. Um, it's truthful, it's honest, it's straightforward, um, but it's also, the the inference is there, the um, it it's the um it's a pejorative statement, isn't it. It's a pejorative question. So. Yeah.
> (UK3c, estate agent)

D7, on the other hand, stated repeatedly his concern over the use of certain advertising material. He was particularly concerned about advertisements that in his opinion manipulated customers and put them under pressure – something that he did not want to do.

> *D7:* Everything that is to do with controlling and manipulating others I find very dangerous.
> *Interviewer:* What ways can you manipulate things?
> *D7:* [Pause] You can manipulate, I think, [pause] with half-truths, for example, to say 'Now it's this and this much, and later only such and such'. But 'later' is so abstract, it doesn't really exist. That means I put the customers sort of under pressure to make a decision. And uh, as I've said, it is a tightrope walk. There are some things that are still OK. You've seen the poster we have in the shop window.[150] (D7b, optician)

[150] *D7:* Alles, was mit Kontrolle und Manipulation zu tun hat, finde ich sehr ähm, sehr gefährlich auch, ja.
Interviewer: Wo kann man denn manipulieren?

In the second interview, he said that his concern over certain advertising material was also one of the reasons that led him to refuse an offer to partner up with a large optical chain - which would have improved his position in the market - as he would have been forced to make use of their promotional materials.

D8, finally, repeatedly referred to the Christian principle of forgiveness and how it should shape his behaviour towards others – even though people might exploit this in a business context (see section 4.5.5).

> They know um that I think as a Christian, and then this, it gets exploited more or less, or they try to exploit it. My good-naturedness or my willingness to forgive others. And then they, I think, say to themselves 'Well, he's one of that sort, he'll surely overlook this.' *Um, but that is what you should do, shouldn't you.*[151]
> (D8b, building)

He reported that he displayed this attitude of forgiving others in a range of relationships, and, as shown in section 4.5.5, even to those people that had cheated him out of money.

All those examples show how some Christian owner-managers might be considerate of others in their business even though it might be considered legitimate if they were not and even though such behaviours might put them at a disadvantage.

In comparison to sections 6.1.4 and 6.1.5, the practices described in this section occupy a middle position in terms of the impact of the Christian faith. Firstly, the wide-ranging application of Christian-based concepts such as stewardship and service for the community follows rather closely the attitudes as described in section 6.1.4. Secondly, the rather extensive application of Christian values such as 'considering the interests of others' to specific aspects of business practices might be an intensified version of behaviours described in section 6.1.5. One could particularly argue here that the 'cost' of such behaviour is higher (although the respondents might not consider it such).

6.1.7 Comment

This section has given some insight into the different kinds of attitudes and behaviours that Christian owner-managers might display and that might be influenced by their faith. The first group related to specific Christian practices, and there were only very few practices that could be described as such. The examples mentioned here referred to practices relating to licentious sexual behaviour, Sunday trading and 'new age' philosophies. The second and third type related to morally correct behaviour and the provision of a good service, practices that are not specifically Christian and might be equally pursued by non-Christians. The remaining three sections looked at attitudes and behaviours where Christianity might make more of a difference, even though the results were not exclusively Christian.

Section 4.1.4 looked at some fundamental attitudes that were distinctly shaped by Christian beliefs and that had quite a considerable effect on their interaction with others in the business. Section 4.1.5 looked at some 'other-regarding' behaviours where they showed themselves to be considerate of others, offered active help to others or implemented some environmentally friendly practices. Here the Christian faith may have made some difference, although not in such a fundamental way as in section 4.1.4. Section 4.1.6, finally, occupied a middle position between the preceding two sections and listed some examples where respondents either sought to apply Christian concepts such as stewardship and

---

D7: [Pause] Mh, [Pause] man kann manipulieren, denke ich, über [Pause] auch so mit Halbwahrheiten, zum Beispiel, so zu agieren, mh, ‚Jetzt so und so viel, später nur so und so viel' Das ‚später' ist aber so abstrakt, dass es das eigentlich nicht gibt. Das heißt, ich setze den Kunden damit künstlich unter Druck sich zu entscheiden. Und ähm [Pause] und, ja wie gesagt, es ist, es ist 'ne Gratwanderung. Es gibt auch, ähm, Dinge, die die sind für mich noch so im grünen Bereich. Sie haben ja gesehen, wir haben jetzt selber ein Plakat außen dran.

[151] Die wissen äh, ja, dass ich vielleicht christlich denke und dann wird das, wird das mehr oder weniger dann so ausgenutzt oder versuchen das auszunutzen. Diese Gutmütigkeit oder dieses Verzeihen oder da wird das, denke ich mal, schon ‚Naja, der ist ja einer von der Sorte, der wird da schon drüber hinwegsehen.' Äh, aber soll man ja auch, nicht.

service to the community to a wide range of business practices or where they extensively considered the interests or circumstances of others – even though that might have placed them at an disadvantage.

Although Christian owner-managers are very likely to engage in a 'mix' of those practices – as it was the case with the people in the study - those different categories of attitudes and behaviours are also a good basis to look for differences among Christian owner-managers. Some Christian owner-managers, for example, might primarily relate their faith to 'morally correct behaviour' and specific Christian practices such as the refusal to trade on Sundays, whereas others might take it further and, for example, consider their general attitudes towards people they interact with in their business from a faith perspective, consider the interests of others in their business or seek to apply their faith to a wide range of business practices.

Another interesting aspect is the 'cost' that Christian practices might entail. It might be relatively easy, for instance, to apply Christian values if Christian behaviour is in line with self-interested behaviour, for example, if it enhances the reputation of the business (see section 6.1.3), or if Christian behaviour does not impose a very heavy 'cost' on the owner-managers and their business (see examples in section 6.1.5). But what about those situations when adherence to Christian values would impose quite a considerable 'cost' on the owner-managers and their businesses? This is not just about the problem when owner-managers operate in environments where 'normal' moral constraints such as tax paying are no longer recognised (see examples in section 6.1.2), but, more importantly when it is about situations where business interests (supposedly) clash with consideration for others. Section 6.1.6 listed some examples where people prioritised their consideration for others over business interests and where some considerable 'cost' was entailed (although the respondents themselves might not recognise it as such). Yet not all respondents would provide such examples,[152] which is an indication that whereas some Christian owner-managers might be prepared to take it quite far when it comes to applying other-regarding values to business, others might not.[153]

This section also considered the presence of other motivations besides Christianity. Section 6.1.3 particularly addressed this problem and listed a number of additional or alternative motivations that respondents mentioned when they talked about the provision of a good service: perfectionism, professionalism and self-interest. It might be difficult to make out which motivation has greater bearing here – the non-religious or the religious motivation – but one might assume that the co-presence of two motivations that lead to the same result might be mutually reinforcing. So even if the religious motivation is not the only or not even the primary motivation – it might still contribute to the owner-managers' aspiration to display certain behaviours.

[152] Despite specific and repeated probing.

[153] Self-interest or business interest might be prioritised then.

6.2 Attitudes to and treatment of employees

In this section we will look at the practices that the respondents reported in relation to their employees. This particular stakeholder group is singled out because most respondents regarded them as the primary group to whom they had (social) responsibilities and they extensively referred to their employees in their accounts.[154]

The aim of this section is to explore the issues and themes that were raised in section 6.1.4 to 6.1.6 further, but also to highlight some differences of framing among the people in the study.

6.2.1 Christian beliefs and concepts shaping attitude and behaviour

As outlined in section 6.1.4 a number of respondents referred to specific attitudes that were marked by Christian beliefs and thus may make a difference in the way they interact with others. In the following two sections we look at some attitudes several respondents referred to in relation to their employees.

Regarding employees as persons

Firstly, some respondents stated specifically that they wanted to regard their employees as people. Similar to some respondents in section 6.1.4 they alluded here to the Christian belief that every person is valuable as they are made in the image of God.

UK2 was one such respondent. In the first interview he stated how important it was for him to regard his employees as people and not just as numbers.

> Um, [pause] and I think, you know, just just the general, perhaps, ... responsibility towards one's employees, really. Um [pause] *I I think it's important that that they're regarded as people. You know, and not just, not numbers and so on. So, the employees are known by name and all those sort of values.* So I think that's, you know, again an important part of of running the business. And particularly if you're still old-fashioned and call somebody's first name their Christian name. And it has an important value.
> (UK2a, manufacture of metal parts)

In a later interview he further elaborated on this responsibility. He particularly pointed out that he sought to take a genuine interest in his employees' lives.

> And, you know, being being British with the sort of British reserve, you don't sort of like to say something 'Well, you know, what's up with you?' But I always, personally, I've always done that. Because when I see somebody who is behaving out of his norm, I'll always say to him, you know, 'What's up?' You know, and they'll say 'Oh, everything is fine.' That magic phrase 'It's all fine.' But then you begin to see, you begin to probe that further, and you see it's not all fine and his marriage is breaking up or, you know, he's worried about his health or something. *Um, and behaviour is is something, which a a lot of people are shy to to express an opinion about and how it relates to business. ... And so I think that that is, to my way of thinking, one of the one of the marks of of Christian behaviour within a business. You have, you don't really have to seek permission of somebody to ask them something personal, um because you're actually showing an interest in them.* ... 'Cause most people, this is one of the things about the owner-manager, I think, he's got to be able to inspire his people. And you can't do that unless

[154] In this respect they are not different to SME owner-managers in general, according to some empirical studies. Spence (2000), for example, found in her research that SME owner-managers generally tend to regard responsibilities towards their employees as one of their main social responsibilities.

you've got a relationship with them. And so if you talk with the people, um, and you do so in such a way as I've described, then they are inspired by that. And they, you know, they feel happier.
(UK2c, manufacture of metal parts)

D5 also considered it his Christian responsibility to regard his employees as people and to take some interest in their personal lives as a way of showing his regard for them.

> Well, what else about employees? That you are a bit interested in their personal affairs. That you from time to time go up to one or the other and ask them how things are going at home. So that you know a little bit what's going on. That you show some interest, *that they're not just a task force who you suck dry for eight hours.*[155]
> (D5a, printing)

Lastly, D7 repeatedly mentioned in his account how important it was for him to give his staff recognition not only for their contribution to the business but to show them some appreciation beyond that.

> Another thing that's important is to really value your employees, uh, not simply recognising when things have gone well - you'd do that as a matter of course – but simply to value them as people.[156]
> (D7a, optician)

In all three accounts the respondents found it important to regard their employees as people beyond a strict contractual work relationship, but they described it in slightly different ways. In UK2's account we find some indication that, although he seemed to regard his attitudes towards his employees as being of intrinsic value, it was also in the back of his mind that this was actually good management practice, as his phrase "the owner-manager, I think, he's got to be able to inspire his people" implied. For UK5 and D7, on the other hand, it seemed to be more important to regard their staff as persons beyond and independent of their contribution to the business.

Regarding employees as equals

Other respondents alluded to the Christian belief about the equality of people in their accounts, which shaped their attitudes and practices towards them.

UK1, for example, talked about the Christian virtue of 'humility' – which means not to regard others better than oneself [157]– and how this should shape his relationship to others. Being asked for an example, he related that he sought to treat his employee in a respectful manner.

> Um, in practical terms it's to do with [pause] respecting other people's [pause] contribution to the, for for example, with the birthpool liners. Um, we have a, one, I employ one person for that. And she is my age. ... Um, but she's what we would call a past working class. But [pause] I respect her very much. And I ask her opinion. And to me her word is law. If she says 'This can be done' it can be done. If she says 'It can't be done.' I don't argue. ... And um and the other is, yes, one aspect of humility is is not to control, not to control too much. So I ring her every week, and I say 'How many have

[155] Ja, was noch an Mitarbeitern? Dass man sich ein bisschen für ihre privaten Sachen interessiert. Dass man öfter mal, sich mal den, mal jenen vornimmt und mal ein Gespräch führt, wie es zu Hause geht, also dass man bisschen weiß, was los ist. Das man Interesse, dass sie nicht nur nicht nur Leistungsträger sind, die man acht Stunden auslutscht.
[156] Was auch wichtig ist, ist einfach Wertschätzung. Also nicht nur äh Anerkennung zu geben, wenn mal irgendwie was gut gelaufen ist, das natürlich auch, aber da einfach ein bisschen persönliche Wertschätzung.
[157] Philippians 2:23

> you made?' Because she is paid how, so much for each piece. And she tells me. I don't question it. I say 'Ok', then we pay. *So, she doesn't think of me, I hope, as a powerful boss in any way. Uh, she thinks me of equal, I hope. So that's the, that is humility in practice.*
> (UK1a, ceramics industry projects and manufacture of birthpool liners)

For UK7, in contrast, the theme of treating employees as equals ran through quite a number of practices, which he often described as giving his employee 'ownership' in the business. He also alluded here to the more specific Christian belief that wealth should be distributed equally (Van Buren and Agle 1998, 164, 166).[158]

For instance, he stated that one decision that he and his co-owner had made was to give thirty percent of the company shares to employees. In the following quotation he also explained a bit more about his attitude behind this.

> *UK7:* And the rest is um is divided up among all the guys in the in the office. They are all shareholders. They they're very small shareholders. But we think it's very important for them to have a um a stake in the business.
> *Interviewer:* Why do you think that's important?
> *UK7:* Um, I I think to to me one of the very important principles in running a business is to get ownership. And by that I mean literal ownership. I mean to get the people believing that this is their company and what they do here matters. Um, any business will have as a strap line in its corporate statement that, you know, 'look the most important people, the thing in our business is people'. Very few of them believe that. We practice that. ... Um and the best way to do that is not just involvement in any part of the business, but but have, let them have genuine ownership of parts of the business. And ideally ... that means real ownership.
> (UK7a, engineering)

Another aspect of giving his employees 'ownership' in the business was to let them select the charities that they wanted to support as a business. Furthermore, said that he felt it was important to be open and transparent to his employees about what was happening in the business.

Lastly, he talked about a current building project, which involved that some of his workers had to work night-shifts. He explained that he felt it was important to go out and help the workers for a few nights – which could be another indicator of his belief about the equality of people.

> Because this is something like a um a three and a half month building programme, so um, and I I will at some point um go and work there for a couple of nights. Because I think it's important to, well, that everybody is prepared to to um to help.
> (UK7b, engineering)

UK1 and UK7's accounts show that the extent to which a certain belief is translated into practices may differ. Whereas UK1 mainly translated the attitude of treating employees as equals into respectful behaviour towards them, UK7 applied it to a range of practices: giving his employees a say in where the charitable contributions of the company should go, keeping them informed about what was happening in the business, helping the shop-floor workers out and, most remarkably, giving employees 'real' ownership in the form of share ownership in the company.

[158] Van Buren and Agle (1998) particularly refer to the practice of early Christians who shared their personal possessions (Acts 2:44).

Developing the employees' gifts and potential

In section 6.1.6 it was mentioned that the reference to certain Christian concepts (such as stewardship) may strongly shape a number of business practices and so make a difference in the way the owner-managers run their business. Several people in the study referred to their concern about the development of their employees' gifts and talents (see section 4.2.4) or potential (see section 5.3.2), and this may make a difference in the way they treat their employees.

Now, business people who do not explicitly follow the Christian faith may also talk about the responsibility to develop their employees' potential. Corporate codes of ethics, for example, frequently make such statements.[159] The difference might be that within the Christian framework of belief the potential and gifts of individuals are regarded as given by God and that therefore Christian owner-managers may have a somewhat different or even stronger motivation to further their employees' gifts and potential.

Another – related – angle with regards to gifts and talents was that of the self-interest of the owner-manager. D10, for example, said that the development of his employees' gifts and talents was to benefit both, the employees themselves but also his business.

> Employees have to serve customers, and employees need to be able to develop through their work for the customers. If it works out that way, we'd have we'd have an optimal solution.[160]
> (D10b, manufacture of measuring instruments)

UK10, by contrast, had a somewhat different outlook on the personal development of his employees. He took a rather altruistic approach towards the provision of training opportunities for his employees, emphasising the importance of his staff's personal advancement over the benefit for the business.

> Um, in terms of staff training we offer them the maximum that they can aspire to achieve. Um, all my staff I encourage to go up to the highest level of training that is possible for them. Uh, what is required by the, you know, the regulations is is that I train some to a minimum level and some to medium level and some to a higher level. *But I actually give more opportunities to train to a higher level. Because it furthers their their sort of personal advancement. Unfortunately it means that some of them leave to get other jobs. So you end up paying for all their training and they they take that elsewhere.* Um, but, you know, I suppose my satisfaction is knowing that they they've actually made something of their lives. ... Um, I've had several who have gone on to much better things. Um, which is great.
> (UK10b, pharmacy)

So even though Christian owner-managers may regard the development of their employees' gifts and potential as one of their Christian responsibilities, some might also be influenced by enlightened self-interest, whereas others might take a more altruistic approach towards it (see also section 4.2.4).

---

[159] Anglo-American's Good Citizenship Business Principles say: "We will provide employees with opportunities to enhance their skills and capabilities, enabling them to develop fulfilling careers and to maximise their contribution to our business." (Anglo-American, p.4). And Unilever's Code of Business Principles states: "We are committed to working with employees to develop and enhance each individual's skills and capabilities." (Unilever)

[160] Also Mitarbeiter müssen Kunden dienen und Mitarbeiter müssen sich bei der Arbeit am Kunden entfalten können. Wenn das funktioniert, dann hätten wir, dann hätten wir eine optimale Lösung.

6.2.2 Other-regarding practices relating to employees

A large number of respondents talked about certain 'other-regarding' practices that related to their employees and that they considered part of their Christian responsibility in business. Similar to section 6.1.5 they either referred to some specific behaviour or to their responses in specific situations.

Being considerate of their employees' circumstances

Quite a few respondents mentioned that they sought to be considerate towards their employees and their circumstances. UK3, for example, said that he felt he had to help one of his employees, who was going through a difficult time, rather than firing him. He gave this response when he was asked where his faith might be in conflict with business.

> Um, usually with regard to um problems that I have where um, if I were completely a businessman, a mercenary I would say 'Right, that was it', you know, 'forget it. Finished, ... go away.' Um, 'I've got to get on and do my job.' I do, spend quite a lot, put quite a lot of effort into, too much effort in, ... into not upsetting um people. I've got a member of staff, for example, who is going through a difficult period. I don't know why. ... Um very difficult. Um, anybody else I'm sure would have just said 'On your bike. Fired.' But I'm not gonna do that. That's really because I I genuinely feel um sorry for him and genuinely feel that I wanna try and help. So I try to help.
> (UK3a, estate agent)

D1, on the other hand, talked at length about how he sought to give his employees the flexibility to balance their work life with their home life. He framed this as 'Considering the interests of others'[161] and also as a 'fruit' of his faith (see section 4.3.3). D1 reported that his approach had even won him an award of being the most family-friendly business in his city borough. In the following quotation he talked about how he met the criteria for winning the award, which also gives some insight into how he tries to put this family friendly approach into practice.

> Criteria were, for example, how you reconcile your work with having a small child. Some of our people sometimes bring their children to work. Uh, they then do some drawing or play or something. Other (employees) have relatives they need to care for. ... So we've got a bit of everything.[162]
> (D1a, pharmacy)

At the same time, he was quite open about the fact that there were also some other motivations, i.e. his own personal experience and his desire to motivate his employees, that had led him to pursue such a family friendly approach with his staff.

> Well, because I used to be an employee myself for a long time, I know how you feel when you're an employee. Uh I also think that what's important to **me** and what motivated **me** to work well, that probably motivates my staff as well, don't you think. This is kind of projecting your own preferences. I mean, I only consider that person to be a good person who behaves in a way that I feel is right.[163] (D1b, pharmacy)

---

[161] This goes back to what the Apostle Paul says in Philippians 2:4

[162] Ja, Kriterien zum Beispiel wie jemand äh mit 'nem kleinen Kind sein Berufsleben unter einen Hut kriegen kann. Wir haben hier Leute, die bringen ihre Kinder auch schon mal mit. Äh, die malen dann oder spielen oder sonstwas. Andere (Angestellte) pflegen ihre Angehörigen. ... Da haben wir eigentlich von allem etwas.

[163] Also dadurch, dass ich eben selber lange angestellt war, weiß ich ja, wie man sich fühlt als Angestellter und äh ich denke auch dass, was mir wichtig ist oder was mich letztlich motiviert hat, 'ne gute Arbeit zu machen, das müsste meine Leute auch motivieren, nicht. Sind ja (..) Ähnlichkeitsphänomene. Nicht, also, ich halte ja nur den für gut, der sich irgendwie in irgendeiner Form so verhält, wie ich das für richtig halte.

Offering active help to employees

Other respondents, again, mentioned that they actively sought to offer help to their employees when they had personal problems. UK8, for instance, reported on one such incident.

> And things like, I mean, one of the guy's wife has been quite poorly. ... She she suffers from something, and nobody seems to be able to figure out what it is. She just faints ever so often. Um, and, you know, I got very little I can do about it other than try and be supportive and if he needs some time off then that is fine. And then if, I keep my ears open if I hear of anything. (My wife) is involved with the National Health Service at work. *So, you know, we try and look out for things that might help.*
> (UK8b, industrial design)

And UK10 stated that he had helped one of employees to pay off her debts, by loaning her money but also by using his personal influence to help her negotiate with the money lenders.

> Um, we actively try to help the employees when they've got problems. Um, we have an employee who was severely in debt. Um, and, I mean, she was on the verge of getting bankrupt and all sorts of things. And there was just no way, no way she was gonna find a way out there. ... But the only ultimate way out of it was to effectively pay off her debts. Um, because otherwise she was just gonna go under. Um, and by by doing that, by being, you know, someone with more influence, more education et cetera et cetera, we actually ... reduced (the debts) quite substantially by paying off early and by negotiating. ...Um, now she would never have had the the power to do that on her own. Um, and she, although she'd been to various people to get advice, again, no one was, no one was able to to give her the money to do it. And we recouped, recued it through her wages to some extent. And ultimately, when she sold her house um she paid us back. But there was a risk. Um, quite a substantial risk.
> (UK10b, pharmacy)

Responsible to provide continued employment

One specific topic that a number of respondents mentioned was their concern about being able to provide continued employment for their employees, and how this in some cases affected their business decisions.

We saw in section 4.2.4 that D4 framed the responsibility to ensure that his employees have a livelihood as a stewardship responsibility.

> A responsibility towards my staff and their families, uh, and that means ensuring that they have a livelihood. And that they do a proper job. And that we've got enough work coming in. ... *And uh this responsibility, I try to make it clear to my staff that I have a responsibility towards them and of course also to God.* If I didn't have this uh but was only answerable to myself, then that would be selfish, because I'm always answerable to God first. Next come my employees. And these two things combined shape my identity. And the way I live.[164] (D4a, heating and plumbing)

[164] Meinen Mitarbeitern gegenüber die Verantwortung und für ihre Familien, äh dafür zu sorgen, dass sie in Brot und Arbeit stehen. Und dass sie ihre Arbeit eben eben ordentlich machen. Und dass wir auch dann auch genügend Arbeit haben. ... Und äh diese Verantwortung äh versuche ich auch den Mitarbeitern klarzumachen, dass ich diese Verantwortung, die ich ihnen gegenüber habe natürlich auch Gott gegenüber habe. Und wenn ich das nicht habe, ähm, sondern dass ich mir selbst gegenüber verantwortlich bin, ähm, dann ist es halt eben 'ne egoistische Sache, weil ich bin an erster Stelle immer Gott gegenüber verantwortlich. Und dann meinen Mitarbeitern. Und aus dieser Situation entsteht eine eine Verbindung, die äh die mich die mich ausmacht. Und in der ich lebe.

And D5 said that he thought his faith impacted on the way he dealt with his employees like this (section 4.5.5).

> How else does my being a Christian have an impact on the company? [pause] Well, OK, the difficulties of not being able to have a callous attitude towards my employees …That you don't dare to' hire and fire'.[165]
> (D5, printing)

In practice this meant for him to make a decision not to move his company to an Eastern European country, although it would have have been easy for him to do and staying in Germany so close to the Eastern European border meant he had to face increasing competition.

> If I bought a printing business in the Czech Republic or, even easier, in Poland, that would be at the expense of the business here. That means I would relocate. I'm not gonna do that. That's where my ethics comes in, you know. I won't make my people redundant because of the because of the EU expansion. If I employed 60 people, I'd say 'OK, 60 people, business is buzzing, we'll work in two shifts. And I could additionally outsource 20 people to Poland for some basic tasks. That would make sense because each would drive up the other. But with a 20 people printing business I'd have to relocate. And they would be made redundant. I certainly won't do this.[166]
> (D5a, printing)

UK8, on the other hand, stated that his concern for his employees' continued employment had led him to make some financial provisions should the business face difficult times:

> We had conversations, I mean, I had a conversation with the accountant the other day. I said 'What I want is a target to put away, tuck away a certain amount of money so that we got two or three months buffer if something went drastically wrong.' And he said 'Well I think that's probably too much because, you know, you'll see it coming and you'll be able to lay people off.' And I said 'But I don't want to do that. I want to have the buffer so that we don't.' Um, 'Well' he said.
> (UK8b, industrial design)

Yet not all respondents considered it their specific responsibility to keep their staff in employment. UK1, for example, explicitly regarded it more his Christian responsibility to tell employees about changes in the market, so that they had enough time to look for different sources of income. He said this about his employee in his birthpool liner business.

> She's paid on piecework. Um, so I will say to her from to time 'Look, continue to make stock. We hope it will improve.' But if you give people plenty of time to find other means of income, as I have with her … And because this is always the case, the employees can see that the orders are drying up. There is nothing to do. … So if you come early and you

---

[165] Was wirkt sich noch aus, wenn ich Christ bin auf die Firma? [Pause] Na ja, gut, die Schwierigkeiten, nicht so kaltschnäuzig mit den Mitarbeitern umgehen zu können…. Dass man eben sich nicht traut, zu heuern und zu feuern.

[166] Wenn ich jetzt bloß eine Druckerei in in Tschechien mir kaufen …, könnte inzwischen oder in Polen vielleicht sogar noch leichter, würde das zu Lasten dieser Firma gehen. Das heißt, ich würde verlagern. Das mach' ich nicht. Da kommt nun wieder mein, meine Ethik wieder rein, nicht. Ich tu' meine Leute nicht auf Straße setzen wegen der wegen der EU-Osterweiterung. Wenn ich eine 60-Mann-Firma hätte, würde ich sagen ‚Ok. 60 Mann, es brummt in zwei Schichten. Und ich könnte für ein paar Primitivarbeiten 20 Leute zusätzlich auslagern nach Polen.' Dann macht das 'n Sinn, weil sich nämlich das gegenseitig hochschaukelt. Aber mit 20 Mann Druckerei äh müsste man verlegen. Und damit wären die hier arbeitslos. Das mach' ich sicher nicht.

say 'You know the situation. Uh, if this continues, I'm sorry, but we're gonna have to cut down' ... Then it gives them the chance to find something else, or and so on.
(UK1b, ceramics industry projects and manufacture of birthpool liners)

Interestingly, he also reported that some people had criticised him for being primarily involved with his other business in setting up manufacturing companies abroad, rather than continuing to provide employment for local people through his original family business.

And I say to them 'Come with me to the tombs outside Cairo and I will introduce you to some of the families who live in the tombs to whom I'm gonna give jobs. And tell me whether I should take jobs away from here or not.' So there is social responsibility in that sense. That it helps me certainly argue my case with those who criticise me what I'm doing. And also my own conscience. And, because I I, my family is a (PLACE NAME) family and go back 300 years. Uh, so uh in in my own conscience as well. ... Uh, [pause] if if a test is often 'What would Jesus do?' and uh I can see in this area, for various reasons, we have very full employment. Actually people have not too much of a problem of getting a job. There are jobs. So that's balances, is ok. Egypt is a poor country.
(UK1a, ceramics industry projects and manufacture of birthpool liners)

6.2.3 Comment

This section gave some insight into the attitudes Christian owner-managers might display towards their employees and how they might treat their staff.

Section 6.2.1 looked at some fundamental attitudes that guided some respondents' interaction with their staff – such as treating them as persons or treating them as equals. Like the responses in section 6.1.4 such attitudes related to Christian beliefs about human beings made in the image of God and human beings being created equal by God. Thus Christianity might make quite a considerable difference here in the way the owner-managers interact with their employees. The same section also mentioned that some respondents sought to develop their employees' gifts and talents or – as some phrased it – their potential. Similar to some respondents' reference to specific Christian concepts such as stewardship (see section 6.1.6) the reference to the biblical concept of gifts might have quite a strong influence on the respondents' attitudes towards their employees. Even though non-Christian business people might also be concerned about developing their employees' potential, the difference here is that Christian owner-managers regard the potential or gifts of others as God-given, which might provide them with quite a distinct motivation to develop their employees' gifts.

Furthermore, the data in section 6.2.1 showed some interesting differences among the respondents. The first difference relates to the motivation of the owner-managers. When the respondents talked of wanting to treat their staff as persons, one respondent was aware that having such attitude towards his staff might also help to "inspire" them, so an element of 'enlightened' self-interest was involved here. Other respondents, by contrast, explicitly stated that their concern for their staff and their recognition of them should go beyond their recognition of the employees' contribution to the business. Similarly, when respondents talked of developing their employees' gifts and potential, some were aware that this also benefited the business. One respondent, however, explicitly stated that he had the personal development of his employees first and foremost in mind – and that he did not mind too much if they left the business and took their training elsewhere. The second difference related to the extent to which Christian values were applied. Two respondents talked of treating their employees as equals. Whereas one respondent mainly translated it into respectful behaviour towards employees, the other one took it quite far and applied it to a range of practices, of which giving employees share-ownership in the business was the most remarkable one. Thus there might be some differences among Christian owner-managers that relate to differing degrees of 'enlightened' self-interest and to the extent to which they apply Christian values.

Section 6.2.2 looked at some 'other-regarding' behaviours that the respondents mentioned in relation to their employees. They talked about how they sought to be considerate of their employees' circumstances, how they sought to offer them help if the employees had personal problems or how they felt responsible to provide continued employment for them. Such behaviours may also be pursued by SME owner-managers who do not explicitly follow the Christian faith, as other empirical studies indicate (e.g. Spence 2000), and the question arises to what extent Christianity has an impact here. One could simply argue that the physical proximity of SME owner-managers to their employees results in moral proximity (Spence 2004) and thus Christian owner-managers may use Christian language simply as a resource to verbalise their behaviour. People in the study also sometimes offered additional or alternative explanations regarding their behaviour, such as D1's alternative explanation as to why he sought to arrange family-friendly working hours for his employees. We further saw in section 4.1.5 that the display of love and consideration may have also been influenced by the respondents' character. With regards to the continued provision of employment, the national context may have played a role as well for the German respondents, as here the provision of employment might be regarded more of a social responsibility than in the U.K. (Donnelly et al. 2001, Charkham 1994). This might also explain UK1's stance, as he explicitly did not consider the provision of continued employment a Christian responsibility, but justified his behaviour with 'doing good' elsewhere.

At the same time, Christian framing of behaviour may make the motivation of Christian owner-managers to help and be considerate of their employees stronger. For example, if behaviour is explicitly framed as fruit of faith, as a stewardship responsibility or regarded as a Christian responsibility, this may provide the owner-managers with additional reasons to behave in a certain way.

6.3 Engagement in wider society

This section will explore the respondents' framing of their engagement in wider society. This aspect of SME owner-managers' practices might play a relatively minor role compared to their day-to-day business activities. But if we regard Christianity as an institution that has potential impact on wider society, it is also interesting to explore the influence of Christianity on the respondents' practices beyond their day-to-day business life, as well as consider additional motivations that might have led the respondents to be engaged in civil society activities. This section will look at the two aspects that are generally associated with involvement in civil society, charitable giving and active participation (Hems and Tonkiss 2000, 8), and will investigate them in the context of the faith community, local communities and professional communities.

6.3.1 Influence of community of faith on the respondents' civic engagement

It was pointed out in section 5.1 that the community of faith played quite a considerable role for most people in the study. Most respondents would regard the community of faith as the main recipient of their charitable giving (see section 5.1.2), but they also often reported on at least some sort of active engagement in the community of faith. This may have related to their business activities, as we saw in section 5.1.2, or may have been more disconnected from their business, but nevertheless took up the respondents' time and commitment. This more general engagement ranged from more administrative tasks such as being a church warden (e.g. UK1, D3) or the church treasurer (e.g. D1, D2) to representative tasks such as being a welcomer (UK2) to 'spiritual' tasks such as preaching (e.g. D9, D10), pastoral care (e.g. D7) and youth work (UK5). Some respondents even reported on extensive leadership responsibilities within the church (e.g. D4, UK4, UK10). Others reported to be actively involved in organisations that sought to connect faith with business, either by seeking to communicate the Gospel to other business people or by looking at how Christian values can be applied to business or a combination of both (e.g. D2, D3, D10, UK1, UK7).[167]

For some respondents, their civic engagement in the church took up so much time and/or played such a central role for them that they did not actively participate in other communities such as the local or the professional community. UK4, for example, explained that he would not get actively engaged in the professional or the business community, because his main interest lay with his church activities. The quotation also interestingly indicates that he regarded business activities primarily as a means of making money rather than linking it with wider societal and or perhaps even spiritual responsibilities.

> But I don't I don't have the time. Um, I mean, ob- obviously being active in the church um and my free-time goes into goes into stuff like that. So, uh ra- rather than finding some cause to to um to champion or or something like that, um it doesn't really have any any interest for me. *I mean, [pause] my business, if you like, is [pause] um is not my main interest. It is my main interest but it's not my main interest, OK, really. I'm I'm more interested in the Christian faith and in the church than I'm really um in making money.* But at the same time, I mean, obviously this is the way we make our money, OK, so that's why we do it to the best of our ability. ... I'm *I'm happy for it to play to play a supporting role. Rather than being an all all enveloping role.*
> (UK4a, car rental)

For others, their financial support of the Christian community and specific Christian causes precluded them from giving money to 'secular' causes. D9, for example, said that he found it more important as a Christian to support organisations that have an overt Christian connection than non-Christian ones.

---

[167] The fact that so many respondents were involved in Christian business groups was no surprise given that most of them were actually approached through such networks.

All initiatives (I support) are all Christian. I mean, the non-Christian ones, that is where non-Christians would give their money. Uh, that seems reasonable to me.[168]
(D9b, security analysis)

6.3.2 Engagement in civil society through Christian charities

Nevertheless, even though a lot of the respondents' charitable giving and active engagement was directed towards the faith community, a number of the Christian projects they supported had a more 'social' dimension, i.e. they sought to alleviate particular societal problems. However, the respondents gave different explanations as to why they supported such projects.

Some respondents gave specific spiritual reasons as to why they supported Christian social action. UK2, for example, said that he had decided to set a proportion of his company shares aside to establish a charitable trust that specifically support Christian-led social projects, particularly in inner cities and deprived neighbourhoods, as it was important for him that God benefited from his business.

> *UK2*: And we we probably give grants of, well, say about 25,000 pounds a year. Something like that. *So um God is a shareholder.* [laughs]
> *Interviewer:* So why did you decide to do that?
> *UK2:* Because I wanted [laughs] um I could have I could have formed a trust um I could have done it in, you know, a charitable trust for any number of sources or any number of purposes. *Um but I felt it was really important that I actually wanted God to have a direct benefit from the business.*
> (UK2a, manufacture of metal parts)

The spiritual connection to the charitable work he supported was very important for him, as he expressed his belief that people may be transformed through the help that these Christian workers offer. He said this about the work of the Church Army, one of the main recipients of his trust.

> *UK2:* The Church Army deals with people on on the housing estates. And you know, that's more interesting to me. Um, that's where that's where Jesus has more work to do and these people, on Sundays they wear um a Church Army T-shirt. Um, and they'll take the service. Like that. Rolled up sleeves, tattoos, because he's probably been a welder or a bus driver or something. Um, and they're wonderful people. And um they're inspiring. And they inspire middle class white people as well. And they inspire all communities of different different races, different ethnic origins, um and, you know, to worship the Lord.
> *Interviewer:* So their projects, their purpose, is that evangelistic, social, both?
> *UK2:* All of it. All of those. And and, you know, people who are, this big word of poverty. *Um, they don't want Satan to get these people. They they want these people to be a light. And so they will do anything they can to to help them.*
> *Interviewer:* For example?
> *UK2:* To try and settle debt, for instance, 'cause these people are often in debt. So they put them in touch with debt counsellors, sometimes, often with Christian debt counsellors. Um, and there are lots of ways and means. So they will try and put these people back on on a life with a purpose. ... Um, ... they they will deal with families, with disaffected members of families. Drug people. Um, violence in families. They will deal with all of that. It's brilliant.
> (UK2b, manufacture of metal parts)

[168] Ja, das, also äh die Initiativen sind alle christlich. Ich mein' äh die nichtchristlichen, da würden halt die Nichtchristlichen dafür spenden. Nicht äh, das liegt irgendwie nahe.

UK9, on the other hand, stated that it was important for him that all giving was "Gospel-based" (see section 5.1.2). He reported, for example, that he was heavily involved in an international Christian children's charity - through being a member of the charity's board and through financial contributions - which provided both physical and spiritual care for children. The "Gospel base" of his involvement here may have particularly referred to the spiritual teaching that the children received alongside practical care.

> Um, (NAME OF CHARITY) is um um it's um it's a Christian-based charity. Uh, providing um holistic care for um children at risk. So we, unlike a lot of agencies like this, we we provide 24 hour care. So we will look after um their physical needs, um their spiritual needs. So we will um teach them about about Jesus Christ. And um, and the hope they can have in Him. We will provide them with education, their health care, um, and just prepare them to be adult citizens in their own communities. ... Um, and uh, the whole idea is is is to just give these kids hope.
> (UK9a, building)

For other respondents, the community of faith may have been the 'natural' context to be involved in social action with the spiritual motivation remaining more in the background. D8, for example, reported that he helps a Salvation Army project that provides schoolchildren in a deprived neighbourhood with warm meals and a safe place where they can spend the afternoon. He said that in his capacity as a builder he had helped to build several facilities there, such as a beach volleyball court. He did not offer an explicit spiritual reason as to why he was involved in this project but stated that the trigger to get involved there was his wife, who he said was very heavily involved in various church activities; she knew the minister who runs the project and suggested that they should help there.

Finally, D5 offered a more personal reason as to why he was engaged in Christian social action. Although he primarily supported missionary organisations, he said that he had decided to sponsor six children in a Third World country through a Christian organisation out of gratitude for his own six children.

> I've got, I've got, for example, I started to sponsor children, because I thought, hey, you've got six children. They are in good health, clever, beautiful, God-fearing, what else do you want? You've got to, you've got to do something, haven't you, everybody says 'What's wrong with you, you're doing so well with your children.' Two children are already married and the third one wants to marry, too. ... Then I thought, I'd also like to give six, six other children a chance. And then we picked six, through World Vision, and started to sponsor them.[169]
> (D5a, printing)

6.3.3 Engagement in local communities

There is a traditional assumption that SME owner-managers act as beneficiaries for their local communities (Spence 1999, 164). This assumption has been challenged somewhat by recent studies that found that a number of small businesses do not assume any particular responsibility for their local surroundings (Curran and Blackburn 1994, Curran, Rutherfoord and Smith 2000). Nevertheless,

[169] Ich hab', ich hab' das zum Beispiel mit den Kindern, mit den Patenkindern angefangen, einfach als ich mal gedacht hab', mensch, du hast sechs Kinder. Die sind gesund, klug, schön, gottesfürchtig, was willst du denn mehr? Ja? Musst du, irgendwas muss man doch mal tun, das geht doch nicht, dass einfach so, alle Leute sagen 'Was ist denn mit dem, euch geht's so gut mit den Kindern.' Da hab' ich nun zwei Kinder schon verheiratet, der dritte will auch noch heiraten. ... So, da hab' ich gedacht, so will ich wenigstens sechs, sechs andern Kindern noch 'ne Chance geben. Und da haben wir da sechs rausgesucht, über über World Vision, und hab' mir die verpatet.

engagement in the local community still remains an interesting aspect of the involvement of SMEs with civil society.

Not all respondents reported on being involved in the local community, and the reasons for this might have varied – either they were too heavily involved with the community of faith, or other reasons, such as lack of time or interest, might have prevented them from getting involved. In this section we will look at those respondents, who did report on some engagement in the local community and investigate to what extent this was influenced by their Christian faith.

Some respondents reported that they were supporting local charities and community activities through their business, but not all of them offered a distinct spiritual motivation. They may have supported charities etc., for example, because they had simply been approached for help or because they regarded it as part of their civic duties to their community.

D4, for example, stated that he sponsored a youth football club in his town. He said that he had been approached by people who had asked him whether he would consider doing this and but he also positively regarded it as a contribution that he could make to the local community.

> I see that this is an opportunity to do something as a businessman for our city, and to support popular sports there. And it hasn't got a 100 percent Christian uh motivation. ... But it was my motivation not to focus completely on Christian causes but also to do something in other areas.[170]
> (D4b, heating and plumbing)

UK4, on the other hand, talked about the discounts that his business offered to charities. He said that he had decided to offer discounts not only to Christian charities; but that every charity that did business with him was entitled to a ten percent discount – simply because that was an easier way of handling the 'problem'.

> We'll give discount for any charity. ... Um, it's difficult to distinguish between one another. Uh, if you know what I mean. Perhaps some charities you might not ordinarily um be interested in, but it's easier to say 'We'll give a discount for all charities.' Um, and otherwise your staff would be always going 'Shall we give one to this? Shall we give one to that?' [laughs] So, it's easier we're just open-handed and say 'If they are a charity you can give them, it's just 10 per-, it's standard 10 percent.' So they don't have to ask what it is. It gets far too complicated if you (say) 'Do not give anything to anybody who is Buddhist' [laughs]. Or whatever, whether, you know, whether you agree with what they're doing or not. You just um, if you like, you just hope that they will, that they're doing something useful with it.
> (UK4b, car rental)

Other respondents framed their charitable giving in a more distinct Christian way. UK11, for example, said this when she was asked why she supported a number of community activities and local charities through her business:

> I guess I feel I should support **somebody** because I'm a Christian. I expect that's that, you know, ... you should give. ... But I don't know, I just feel like, you know, *God's given me the business, and it's doing really well, really this is ideal. And I think I've got to give something back. But I don't necessarily think I've got to give it all back to a Christian charity.* You know, we support Christians sort of separate to the business.
> (UK11b, optician)

[170] Hier sehe ich auch den den Vorteil einfach, auch als Unternehmer in der Stadt irgendwas zu tun, und so den Breitensport auch so ein bisschen zu fördern. Jetzt nicht äh den 100prozentig christlichen äh Anspruch, ... Aber das war so meine Motivation, nicht jetzt nur alles äh zu fixieren auf christliche Dinge, sondern auch an den Stellen auch ein Stückchen weit etwas zu tun.

She was one of the few respondents that made a separation between what she gave through her business and what she gave personally.

UK3 also offered a spiritual reason when asked why he financially supported various local community projects and events. At the same time, he was aware of the potential benefit for his business.

> *Interviewer:* Why do you do that?
> *UK3:* [pause] Because it doesn't cost me anything. It cost me maybe a few hundred pounds. Mh, but every two or three years, someone will sell their house through me instead of selling it through somebody else as a result. *So, you know, it's one of my favourite sayings 'What goes around, comes around.' You 'cast your bread upon the waters, and it will come back to you manifold'.* Doesn't do any harm. [laughs]
> *Interviewer:* Um, do you think that is in any way to do with you being a Christian or would you say you would be doing it, even if you were not a Christian?
> *UK3:* [pause] *In truth it's because I'm a Christian and in truth it's because I take God's promises seriously um that we should try to be a blessing to the people around us.* Um, but I can also make a good secular argument, that it's good business. Um, uh if it was just good business I wouldn't do it. Because there is, there is more effective ways of making money. But it's, the truth is that even from the secular point of view it doesn't really cost anything because you get, you get, it does come back.
> (UK3a, estate agent)

UK3 offered furthermore two different explanations as to why he liked to offer practical help to organisations and people in the local community. In the first interview he said

> We tend to um, we tend to have people calling in here. If somebody wants the photocopying done for something for a church thing or a school thing, they come in here and they do it and we don't charge them. Um we tend to encourage people who are having a tough time to pop in here round the corner and have a cup of tea. We like, we like to [pause] we like to [long pause] we like to be nice. It's a little bit weak, I know, but that's that's what it is. We we enjoy it. It gives, you know, it gives us a sense of satisfaction as well. We haven't sold a house for a fortnight but at least we made, you know, made loads of people happy. There is some satis-, some satisfaction.
> (UK3a, estate agent)

In the second interview, however, he framed this engagement more in terms of 'being a witness', rather than just in terms of "being nice" and the satisfaction that it gave him.

> Motivation is um really that I don't want people pointing the finger at this office and saying 'Oh well, they they call themselves Christians but…' 'Cause I hear it all the time. I mean, all the time on the television, on the radio and so on. 'Oh they call themselves Christians but …' Um, and I'm sure people say it about me. But I hope not to give them the opportunity of doing so.
> (UK3b, estate agent)

The motivation to participate more actively in the local community was not necessarily motivated by the respondents' Christian faith, either.

For example, D5's motivation to become involved in local politics was distinct from both being an owner-manager and being a Christian. He said he became a local councillor because at one time "sensible people … who were able to think clearly and, above all, were willing to get involved"[171] were required to be put on the list of an independent political group. He further said that his active engagement in a local business group was not motivated by his Christian faith, either, but rather by his desire to network and socialise with other owner-managers in the local area.

---

[171] vernünftige Leute, ... die in der Lage sind, ein bisschen klar zu denken, und vor allem, die mitarbeiten.

Other respondents applied more strongly a Christian framing to their active engagement in the local community.

We saw in section 4.1.4 that UK10 reported on being involved in a local panel that made decisions about building projects in the area because he was concerned about the well-being of the community. He framed his engagement for the local community in very strong Christian terms.

> Because, I mean, you know, as a Christian part of your mission is to to care for and love other people. And um, and therefore caring for those people you want things to be good for them. Um, and, you know, ... justice to be done for them.
> (UK10b, pharmacist)

Lastly, UK2 reported that he was involved as chairman in a local charity that provides training and employment opportunities for unemployed young people. He, too, regarded engagement in the community as a specific spiritual responsibility.

> Um but that's my um commitment I suppose to, you know, a) to explore more about myself, um and b) you know, *doing something for for the community. And and the third point as well certainly is um, you know, the whole question that if you are if you are a Christian you can't hide, you know, there is no hiding place.* Um a wonderful Psalm 139, isn't that. Um, you know, where David is saying to God 'You're everywhere. And there is no way I can escape. You know where I am. And You know what my thought is. And You know what I'm going to say.' Um, and, you know, I'm sort of I've learned that if you're a Christian, you can't hide. And if you are a hiding Christian, you're not much use. Really. You had to do something about it.
> (UK2a, manufacture of metal parts)

Being asked what motivates him to be involved in that charity he reiterated his belief that people can be transformed through developing their potential (see section 5.3.2).

> Um, well originally I never asked that question. [laughs] More recently I **have** asked that question, um and I've just been very interested in, I always have been interested in in people ... I believe people have far more potential in their lives than they ever dream of. Um, God can find it and switch it on to a whole range of fruit. Of the spirits. Fruit of the spirit. In, which lies within everybody, if you can tap it. But even if you don't, um there are lots of things, which people can do with their lives. Um, which opens up their lives.
> (UK2a, manufacture of metal parts)

6.3.4 Engagement in professional communities

A number of scholars who have written about the role of civil society in relation to economic activity have emphasised the necessity of structural arrangements to keep economic activities in check. As stated in section 2.1, Durkheim (1957) already argued back in the 19th century that economic activity should be regulated through professional bodies and professional codes of ethics. And other scholars have pointed to the possibility and – in some cases – responsibility of economic actors to 'positively' influence economic activities through engagement in professional associations and rule-making bodies (e.g. Herms 1991, 98; Ulrich 1997).

Active involvement in professional or other rule-making bodies was rather rare in the sample, which may have – again – been influenced by the respondents' engagement in faith community activities or by other things such as lack of time and interest. However, if respondents reported on such kind of civic engagement they did not always relate that to their faith but argued, for instance, that they were primarily engaged out of professional interest.

D8, for example, reported on being involved in a government-linked committee that had helped to draw up environmental guidelines for his sector. He said that he had always been interested in environmental matters and thought that it was better if businesses got involved to help draw up 'sensible' guidelines rather than leaving those matters to civil servants alone. However, he also made a tentative link to the spiritual traditions of his trade (see section 5.3.1).

UK3, on the other hand, strictly separated his faith from his involvement in professional bodies. He mentioned that he had got involved, alongside other professionals, with a professional body to prevent regulations that he considered to be 'unsensible' from coming into force. He said that he got involved because he liked "things to be done properly" and therefore felt a responsibility to speak up in his capacity as a professional, but not as a Christian.

> I think far too many Christians take it upon themselves and think it's their responsibility to point out other people's problems. ... And I think as an estate agent, you know, if I if I see someone meddling with my business and and screwing it up, I think it is my responsibility to tell them, you know. There is far too many interfering Christians with an opinion on things that they don't need to have an opinion about.
> (UK3c, estate agent)

UK7, by contrast, related his spiritual beliefs also to his civic engagement. It was already mentioned in section 4.1.3 that his strong beliefs about Christian stewardship – particularly environmental stewardship - had led him to be involved in committees of industry bodies that look specifically at environmental sustainability and renewable energy. Thus his faith may have had made an important difference in terms of his engagement for structural change in society.

Finally, D9 made some references in his account to some structural aspects of society, both from a Christian viewpoint and from his professional perspective as a security analyst.

> When I read in the book of Revelation, we have figures there that operate on a global scale. Like the Anti-Christ. Or the two witnesses on our side. And uh that's why I have the impression that globalisation, which worldwide, which practically turns the entire earth into one single entity, uh, is perhaps inevitable, but it's like what the Bible says about the end-times. And I don't know whether we ought to want this. I sometimes think that we should not artificially induce those 'last labours'. And I can imagine that if you regard decentralisation as a value; that could be better for society.[172]
> (D9a, security analysis)

He said that he had thought about possible solutions to the difficult problems that globalisation has created. He argued, for example, for decentralised economic systems or for transport trading certificates, a system similar to carbon emissions trading, in order to counter-balance effects of globalisation. However, he stated that he did not seek to promote these ideas through engagement in professional or other political bodies; and said that at best he would write letters to the editors of well-known national newspapers and magazines to tell others about his ideas. This decision to stay more inactive may have been partly influenced by his choice to be primarily engaged in his church.

6.3.5 Comment

This section has given some insight into different kinds of Christian owner-managers' engagement in wider society by looking at three types of civic engagement: engagement in and through the

[172] Wenn ich äh so gucke in der Offenbarung, da haben wir so Gestalten, die weltweit wirken. Wie den Antichristen. Oder auf unserer Seite die zwei Zeugen. Und äh deswegen habe ich den Eindruck, 'ne Globalisierung, die praktisch äh weltweit, die ganze Erde praktisch zu einem Gebilde macht, äh, die ist vielleicht nicht zu vermeiden, aber sie hat was Endzeitliches an sich. Und äh ich weiß nicht, ob wir das wollen sollen. Ich denk' mir manchmal, dass man diese 'letzten Wehen' nun nicht unbedingt noch künstlich herbei rufen muss. Und ich kann mir vorstellen, dass man sagt, wenn man Dezentralisierung als 'nen Wert begreift, das könnte für die Gesellschaft besser sein.

community of faith, engagement in the local community and engagement in professional and rule-making bodies.

Section 6.3.1 followed up the context of the community of faith, whose importance was already discussed in section 5.2. It was argued there that some owner-managers might regard their engagement in the community of faith as a natural part of being an active Christian. This is not only the case for business-related civic engagement and charitable giving but also for wider, more general civic engagement. Section 6.3.1 listed the different kinds of community of faith-related civic engagement in which the respondents got involved.

Whereas for some Christian owner-managers this might just be one form of civic engagement among others, for other respondents this might be the only kind of civic engagement that they might be involved with. Time constraints may not permit them to get involved somewhere else but – as it was pointed out in section 5.2 – they might also regard their engagement for the community of faith as having particular spiritual importance and/or something that is more in line with their Christian identity, which makes them focus exclusively on Christian-based civic engagement. This may have been the underlying rationale for UK4 and D9, who reported that their active civic engagement and their charitable giving respectively had an exclusive Christian focus. Thus Christianity may actually sometimes prevent believers from getting engaged in wider society.

But section 5.2 also mentioned that despite the strong focus on community of faith related activities, a number of the Christian initiatives that the respondents reported on being engaged with had a social dimension. Here the Christian faith made a difference in that the respondents benefited wider society through their engagement for Christian charities. Interestingly, the respondents offered different explanations as to why they were involved in such kind of Christian activities. For UK2 and UK9 the spiritual context of the initiatives they supported seemed to be very important although they talked about it slightly differently. It seemed that it was rather important for UK2 that the end recipients of his help were 'transformed', i.e. that the help they received through Christian workers helped them to live a better, 'transformed' life (see section 5.3.2). UK9, on the other hand, emphasised the importance of explicit spiritual teaching that went alongside the provision of practical care. Those slightly different 'priorities' may link to different theological understandings (see section 5.3). D8, by contrast, did not offer a distinct spiritual rationale for his faith-related social engagement. Thus it might have been rather physical 'proximity' that made him get engaged in Christian social action, with the spiritual motivation remaining more in the background. And D5 supported Christian social action for a rather personal reason: out of gratitude for his own children.

Section 6.3.3 looked at some respondents' engagement in their local communities and highlighted that respondents had a number of different reasons to be involved there. For some respondents their Christian faith provided a distinct rationale as to why they were involved in their local communities. UK11, for example, talked about wanting to give something back out of gratitude to God for giving her the business, UK3 talked about wanting to be a blessing to people around him and also about wanting to be a witness, UK10 considered his involvement to be part of his mission to 'care for and love other people' and UK2 said that he was involved in a local educational charity because he did not want to hide as a Christian and also because he believed that young people should be able to develop their God-given potential. Other respondents, however, reported that they sponsored local charities (D4 and UK4) or actively participated in the local community (D5) without giving a distinct spiritual reason for their involvement.

Interestingly, UK2's and UK3's account highlighted the fact that people often may have more than one motivation for being engaged in wider society. UK2, for example, said that his involvement in an educational charity was also influenced by his desire to explore more about himself. And UK3 stated that his financial support of local community activities also contained an element of self-interest, and that his desire to help people out in the local community simply gave him personal satisfaction. One could argue more generally here that the respondents' engagement in local communities might be influenced by a number of other factors, for instance, by self-interest or by their proximity to the local situation – particularly when owner-managers have a local customer base[173] or when they also live in

[173] Schmidpeter and Spence (2004), for example, found that garage owners who run their business in a local community context are likely to be more interested in local community activities than small marketing firms that serve a national or international customer base.

the local community. At the same time, the Christian framing of local civic engagement – even though it might only be an additional motivation - may make their involvement stronger.

Finally, section 6.3.4 investigated the respondents' engagement in professional communities or rule-making bodies. Such kind of involvement was rather rare among the people in the study and, similar to section 6.3.4, the respondents offered a range of different motives as to why they were engaged there. UK7 was the only respondent for whom his faith provided a distinct rationale for his engagement. He translated his spiritual beliefs about environmental stewardship into active involvement in industry bodies. D9, on the other hand, even though he considered societal problems from a spiritual point of view did not get actively engaged - presumably because of his strong engagement in the church. (This, again, illustrates the prioritisation of community of faith activities over 'secular' ones.) At the same time, D8 stated his personal interest as the main reason to get engaged in a rule-making body, and UK3 even strictly separated his faith from his engagement in professional bodies. This demonstrates that involvement in professional and rule-making bodies does not need to be linked with spiritual motivations; indeed, respondents like UK3 even rejected a spiritual link to their involvement in the professional community. At the same time, UK7's Christian framing of his civic engagement may have provided him with a rather strong motivation to get civically engaged.

In summary, the data has shown that Christian owner-managers may have all kinds of different motivations that influence their involvement with wider society – distinct Christian motivations, a range of 'secular' motivations or a mix of both. Paradoxically, the Christian influence can work two ways. It can either prevent people from getting engaged in wider society as it leads them to focus on community of faith related activities only; or it can provide a distinct rationale for wider civic engagement, either through the community of faith or in the local community or even in professional or rule-making bodies. Whether Christian owner-managers apply a Christian rationale to community of faith related activities only or also to other 'secular' civic engagement may depend on what areas of social action they perceive to be of spiritual significance (see discussion in section 5.3). At the same time, the data showed that the respondents did not always require a spiritual motivation to be civically engaged as they had other reasons for their engagement. Moreover, even though some respondents framed their engagement in distinct spiritual terms, they were aware that they were also influenced by other factors. Specific Christian framing of civic engagement may nevertheless make the motivation to be engaged stronger – even though it might not be the only motivation.

7. Discussion and Conclusions

7.1 Main findings and contributions

Using a socio-psychological approach, this study set out to investigate how one specific civil society institution – Christianity – might impact on the way a specific group of economic actors – owner-managers of small to medium-sized enterprises – carry out their business activities.

The main finding of the study is that the active Christian context provides Christian SME owner-managers with distinct conceptual and linguistic resources, resources which are not available in that way to non-Christians. These resources lead them to frame their practices in a highly distinctive way, which can and probably will have far-reaching implications for the way they carry out their business activities.

By employing an inductive approach, the researcher identified from the respondents' interview accounts what faith-related resources have meaning for Christian SME owner-managers, and showed how these resources can influence their attitudes and behaviours. These findings contribute to a better understanding of how the influence of Christianity on business activity 'works'. The insights gained from this study may be particularly useful for academics (business ethicists, sociologists etc.) and other people who are interested in this particular phenomenon or, more generally, in the influence of civil society frameworks on economic activity.

The first two data analysis chapters (chapters 4 and 5) outlined the various 'Christian' resources to which the respondents referred in their interview accounts, and showed how they provide distinct 'constraints' and 'enablers' for action (Giddens 1984, 25). Chapter 4 listed five faith-related concepts that have distinct 'significations': 'calling', 'stewardship', 'witness', 'holiness' and 'general moral tenets'. It mapped out what implications these concepts have for Christian owner-managers' conceptualisations of practice. Whereas the concepts that were listed in chapter 4 could be loosely regarded as different 'types' of identity that respondents used to conceptualise their business practices, chapter 5 focused on the 'constraints' and 'enablers' that arose from specific contexts that are related to Christianity. These contexts referred to the community of faith, the (imagined) presence of God in one's working environment ,and the spiritual significance that respondents ascribed to various aspects of their business context.

Finally, chapter 6 focused on the different types of attitudes and behaviours that the respondents related to their faith, thereby giving insight into the different areas of practice, where Christianity might make an impact:

- Some behaviours that can be regarded as specifically Christian in the context of a secularised society, such as the refusal to trade on Sundays.
- Some 'commonplace' practices, such as honest and reliable business conduct. Here the Christianity impacts primarily in the way these practices are framed and described.
- Some attitudes and behaviours that 'make more of a difference', such as some 'egalitarian' practices. These might not be exclusively Christian and may thus be pursued by non-Christian owner-managers as well, but they are distinctly motivated by Christian discourse.

Section 7.3 will discuss the research findings in more detail.

The structure in which the data was presented in the three data analysis chapters was the outcome of a long, interpretative process on the part of the researcher (Symon and Cassell 1998, 6), as she felt that this particular structure best captured her data (see section 3.2.3). It may need some further discussion and debate as to whether some of the contexts could not have also been conceptualised as concepts. However, the concepts-contexts-practices structure can be a used as a framework for conceptualising the influence of civil society institutions on economic activity, and thus forms another contribution of the study. Section 7.6 will make some suggestions as to how the concepts-contexts-practices structure could be used to investigate other civil society frameworks.

The study did not only identify the Christian concepts and beliefs that are likely to be relevant for Christian SME owner-managers, but also drew attention to the fact that the way Christian owner-managers engage with the Christian context is a rather individual matter. For example, the study found that the owner-managers in the sample used different 'combinations' of faith-related resources in their accounts, as well as showed differences in the interpretation, application and exploitation of these resources – resulting in different attitudes and behaviours. Section 7.4 will look at this diversity among Christian SME owner-managers in more detail and seek to explain as to why such diversity exists.

Finally, the study also provides an understanding of how other discourses might influence the way Christian SME owner-managers conceptualise their worlds of business practice and how these discourses might interact with a more specific Christian motivation. First, the researcher identified a set of alternative motivations for certain behaviours. These were often provided by the respondents themselves or were implied in their accounts. Secondly, the researcher also identified how the contexts in which the research was embedded – the context of small to medium-sized businesses and the two distinct national contexts – might influence the owner-managers' conceptualisation of practice. Section 7.5 will look at the impact of these other influences in more detail.

7.2 Limitations of the study

No claim about research findings can be made without the acknowledgment of the limitations of the study. The researcher felt that limitations arose particularly from the choice of the research method and the sample size. These limitations will be discussed in the following.

7.2.1 The limitations of interview-based studies

Section 3.1.3 already explained that interview-based studies have a number of limitations and outlined some potential weaknesses such as the social desirability effect, the influence of the interviewer's shared member status, deliberate or unintentional inaccuracies and selectiveness on the part of the interviewees, but also some limitations on the part of the researcher etc.

More crucially, however, one needs to realise that interviews are indeed highly specific and somewhat artificially created situations: People are asked to stop in the flow of their day-to-day activities and to reflect about their activities (Weick 1995, 25; Watson and Harris 1999, 20) and, in the case of this study, to reflect about the possible influence of a particular discursive context. As such, interviews can – notwithstanding the limitations that were mentioned above - at best capture how people *rationalise* their actions using certain linguistic and conceptual resources.

To what extent the respondents' rationalisations are not just 'nice stories' that they tell the researcher and also have implications for their actual practices is an open-ended question. However, people who read the accounts that were presented in this study will be in the position to judge whether these can be considered to be 'authentic' enough to conclude that the respondents' rationalisations of their practices also will make an impact on their actual behaviour. Furthermore, the open-endedness of the research findings might be overcome by carrying out further research. For example, one could seek and 'triangulate' the findings by interviewing the respondents' 'stakeholders' (see section 7.6).

At the same time, we must keep in mind that the accounts were produced at a particular point in time, and that, because persons and their worlds are continuously in process (Watson and Harris 1999, 18), the respondents might produce different accounts were they interviewed today. Their knowledge about their circumstances may have changed (and their circumstances themselves) or they may have come to understand their Christian faith in a different way.

Yet, even if the respondents' outlook on their worlds of practice was different today, their accounts can still teach us how Christianity might influence the behaviour of SME owner-managers.

7.2.2 The limitations of the sample

There were further limitations with regards to the sample size and make up. A sample in a qualitative study does not need to be representative to gain insights, as the researcher does not primarily seek to produce generalisable, quantifiable statements (Bryman 2001, 99). But the question arises how well the data covers the phenomenon that the researcher set out to study.

It was pointed out in section 7.1 that one finding of the study was the diversity in which Christian SME owner-managers drew links between their faith and their business practices (see sections 7.1 and 7.4). This diversity demonstrated the 'richness' of the possible Christian influence on Christian SME owner-managers' conceptualisations of practices. But one might ask if there was such diversity in the sample, whether there is more 'out there', and whether talking to more people would have provided additional or even completely new insights into the phenomenon. Of course, each 'story' of an SME owner-manager is unique, as they operate a particular business in a particular sector and bring their own life experience and understandings of the Christian faith to the interview, and each additional interview would perhaps provide some new insights. However, the data did not only capture diversity but also showed that Christian concepts and beliefs were repeatedly used across the sample. Therefore the researcher assumes that more interviews would have primarily yielded different 'combinations' of concepts and beliefs and different 'variations' of how they were translated into, and linked with, practices. Furthermore, theoretical and empirical literature that deals with this phenomenon does not suggest that there exist a significant number of further Christian concepts and beliefs (Van Buren and Agle 1998, Roels 1997, Nash 1994, Childs 1995) that might be relevant for 'conservative' Protestant owner-managers.

Therefore, whilst the researcher cannot be sure that everything relating to the phenomenon was covered she expects that a good part of it was.

In the following three sections, the specifics of the research findings will be outlined and discussed.

7.3 The distinctive influence of Christianity

This section will outline and discuss what can be learned from the research findings with regards to Christianity's distinctive influence, and will relate the research findings to the literature.

7.3.1 Specific Christian behaviours

First, the 'distinctiveness' of the Christian influence may show itself in a few specific behaviours, which are easily observable and which could easily be ascribed to the owner-managers' Christian faith. Section 6.1.1 mentioned a few specific business-related practices where the respondents' Christian faith offers the most likely explanation for their behaviours: the refusal to trade on Sundays, the refusal to engage in practices that would promote sexual licentiousness and the refusal to promote products that are based on a different 'spiritual' philosophy. Other behaviours related to the owner-managers' membership in the faith community (section 5.1), such as preferred trading with and recruitment of fellow Christians, and business-related civic engagement in the community of faith. Finally, some respondents would regard it their responsibility to share their faith with others in their workplace (see section 5.3.2), which would again be something specifically Christian.

If we look at these 'specific' Christian behaviours, it seems that even though they are important to the owner-managers, they seem to make less of an impact on wider society. The focus on the community of faith, for instance, restricts the owner-manager's focus to a particular societal group with whom he shares an identity. Also, even though it depends on what the respondents understand by 'sharing one's faith' (see discussion in section 5.3.3), witnessing by word does not seem to have a direct impact on wider society. With regards to the practices that related to specific Christian moral values, however, one might want to debate whether less sexual licentiousness and the observance of Sunday as a public day of rest could not be positive for society.

The strong, and at times exclusive, focus on the community of faith was a rather peculiar finding. Whereas Christian doctrine tells believers to 'love one another', and therefore provides a spiritual reason to be concerned about the well-being of the community of faith, there is also the more universal commandment to 'love one's neighbour', which should encourage Christian to help and love people no matter what identity they have. The findings would, however, confirm Münkler and Fischer's (2000a) observation that civil society activities are usually bound up with people's own life-worlds (see section 2.1.1) and they also echo Bellah et al.'s (1996) findings about evangelical Christians being primarily focused on the well-being of their community (see section 2.2.1). In this respect – even though it is a practice that marks owner-managers out as Christians - they would not be different to any other group in society that recognises a common bond due to a shared identity. Section 5.4.1 outlined possible reasons for such behaviour, starting from the fact that the owner-managers' behaviours arise naturally from the physical proximity to people and needs within the faith community to the possibility that engagement for the faith community has particular spiritual significance for the owner-managers. The frequent reference to the Christian practice of 'tithing', for instance, underlined their commitment to supporting the community of faith and spiritual causes. Another explanation for some of these behaviours might be, however, that it is the increasingly secularised environment that might make practising Christians more conscious of their religious identity, which might lead to the curious fact that the focus of their 'other-regarding' actions are often geared towards the community of faith and their members rather than towards other communities.[174]

[174] As pointed out in section 5.1, a number of faith community related causes that the respondents supported are also meant to 'reach out' to others, and so the focus on the faith community might also indirectly benefit wider society. However, the effect on wider society depends on whether 'outreach' is interpreted in terms 'helping others' or 'seeking to convert others', with the latter having rather little direct impact.

7.3.2 Distinct motivations

Yet the data also revealed that the Christian context can have quite a considerable impact on more 'general' business practices, with this impact relating to the linguistic and conceptual resources that arise from Christian discourse and refer to the presence of and the relationship with the 'transcendent'. A number of these distinct motivations – 'constraints' as well as 'enablers' – were part of the concepts or frames that were reported in chapter 4.

Several respondents drew on the concept of calling, whose distinct motivation lies in the belief that God has called the owner-managers to their place of work. Even though the concept of calling was interpreted differently by the people in the study, it can provide a rather strong motivation to engage in a range of business practices that consciously take the good of others into account. Whereas non-religious people may at times also talk about their calling – often to rationalise life choices in line with their abilities or preferences - a 'divine' calling may make an individual's motivation to engage in certain practices particularly strong (section 4.1).

A concept that was rather frequently used across the sample was the concept of stewardship. The distinctiveness of the stewardship frame is the strong sense of responsibility and accountability to God that arises from the belief that God has entrusted the business to the owner-managers or that God/Jesus is the actual 'Lord of the business'. This can provide Christian owner-managers with a strong 'constraint' not to do anything irresponsible in their business, but can also, more positively, motivate owner-managers to take an active interest in developing the potential of their employees or to engage in environmentally friendly practices. Non-religious business people might also use stewardship discourse to frame their business practices - and in that stewardship is not a unique Christian or religious concept - but they, by contrast, would not feel accountable to a 'divine' authority (section 4.2).

Some respondents referred to the concept of holiness. This concept provides motivation to engage in practices that are in line with the holiness of God or the moral qualities of Christ as the pattern of holiness. This very distinct religious motivation can, again, place particular 'constraints' on an owner-manager, e.g. lead him not to engage in fraudulent behaviour, because he has a sense of accountability to a 'holy' God. At the same time, the concept can positively 'enable' him to engage in other-regarding behaviour, e.g. to show 'acts of kindness' and so emulate Christ's example. The question 'What would Jesus do?', which was mentioned by a number of people in the sample, seems to be a particularly strong internal 'control mechanism' that can make them stop and think how they should be treating others in reference to Christ's moral example (see section 4.4).

The witness discourse – to which several respondents related - goes beyond the 'internal' motivations relating to the relationship with the 'transcendent'. It provides owner-managers with a strong 'external' motivation as it relates to how other people would perceive their behaviour in the light of their faith. This can exert a strong discipline on the respondents not to do anything wrong. At the same time, the motivation to bear witness about one's faith can also result in wanting to positively communicate something about the Christian faith through one's actions. The phrases 'fruit of faith' and 'Christ in you', that some of the respondents used, are examples of how Christian discourse provides some 'enablers' to engage in such 'positive' behaviour (see section 4.3).

Lastly, a number of respondents referred to general moral tenets that are linked with the Christian faith. Such engagement with Christian discourse seems to have the least distinctive impact, as the practices framed in this way are not linked to a distinctive spiritual motivation, and a lot of non-religious people or people that adhere to other religions could also refer to the same or similar 'principles'. Still, there could be some underlying spiritual motivations for the owner-managers' actions even though they are not verbalised, and some of the practices that were mentioned in the study such as the obligation to show love and forgiveness to others – which are more peculiar to Christian doctrine – would mark owner-managers out as Christians (see section 4.5).

Similar to the frames, section 5.3 identified some other conceptual resources that the respondents used and that are linked with the Christian discourse, and that the researcher conceptualised as relating to the spiritual significance of the business context. These resources can create strong motivations for Christian SME owner-managers to engage in particular practices. The belief that the work that is done through the business is done 'for the Lord' and the belief that God is 'Lord of all creation' as well as the reference to the values of the 'Kingdom of God' can be powerful motivators for Christian owner-managers to engage in practices that benefit others and that also go beyond social expectations (see section 5.3.1). Likewise, section 5.3.2 pointed out that if owner-managers hold in one way or another the belief that the Christian faith can 'renew' or 'transform' a person and apply it to their business context, this has far-reaching implications on the way they seek to deal with people they interact with through their business (employees, customers etc.). For instance, they might consider it their spiritual responsibility to 'positively' influence other people's attitudes and behaviour towards themselves and in relationship with others.

Section 5.2, finally, listed some Christian spiritual beliefs that several people in the study mentioned and that can impose some powerful 'constraints' on Christian owner-managers' behaviours. For example, some people in the study said that their belief that God would sustain and provide for the business would lead them to refrain from practices that were illegal or that they perceived to be unethical (see section 5.2.1). Similarly, some respondents reported that they felt that their faith imposed a 'control mechanism' on them, which kept them from giving into temptations (see section 5.2.2). Lastly, the belief that prayer or spiritual texts can provide guidance might have led some respondents to make more ethical decisions in their business (see section 5.2.3).

Two things should be noted here. First, section 2.2.1 mentioned the Protestant Work Ethic as a potentially relevant concept for Protestant Christians. The people in the study, however, very rarely alluded to the Protestant Work Ethic as conceptualised by Weber, and if they did they alluded only to certain parts of it, but not to the whole 'philosophy' that underpins the Protestant Work Ethic. The strongest reference was made by D5, who particularly alluded to the notions of calling that are ascribed to the Calvinistic tradition (see section 4.1). No respondent in the sample, however, expressed anxiety about their salvation, which could have been a strong spiritual motivation to seek success in business and so to be able to 'prove' one's salvation. We may thus conclude that the Protestant Work Ethic, although we cannot rule out that it has completely lost its significance, has less relevance for contemporary conservative Protestants who run SMEs.

Secondly, we may also compare the findings of this study with previous studies that have sought to identify concepts that are part of Christian discourse and that are potentially relevant for Christian business people, such as Roels' (1997) observations on evangelical SME owner-managers in the U.S. (even though the author focused on conservative Protestants as a somewhat wider group) (see section 2.2.2). Roels argued that evangelical business people would primarily draw on general Christian concepts and she referred to them as 'piety' and 'witnessing'.[175] 'Piety' seems to be the corresponding 'general' concept to holiness and general moral tenets. 'Witnessing', however, was in this study identified as not only relating to overt sharing of one's faith – as Roels did – but also as a concept that provides distinct 'constraints' and 'enablers' for action. This study, moreover, identified two concepts in the respondents' accounts which were more business or workplace related: calling and stewardship. Even though they were interpreted differently by respondents, these two concepts have the potential to make a direct impact on a number of business practices. We must therefore disagree with Roels when she states that evangelical business people would not go beyond 'general' Christian concepts and would not consider business-related Christian concepts. At the same time, the findings of this study would be in line with Nash's (1994) findings, who stated that a number of respondents in her study referred to the stewardship concept.

7.3.3 Linking motivations with practices

Finally, how are the distinct motivations that arise from the Christian context linked with the owner-managers' practices?

[175] She further identified 'tithing' and 'neighbourliness' as relevant concepts. 'Tithing' and 'neighbourliness' were also of relevance for the people in this study. Whereas 'tithing' and some interpretations of 'neighbourliness' had particular relevance for the way respondents related to the community of faith (see preceding subsection and section 5.1), some aspects of 'neighbourliness' were also expressed in the respondents' practices (see next subsection).

Most often, people in the study linked their Christian motivation with practices that are not specifically Christian and may be considered rather 'commonplace', such as morally correct behaviour or the provision of a good service (see sections 6.1.2 and 6.1.3). Here the distinctiveness would primarily lie in the way owner-managers frame these practices. For example, they would say that they cannot afford to do anything wrong in their business because they do not want to "bring shame upon God" or that they seek to provide a high-quality service because they "worked for the Lord". In a number of instances, however, such 'commonplace' behaviour might become 'extraordinary' behaviour, for example if adherence to certain moral principles is punished rather than rewarded, or if other firms in the sector do not have the same standards. It was difficult however to tease out if and when this behaviour might be more 'extraordinary' in the context of this study, as it included no comparative element, and this might be an area for further research (see section 7.3.1).

In other instances, though, distinct Christian motivations were also translated into more or less distinct practices, practices that regard the good of others. These practices may be shared with other frameworks to varying degrees, but the Christian framework of belief provides a strong rationale for engaging in such practices (see sections 6.1.4 to 6.1.6, sections 6.2.1, 6.2.2 and section 6.3.2 to 6.3.4).

Section 6.1.4 and 6.2.1 listed some examples where the Christian faith might have a particular important influence. The Christian context, i.e. because the respondents felt that they were accountable to God in their business, that they worked "for the Lord", that they wanted to "live out Christian values" in their business etc., led a number of respondents to engage in 'egalitarian' practices and in practices that regarded people beyond the transactional relationship. The underlying rationale for such attitudes and behaviour lies in the Christian beliefs that everyone is made in the image of God and everyone is created equal (see section 6.1.4). 'Egalitarian' practices ranged in the sample from treating each customer equally well to sharing profits with employees. The attitude to treat others 'as people' was particularly applied in personal interactions with customers, employees etc.

Other more distinctive practices came from the application of Christian-based concepts such as stewardship, service for the community, and gifts and talents (see sections 6.1.6 and 6.2.1). Even though these concepts are not exclusively Christian, each of them has a specific Christian rationale and provides distinct motivations, for instance, for engaging in environmentally friendly practices, for putting service before profit and for being concerned about the use and development of employees' gifts and potential.

Finally, sections 6.1.5, 6.1.6 and 6.2.2 listed some examples where the Christian framework of belief translates into some specific practices that concern the good of others. Although the Christian influence is not as distinctive here as with the practices mentioned above, the Christian faith would still make some difference. Some people in the study engaged, for instance, in practices that related to what Roels (1997) called 'neighbourliness', such as some respondents' willingness to help disadvantaged people through their business. Other practices related to the consideration of the interests of others, customers and employees. In some cases, however, other-regarding behaviour that some respondents reported was of such 'intensity' that it would impose quite considerable cost on them and possibly put them at disadvantage. Examples included the consideration of the interests of competitors or the refusal to use 'manipulative' advertising material (see section 6.1.6).

Section 6.3, on the other hand, showed how the Christian context can provide a strong rationale to engage in the wider community. Some respondents offered some distinct spiritual rationales for supporting Christian social action, such as to give others "hope in Jesus Christ" or to help people "to be a light" and not be "caught by Satan". Others offered spiritual rationales as to why they were engaged in the local community: because of "wanting to be a blessing to people" or because it was the "Christian part of one's mission to care for and love other people". Finally, the Christian beliefs about stewardship and 'care for creation' also provided a rationale for one respondent to get engaged in professional bodies.

7.3.4 Conclusion

This section discussed the various resources arising from the Christian context that the study identified as having an impact on Christian SME owner-managers. Some of these resources are more, others less distinctive; some are more business-related, others more 'general' but they all have the potential to make a significant impact on the way Christian owner-managers conceptualise their worlds of business practice.

The primary purpose of this study was to identify how Christianity might distinctively influence the activities of Christian SME owner-managers - by mapping out the range of faith-related sources that have meaning for them – and not to produce generalisable statements (see sections 3.1.2 and 7.2.2). However, if one considers both the 'strength' of motivation that was implied in each concept as well as the frequency in which the respondents referred to particular concepts across the sample, one may conclude that 'witness' (as a 'general' concept), 'stewardship' (as a business-related concept) and to some extent 'calling' (also business-related) have particular relevance for Christian owner-managers. These findings have, among others, implications for potential action research (see section 7.6.1).

To what extent these resources are 'effective' in the context of wider society, however, depends on how these resources are linked to actual practices. Often they would simply provide a distinct and strong motivation for 'commonplace' practices, or for specific Christian practices (that do not always necessarily benefit wider society or whose benefits might be a matter of debate), whereas in other cases they would provide a rationale for practices that 'make more of a difference'.

At the same time, it needs to be acknowledged that some of the respondents' behaviours may not be influenced by the Christian context alone, but that other interacting influences play a part as well. These other influences will be discussed in section 7.5.

7.4 Differences among Christian SME owner-managers

The study did not only identify the areas where the Christian discursive context might have a distinct influence on SME owner-managers' conceptualisation of their worlds of business practice, but also found that the respondents linked their faith to their business in rather different ways.

For example, the respondents would draw in their accounts on different combinations of the Christian frames or concepts that were outlined in chapter 4. Some would draw on up to four concepts, whereas others drew on one or two only. Furthermore, the concepts were exploited in rather different ways. For instance, the witness frame was by some interpreted in terms of not wanting to do anything wrong, whereas others used it in terms of wanting to communicate something positive about their faith (see section 4.3). Specific conceptual resources were also interpreted differently. 'Working for the Lord' would mean for some to strive to provide a high-quality service, whereas for some other respondent it meant to raise money for Christian causes through the business (see section 5.3.1). Moreover, whereas some respondents focused their civic engagement almost exclusively on the community of faith, others would – despite being involved in the Christian community – also be involved in the wider community (see section 6.3). There were also differences between the owner-managers in terms of the degree to which their faith was integrated into business practices; i.e. for some faith was related only to a few specific aspects of their business activities, whereas others linked their faith to a range of business practices, sometimes even to the extent that faith was prioritised over business considerations (see chapter 6).

This section explores this diversity and seeks to offer some explanations as to why this diversity might exist.

7.4.1 Differences in framing and engagement with Christian concepts

An obvious explanation for the diverse use of the Christian concepts would be the teaching that the owner-managers have been exposed to. Owner-managers who attend a church that teaches how important it is to be a witness of the Christian faith would presumably primarily draw on the witness frame and perhaps also seek to witness by word to others. Those who come from a church background that teaches more the importance to follow the Ten Commandments and the moral teachings of Christ would primarily draw on the 'general Christian moral tenets' frame. Others again would draw on the 'stewardship' frame as a business-related concept because they have been exposed to specific teaching on how business and faith interrelate.

The same applies to the way these concepts are interpreted and linked to particular practices. Owner-managers who do not receive any specific teaching about the spiritual significance of business activity might relate their faith only to practices that they can easily link with Christianity such as to certain moral behaviours (not cheating, not lying, paying taxes etc.) or to specific Christian practices (such as no Sunday trading or witnessing by word). Those who have been exposed to teaching how business and faith interrelate may perhaps actively link their faith to the way they engage with people with whom they interact in their business (e.g. apply the Christian concept of gifts and talents to their employees), or even to practices that relate to the 'care for creation'. Furthermore, the teaching and practice in the community of faith would probably also have an impact on Christian owner-managers' civic engagement. If the community of faith encouraged their members to get engaged in wider society, either through Christian social action or through other forms of engagement, this might encourage the SME owner-managers to get engaged in social action themselves. If, on the other hand, the community of faith conveyed in one way or another a sacred-secular divide, i.e. that engagement in and for the church and evangelistic outreach only are considered to be of spiritual significance, then this might equally influence the owner-managers' conceptualisations of practices.

The use of frames may also be influenced by the sector in which Christian owner-managers operate. The fact that two people in the study felt "called to serve the community", for instance, was clearly influenced by the fact that they ran businesses whose 'service' character was rather obvious (see section 4.1.4).

However, even though the difference among Christian owner-managers might be partly explained by the exposure to specific Christian teaching and by the influence of their sector, they do not determine the conceptualisation of practice alone. In the study, for instance, people who drew on the witness frame would also at times draw on the general moral tenets frame (e.g. D5, see sections 4.3 and 4.5). Section 4.3 moreover pointed out that respondents would engage with the stewardship frame without having been explicitly exposed to teaching on Christian stewardship. Finally, even though UK10 and UK11's conceptualisations of practice may have been influenced their sectors, their German counterparts would not apply the same frame to their practices.[176]

The data also showed that owner-managers' exposure to specific teaching does not necessarily result in uniform responses. As pointed out in section 2.2.1, some people in the study attended the same church, which the researcher perceived to have some strong teaching about witnessing to others. Those respondents, however, applied the witness concept in quite different ways, in other words, they adopted different 'positionings' within the witness discourse (Harré and Gillett 1994, 140). D3, for example, sought openly to witness by word through his business (section 5.3.2), D7 referred the concept of 'Christ in you' to explain how he wanted to be a witness through the way he interacted with others, and D1 talked about the 'fruit of faith' that people should see in his business but openly rejected the idea of 'advertising' his faith (section 4.3.3). Likewise, people who had been exposed to teaching on stewardship applied the concept to their business practices in diverse and sometimes rather idiosyncratic ways (see section 4.2). It was pointed out in section 4.2.5 that the differences in the conceptualisation of the stewardship concept might have also depended on the co-presence of other Christian frames (such as the witness frame) or that it was simply adapted according to the respondents' own plans and preferences.

Furthermore, despite some trends and tendencies, the researcher further felt she could not put the respondents 'in a box'. She could not, for example, follow Bellah et al.'s (1996, 231) observations that 'evangelical' Christians would be interested only in the well-being of the faith community and in evangelising (see section 2.2.1). Despite the fact that the community of faith was the focus of a number of respondents, others reported on some 'wider' engagement. UK9, for instance, who said he attended an evangelical church, had decided to take on a disadvantaged young person as an apprentice and offered a spiritual reason for doing so (see section 4.4.2). He was moreover strongly engaged in a Christian children's charity (see section 6.3.2). UK3, who also attended a strong evangelical church, reported on extensive charitable engagement and on how he tried to be a good neighbour in his local community. Even though he stated that there was a mix of motivations for his behaviour, he also recognised a 'spiritual' responsibility there (see section 6.3.3). Those findings would have been in line with some of Roels' (1997) observations about the 'neighbourliness' of evangelical business people. She had observed that a number of evangelical business people would apply 'neighbourliness' not only to helping fellow Christians but also to helping disadvantaged people and the local community (see section 2.2.2). Finally, the fact that a number of respondents came from evangelical backgrounds did not automatically mean that they sought to evangelise others in their business, as some of them considered this an inappropriate practice in a workplace context (see section 5.3.2).

Furthermore, the fact that some respondents focused very much on 'other-worldly' things did not mean that they rejected more 'mundane' responsibilities. D5, for example, who regarded his business first and foremost as a means to raise money for Christian causes and applied particular spiritual significance to his 'practical' contributions to the community of faith (see sections 4.1.1 and 5.3.2) showed himself very strongly concerned about the well-being of his employees (see sections 4.2.3, 6.2.1 and 6.2.2) and would also engage in some kind of Christian social action (see section 6.3.2).

Interestingly, the study also found that people who came from different traditions would hold similar ideas and people from the same tradition different ones. For instance, D8 and UK1, whose church backgrounds were more 'traditional', and UK9, who came from a strong evangelical church, would all apply the concept of 'working for the Lord' to the provision of a high-quality service, whereas D5 who also came from a more 'evangelical' tradition would apply the concept to his contributions to specific spiritual causes only (see section 5.3.1).

---

[176] As the environment in which German pharmacists and opticians operate might be somewhat different, it would be interesting to explore whether other British pharmacists and opticians who are Christian would also refer to the 'service to the community' frame.

Lastly, some respondents would engage with Christian ideas that were not immediately part of their own faith tradition. D7, for instance, drew on Franciscan ideas (see section 4.1.1), and the teachings of St Francis are a pre-reformist source rather than a central part of the Protestant tradition. UK10 and UK11, as another example, applied the 'serving the community' frame to their practices. As explained in section 4.1, this concept is central part of the Lutheran tradition, however, neither of them came from a Lutheran background (they both had a Methodist background).

7.4.2 Varying degrees of integrating and prioritising faith

The respondents did not only differ in the way they drew from and interpreted Christian discursive concepts but also in the way they sought to integrate their faith-related values into their business. This sub-section will explore some of these differences.

Sections 6.1.7 and 6.2.3 discussed some aspects that relate to this question. The first aspect relates to the kind of practices owner-managers might link with their faith. In other words, it was argued that some owner-managers may apply their faith only to moral conduct or to some specific Christian practices such as the refusal to trade on Sundays, whereas others might take it further and apply Christian values to a wider range of business practices (see section 7.4.1). The other aspects relate to the 'intrinsic' value and the 'cost' that is attached to Christian values, and they will be discussed a little further here.

We could think of the way owner-managers integrate faith-related values to their business as a spectrum, with some owner-managers regarding faith-related values as a set of basic moral constraints and/or simply as 'enlightened' management practice on the one end, and others prioritising faith-related values over business considerations on the other end of the spectrum, with a number of nuances between those two extremes.

An interesting example from the study that illustrates these differences among owner-managers is how some respondents considered their employees' gifts and potential. One respondent talked of considering employees' gifts and talents primarily in terms of it being good management practice, whereas another one – even though he regarded it as good management practice as well – was also concerned about how the employees themselves would benefit from such practice (see section 4.2.4). A third respondent, however, took a rather altruistic stance towards the development of his employees' potential and did not show himself too concerned if his employees took the high level of training that he offered to them elsewhere (see section 6.2.1). Another example referred to the respondents' aspiration to treat and recognise their employees "as people" and not just as employees. For some respondents this was a practice that was important for them simply because of its intrinsic value, whereas another respondent was aware that this was also good management practice (see section 6.2.1). Lastly, section 6.1.6 listed some examples of respondents being willing to forego profit opportunities or to be put at a disadvantage because of their concern about the interests and needs of others, whereas other respondents would not offer such examples in their accounts.

What causes these differences is a question that might not be easy to answer. Those at the one end of the spectrum might simply be aware of their business-related self-interest or think that a business setting might not allow them to be too considerate of the interests of others, if they themselves will be put at a disadvantage. Those who are at the other end might be influenced by a high degree of religious devotion or by other – interacting - factors such as by certain character traits. For example, D8's extreme willingness to be generous and forgiving to others could be an extreme application of Christ's commandment to "turn the other cheek" (Matthew 5:39) but might have also been the result of having a very soft character (see section 4.5.5).

7.4.3 Conclusion

From the data in the study we can conclude that the construction of a religious identity in relation to business activity is a highly individual matter. Some trends and tendencies may be explained through exposure to particular Christian teaching and traditions, but the owner-managers' own individual engagement with Christian discourse and Christian tradition does certainly play a part.[177] Furthermore, the engagement with Christian discourse is a dynamic activity, hence Christian owner-managers may change the way they relate their faith to their business activities over time (see UK7's account in section 4.1.3). What part of Christian teaching owner-managers consider to be relevant for their business, how they interpret it and to what extent they seek to apply it to their business practices, however, might also depend on the intensity of their business-related self-interest as well as on a number of other interacting influences, such as certain character traits (see section 7.5).

[177] Based on her own 'inside' knowledge, the researcher assumes that individual engagement with Scripture and Christian thought is particularly prominent among Protestant believers (often due to the 'vagueness' of Protestant doctrine). This would be in contrast to the Catholic tradition, where teaching that gives rather detailed instructions on how believers have to live out their faith, is a lot more prominent.

7.5 Other influences

A final set of research findings related to the presence of other – often interacting – influences that can have an equally important impact on Christian SME owner-managers' conceptualisations of practice as their Christian faith. These other influences that were identified from the research data will be discussed in this section.

7.5.1 Alternative explanations for certain behaviours

A number of behaviours and attitudes that the respondents reported might be ascribed to other aspects of the respondents' identity than their Christian one and people in the study would often themselves offer alternative rationalisations for some of their actions alongside a Christian one.

The data showed, for instance, that particularly with practices that were more 'commonplace', such as the display of morally correct behaviour and the provision of a good service, a number of different influences could have played a part as well.

It was pointed out in section 4.5.3 that respondents often referred to their conscience when they explained why they held certain moral principles or did not want to do anything unethical or illegal. Section 4.5.1 further touched on the possibility that the respondents' moral behaviour was influenced by their upbringing (Christian or non-Christian), i.e. that the values that they had been taught by their parents were quite formative for their behaviour.

With regards to the provision of a good service, several respondents mentioned the influence of their professional ethics. They felt that they had to provide a good, high-quality service because they wanted to be seen as being professional in their business. Their professional identity might be a particularly strong influence as it is a very specific identity that directly relates to the owner-managers' business activity. Other respondents talked about their perfectionism when they explained why they sought to deliver high-quality work (see section 6.1.2).

There might also be some alternative explanations to Christian owner-managers' 'lenient' attitudes towards people they interact with in their business. A number of respondents, for example, talked also about their 'soft' character (section 4.5.4), when they explained why they were often forgiving and generous towards employees and business partners.

Furthermore, one respondent linked his concern about the well-being of his employees particularly to his own experiences as an employee (see section 6.2.2). In other words, even though he phrased his efforts to create a family-friendly workplace a 'Christian' practice, it was equally informed by his own life-experience.

At the same time, a number of the practices that the owner-managers described could simply be regarded as good management practice, and thus be in their 'enlightened' self-interest (see section 7.4.2). Reliability and honesty in the relationship to customers and other business partners (see section 4.5), the provision of a good service (see section 6.1.2), the good treatment of employees including the concern to develop their gifts and talents (see sections 6.2 and 4.2.4), and financial stewardship (see section 4.2.4) would often be beneficial for the business, and perhaps would not always require a specific Christian motivation.

Lastly, some particular behaviours regarding the treatment of employees might also be explained by the owner-managers' physical proximity to them. This physical proximity may result in moral proximity and thus owner-managers might feel that they have a particular responsibility towards their employees. This might lead them to be particularly considerate about their employees' circumstances and to be concerned about keeping them in employment (see section 6.2).

In all those cases it is often difficult to make out which motivation – the Christian or the 'non-Christian' – is more important. These 'non-Christian' motivations might interact with a Christian motivation and they might be mutually reinforcing, but at times the non-Christian motivation might have more of an impact on owner-managers' practices.

In a few cases, moreover, respondents explicitly pointed out that some of their practices that could be regarded to be beneficial for 'wider society' did not come from their Christian identity. For example, it was pointed out in section 4.2.4 that D5's interest in environmental technology did not come from his faith, and presumably his national identity, with Germany being very advanced in environmental standards and technology, might have influenced his engagement there. Furthermore, it was pointed out in sections 6.3.3 and 6.3.4 that some of the respondents' civic engagement was not linked to their faith, but rather to their identities as local citizens and professionals.

7.5.2 The influence of the SME context and the national contexts

This sub-section briefly considers how the two contexts within which the study was carried out, the SME and the two national contexts, might have influenced the SME owner-managers' conceptualisation of business practice.

It was argued in section 2.1.3 that, due to the size and set-up of SMEs, owner-managers would often engage in close personal interaction with the business' stakeholders. Precisely this relational set-up of SMEs seemed to be quite important for the Christian owner-managers in the way they sought to bring their faith to their business. This was particularly obvious in the accounts in section 5.3.2, where respondents talked of how they – through their personal interaction with employees, customers and business partners – sought to 'bring about a change' in them, either by personally seeking to influence their attitudes and moral behaviour or by seeking to contribute to people's personal development. Also, behaviours and attitudes that were based on Christian beliefs about equality and human dignity often related to concrete interactions with customers and employees (see sections 6.1.4 and 6.2.1) and were not treated as more abstract principles. These observations, however, would also be in line with Nash's (1994) findings concerning the 'relational' nature of (evangelical) Christian business people's leadership style, i.e. that the Christian business people she interviewed would conceptualise their Christian responsibilities towards others in terms of individual relationships (Van Buren and Agle 1998, 164).

This more relational focus of the owner-managers' ethics may also explain why hardly any respondent mentioned any 'wider' responsibilities relating to their business activity from a faith perspective. For example, the people in the study generally did not stop and ask whether the business practices of their suppliers were socially responsible. When asked about their responsibilities to their suppliers, they usually seemed to be more concerned about paying their bills on time or perhaps dealing with the suppliers' sales representatives in a respectful and honest manner.

The SME set-up also enabled respondents not just to 'integrate' their faith into their business practices but also to prioritise their faith, even if that meant to forego profit opportunities. This was particularly evident in the accounts of UK11 and UK10, who sought to provide a service to the community, but also in the accounts of other respondents, who sought to consider the interests and needs of others in their business practices (see sections 6.1.6, 6.1.5 and 6.2.2). This opportunity to be able to go beyond 'enlightened' self-interest may be the reason that some Christians might prefer to run a small to medium-sized business rather than seek to pursue a career within a larger organisation.
At the same time, we must conclude that a lot of the practices that the respondents reported may also be displayed by other SME owner-managers, such as the provision of a good, high-quality service, responsibility to employees and honesty in business dealings (cf. Spence 2000). Therefore it might often not be the practices but rather the underlying motivations that would make a Christian owner-manager different. On the other hand, those spiritual motivations might provide a stronger motive to display particular behaviours.

We will now turn to the two national contexts within which the study was conducted. It was argued in section 2.3.3 that even though both the U.K. and Germany can be regarded as welfare states, they have quite different socio-institutional frameworks for economic activity which have resulted in quite different business systems (Lane 1992). Economic activity in Germany is considered to be a 'cooperative' activity, strongly embedded in societal institutions and geared towards the long-term. Economic activity in the U.K. context, by contrast, is considered to be less strongly embedded in societal institutions and to have a more short-term perspective (ibid.). This different set-up of the economic system might also have an impact on how SME owner-manager conceptualise their worlds of business practice.

Of course, the researcher did notice a number of differences in the accounts of the U.K. and German respondents. For example, a number of issues that the German respondents mentioned in their accounts related to particular societal structures within which their businesses were embedded, issues that their British counterparts would not face in that way. Yet as the main focus of this study was on how faith related to business practices, the effect of those differences arising from societal structure were not explored in detail in the context of this study. (This might be done by other studies, which focus on the comparative element only.)

In terms of how faith was linked to business practices, however, the respondents' responses were often rather similar. Respondents in both countries would, for instance, refer to their 'Christian' responsibility to be honest and reliable in their business dealings, to their obligation not to defraud the taxman, to their aspiration to provide a high quality service, to the biblical concept of gifts and talents, and to the social responsibility towards their employees. And it might be difficult to judge whether such practices appear a bit more 'unusual' in one national context than in the other.

The fact that faith was linked with similar practices implies that shared religious identity might be stronger than national identity. At the same time, one might want to argue that their common identity as SME owner-managers might have played an important part as well.[178] As already indicated above, the strong social responsibility towards employees might be something that marks them out as SME owner-managers - in contrast to top-managers in large listed corporations. Moreover, small business researchers argue that not all SME owner-managers seek to maximise their profits (Curran and Blackburn 2001, 45, Spence and Rutherfoord 2001), so that a general assumption made about the focus of businesses on (short-term) profit-maximisation – particularly in the British context - does not necessarily hold true in an SME context. Thus if Christian owner-managers run their business on the basis of profit-satisficing rather than profit-maximising, this would not be an exclusive Christian focus but would also be shared with other non-Christian SME owner-managers.

However, the data found that in some places the national context seemed to make some difference in the way practices were conceptualised from a faith perspective. It was pointed out in section 4.1, for example, that some of the British respondents related the concept of calling to a specific calling to make a 'difference' in the way their business was run, whereas German respondents who engaged with the concept of calling would often relate it to narrower 'spiritual' responsibilities. This might have been due to the fact that the notion of 'serving society' and the expectation and obligation to engage in responsible business practices is already embedded in the German national culture, and therefore the engagement in responsible business practices would not require a specific spiritual motivation. Furthermore, section 4.2, which looked at the different stewardship responsibilities, showed that German respondents would not include in their stewardship responsibilities a strong engagement for environmental sustainability, unlike one British respondent. A possible explanation for this might be that in Germany owner-managers are required by law to adhere to high environmental standards, and environmentally friendly practices are also part of the national culture, and so they may see no need to apply a particular spiritual motivation to environmentally friendly practices. Another example was the reference to Sunday trading. It was pointed out in section 6.1.1 that only British respondents talked about not working on Sundays and that this was probably influenced by the fact that Sunday trading is regarded more of a 'normal' societal practice in the U.K. than in Germany, where the law (still) limits Sunday trading. Lastly, perhaps it would also be possible to argue that the fact that the state provides extensive welfare services in both countries is a reason for some Christian SME owner-managers to restrict their civic engagement to community of faith related causes. They might feel there is no need to be concerned about wider social issues as the state is taking care of them.

We may conclude from these examples that the absence of certain societal structures might make a spiritual motivation to engage in certain practices stronger - if some spiritual significance is recognised there. At the same time, the presence of such societal structures might lead owner-managers not to

[178] The assumption that SME identity might be more prominent than national identity is underlined by Schmidpeter and Spence's (2004) findings in their cross-national study of German and UK SME owner-managers. They found that the differences between industry sectors were likely to be bigger than national differences.

consider particular practices from a spiritual point of view, because the law or cultural practices already cover them, and to rather focus on narrower spiritual responsibilities. If, however, owner-managers also had a strong spiritual perspective on particular issues, this might encourage them to go beyond regulatory standards and 'cultural' practices.

On the other hand, it might also be the case that a Christian motivation can be reinforced by the national context, even though there was only some evidence in the data that confirmed this assumption. The national context may have, for example, reinforced the German respondents' concern to keep their staff in employment, as the social responsibility towards employees is strongly embedded in the German business system (see sections 2.3.3 and 6.2.2).

7.5.3 Conclusion

This section looked at influences other than their religious faith that could impact on SME owner-managers' conceptualisations of practice, thereby highlighting the fact that the actions of economic actors are not influenced by one discursive context alone but that other resources and contexts may play a part as well.

Section 7.5.1 identified a range of alternative explanations for certain behaviours: the respondents' professional ethics, certain character traits, their upbringing, their life experience, local citizenship, physical proximity to other people (resulting in moral proximity), but also business-related self-interest. These other influences might interact with a specific Christian motivation, but sometimes they would provide the primary motivation for action.

But the SME context and the national context may also have some kind of influence on Christian SME owner-managers' conceptualisations of practice. SMEs, for example, provide 'favourable' contexts for the integration of Christian values to business, particularly in terms of their relational set-up, and also because they allow owner-managers at times to prioritise their faith-related values over business considerations. In terms of the national context, however, the presence of particular common-good orientated societal structures (laws, national customs etc.) might at times lead to the curious effect that owner-managers do not consider particular issues from a faith perspective.

7.6 Suggestions for further research

The insights that have been gained through this study merit further investigation. This section outlines the areas into which further research might be undertaken to improve understanding of the specific research problem – the influence of Christianity on business activity – as well as of the more general issue of how civil society institutions influence economic activity.

7.6.1 More research on the influence of Christianity

This study identified which linguistic and conceptual resources that are linked to the Christian context are likely to be relevant for Christian SME owner-managers and outlined how they might impact on their conceptualisations of practice and subsequent behaviour. However, as this study employed only one research method and, as a result, some of the findings were rather 'open-ended' (see section 7.2.1), one might want to conduct some further research on Christian SME owner-managers. For instance, it would be worthwhile to carry out some further studies that focus more on SME owner-managers' *practices*. It might be useful, for example, to carry out interviews with employees and customers to explore whether the owner-managers' faith really makes a difference in the way they interact with them or whether that is just something that only makes a difference for the owner-managers (see sections 5.3.2, 6.1.4 and 6.2.1) - even though carrying out such interviews might be difficult in practice (see section 3.1.2). One could also try and observe the respondents in their day-to-day running of the business, although again that would depend on whether SME owner-managers would be willing to be observed.

In order to explore the extent to which a Christian motivation is a stronger motivation when it comes to the display of morally correct behaviour (see sections 6.1.2 and 7.3.3), one could also conduct a comparative study with people who construct their moral framework without recourse to religious beliefs. It would be particularly interesting to carry out such studies in sectors that do not enjoy a good reputation, such as the building trade. Such studies should ideally not rely on the owner-managers' perspectives only.

At the same time, one might want to study Protestant Christians who occupy top-management positions in larger organisations and run the business on behalf of external providers of capital. One might want to explore whether organisational constraints would have an impact on the way they bring their faith to bear on their management activities or whether they would seek to 'integrate' their faith into their business similar to SME owner-managers.

Furthermore, the research was restricted to conservative Protestant Christians. It might therefore be useful to explore other Christian traditions, for example, the Catholic tradition, and find out what concepts and contexts are meaningful to them and how they are linked to practices. Those findings could be compared with the findings of this study.

Lastly, the insights gained through this study could also be used for action research. This study identified Christian concepts that are likely to be meaningful for conservative Protestant Christians, and researchers and other people (e.g. faith community representatives) who seek to encourage Christian business people 'to make a difference' in business should be building on those conceptual resources rather than use, say, secular philosophical approaches to business ethics (Roels 1997). In other words, if researchers use concepts such as 'witness', 'stewardship' or 'calling' when they talk to Christian business people, they are more likely to 'strike a chord' with them than if they used concepts that have not much meaning for Christians. The concept of stewardship might be particularly fruitful concept, given that it can be directly linked to business activity (as a large number of respondents in the sample did) and given that it can be used to frame a wide range of business practices (see section 4.2). Furthermore, the fact that a number of respondents reported that they found small church-related groups to be a particularly helpful context, in which they could discuss and pray over business issues (see section 5.2.3), might also be a useful insight for those who want to engage in action research with Christian SME owner-managers and their faith communities.

7.6.2 Exploring other religious frameworks

One could also carry out some comparative research with owner-managers that adhere to other religions. Using the concepts-contexts-practices framework (see section 7.1), one could seek to explore what concepts and contexts are meaningful for them, what implications these concepts and contexts have for their conceptualisations of practice, and what practices are linked with these faith-related resources. The findings of such studies could then be compared with the findings of this study. It would be particularly interesting to find out whether the concept of stewardship, which was identified as a concept that Christianity shares with other mono-theistic religions (see section 4.2), is also of the same importance to Jewish and Muslim business people. Given the diverse interpretations of the stewardship concept by the Christian owner-managers in this study, it would also be interesting to explore how the adherents of other religions interpret 'stewardship' and link it to practices.

This study looked at the influence of Christianity in the context of countries where Christianity has once been a very strong cultural institution but has been losing its importance in the light of secularisation processes. Therefore it would be worthwhile to explore the influence of other religions on business activities in countries that have also been undergoing secularisation processes. For example, Turkey is perceived to be a Muslim yet increasingly secular country and one might want to explore to what extent committed Muslims are influenced by their faith in their business activities in this secularised national context. It might be interesting to find out whether their religious identity might also lead them to network with and help out other committed Muslims or their communities of faith.

Comparative studies might also explore what concepts and contexts have significance for 'secular' owner-managers and how they 'constrain' and 'enable' their behaviour. For example, it would be interesting to investigate whether the stewardship concept – which was identified as a concept that is potentially shared with 'secular' business people – is also as prominent among 'secular' owner-managers as it is among Christian ones, and to explore to whom people who refer to the stewardship concept feel accountable.[179]

7.6.3 Exploring other civil society frameworks

The study's focus on the influence of Christianity on SME owner-managers' conceptualisations of practice was embedded in the more general problem of how civil society institutions might impact on the way economic actors carry out their activities.

Subsequent research might therefore also explore what impact other civil society frameworks might make on owner-managers' conceptualisations of practice, using the concepts-contexts-practices framework (see section 7.1). One might want to explore more business-related frameworks, for example, how active (and passive) membership of trade associations, professional bodies but also business groups might impact on their conceptualisation of practice. Given the prominent role that the professional identity played in the accounts of the respondents in this study, one might assume that membership of professional bodies might make a particular strong impact.

One might also investigate how 'membership' (active and passive) of more general civil society contexts such as local or national contexts have an impact. Finally, following Putnam's assumptions about the link between engagement in any kind of associational activity and the development of 'civic virtues' (see section 2.1.1), one might want to explore whether active membership of sports clubs or choral societies might make a difference in SME owner-managers' conceptualisation of practice.

This study found that the distinctiveness of the Christian influence lies particularly in the availability of some distinct significations that relate to the presence of the 'transcendent' and that can be powerful 'constraints' or 'enablers' of action (see section 7.3.2). One might therefore want to explore what distinct 'enablers' and 'constraints' would arise from those other civil society frameworks in terms of concepts and contexts and how they would translate into practices. The

[179] Particularly in the absence of external providers of capital, to whom managers might feel accountable with regards to their stewardship over finances and assets.

question about constraints may be particularly interesting in the absence of a 'divine' authority, yet there might be some strong constraints that arise from the social context.

With some civil society frameworks, it would also be worth investigating is whether membership of these institutions might lead owner-managers to focus particularly on the well-being of fellow members or whether it has also positive 'spill-over' effects in terms of the pursuit of a wider 'common good'.

7.7 Concluding remarks

Durkheim's call for some 'regulating' force that would provide an effective counter-balance for the excesses of economic self-interest and so contribute to societal stability and individual well-being has in our contemporary world, in which free markets proliferate and the moderating influence of the state declines, perhaps more urgency than ever.

This study investigated Christianity as one such 'force' that could channel economic activity in ways that produce beneficial outcomes for society. However, despite the fact that it has a rather strong potential to provide an effective counterbalance to 'unrestrained' self-interested behaviour - as shown in this study -, it is a civil society institution that is in decline in secularised Europe.

To what extent it will continue to be an effective 'force' will depend on whether people will continue to attach meaning to the Christian discourse and on the extent to which they will interpret Christianity as being relevant for 'worldly' activities. This study has shown that the 'effectiveness' of Christian context depends on the way it is interpreted by believers: Some interpretations of the Christian faith and some faith-related practices have hardly any impact on wider society, whereas others can have a rather strong impact. It is an open-ended question as to which interpretations of the Christian faith will survive, and one important factor will be how Christianity will be communicated through, and practised by, Christian faith communities.

Hence it remains to be seen whether Christianity will continue to make an impact or whether in future the 'forces' that regulate economic activity will have to be completely provided by other frameworks.

8. Bibliography

Adler, P., Kwon, S.-W. (2002). 'Social Capital: Prospects for a New Concept.' *Academy of Management Review* 27(1), 17-40.

Agle, B., van Buren, H. (1999). 'God and Mammon: The Modern Relationship.' *Business Ethics Quarterly* 9(4), 563-582.

Ählström, J., Sjöström, E. (2005). 'CSOs and Business Partnerships: Strategies for Interaction.' *Business Strategy and the Environment* 14, 230-240.

Alexander, J. (1998). *Real Civil Societies: Dilemmas of Institutionalization*. London: Sage.

Allport, G. (1985). The Historical Background of Social Psychology. In: Lindzey, G., Aronson, E. (eds.) *Handbook of Social Psychology*. New York: Random House. **1**, 1-46.

Alvesson, M., Deetz, S. (2000). *Doing Critical Management Research*. London: Sage.

Alvesson, M., Karreman, D. (2000a). 'Taking the Linguistic Turn in Organizational Research - Challenges, Responses, Consequences.' *Journal of Applied Behavioral Science* 36(2), 136-158.

Alvesson, M., Karreman, D. (2000b). 'Varieties of Discourse: On the Study of Organizations through Discourse Analysis.' *Human Relations* 53(9), 1125-1149.

Anglo American. Good Citizenship Principles http://www.angloamerican.co.uk/static/uploads/Business%20Principles%200204.pdf accessed 27/07/06.

Aquinas, T. (1969). *Summa Theologiae*. London: Blackfriars.

Argandoña, A. (1998). 'The Stakeholder Theory and the Common Good.' *Journal of Business Ethics* 17(9/10), 1093-1102.

Atkinson, J. (1988). Vocation. In: Ferguson, S., Wright, D. (eds.) *New Dictionary of Theology*. Leicester: Intervarsity Press, 711.

Banks, R. (1998). 'The Protestant Work Ethic.' *Faith in Business Quarterly* 2(2), 5-7.

Bauckham, R., Hart, T. (1999). *Hope against Hope - Christian Eschatology in Contemporary Context*. London: Darton, Longman and Todd.

Bauman, Z. (1993). *Postmodern Ethics*. Oxford: Blackwell.

Bellah, R., Madsen, R. et al. (1996). *Habits of the Heart - Individualism and Commitment in American Life*. Berkeley: University of California Press.

Blum, F. (1968). *Work and Community - The Scott Bader Commonwealth and the Quest for a New Social Order*. London: Routledge & Kegan Paul.

Bockmuehl, K. (1988). Sanctification. In: Ferguson, S., Wright, D. (eds.) *New Dictionary of Theology*. Leicester: Intervarsity Press, 613-616.

Bryman, A. (2001). *Social Research Methods*. Oxford: Oxford University Press.

Burchell, J., Cook, J. (2006). 'Confronting the 'Corporate Citizen' - Shaping the Discourse of Corporate Social Responsibility.' *International Journal of Sociology and Social Policy* 26(3/4), 121-137.

Byron, W. (1988). 'Twin Towers: A Philosophy and Theology of Business.' *Journal of Business Ethics* 7, 525-530.

Carey, G. (1992). Stewardship. In: Harrison, R. (ed.) *Encyclopedia of Biblical and Christian Ethics*. Nashville: Thomas Nelson Publishers, 395-396.

Cassell, C., Symon, G. (1994). Qualitative Research in Work Contexts. In: Cassell, C., Symon, G. *Qualitative Methods in Organizational Research*. London: Sage, 1-14.

Castells, M. (2003). Global Informational Capitalism. In: Held, D., McGrew, A. (eds.) *The Global Transformations Reader*. Cambridge: Polity Press, 311-334.

Charkham, J. (1994). *Keeping Good Company - A Study of Corporate Governance in Five Countries*. Oxford: Oxford University Press.

Childs, J. (1995). *Ethics in Business: Faith at Work*. Minneapolis: Fortress Press.

Christians, C. (2002). Ethics and Politics in Qualitative Research. In: Denzin, N., Lincoln, Y. (eds.) *Handbook of Qualitative Research*. London: Sage, 133-155.

Clark, J., Dawson, L. (1996). 'Personal Religiousness and Ethical Judgments: An Empirical Analysis.' *Journal of Business Ethics* 15, 359-372.

Curran, J., Blackburn, R. (1994). *Small Firms and Local Economic Networks - The Death of the Local Economy*. London: Paul Chapman.

Curran, J., Blackburn, R. (2001). *Researching the Small Enterprise*. London: Sage.

Curran, J., Rutherfoord, R., Smith, S. (2000). 'Is There a Local Business Community? Explaining the Non-participation of Small Business in Local Economic Development.' *Local Economy* 15(2), 128-143.

Daly, H., Cobb, J. (1994). *For the Common Good - Redirecting the Economy toward Community, the Environment, and a Sustainable Future*. Boston: Beacon Press.

Davies, R. (1983). Vocation. In: Richardson, A., Bowden, J. (eds.) *A New Dictionary of Christian Theology*. London: SCM Press, 601-602.

Denzin, N., Lincoln, Y. (2002). Introduction: The Discipline and Practice of Qualitative Research. In: Denzin, N., Lincoln, Y. (eds.) *Handbook of Qualitative Research*. London: Sage, 1-27.

Donnelly, S., Gamble, A., Jackson, G. And Parkinson, J. (2001). The Public Interest and the Company in Britain and Germany. London: Anglo-German Foundation for the Study of Industrial Society.

Durkheim, E. (1957). *Professional Ethics and Civic Morals*. London: Routledge.

Evangelische Kirche in Deutschland (EKD) (2004). Christen in Deutschland. www.ekd.de/download/christen_in_deutschland.pdf accessed 8/9/2006.

Fenton, N. (2000). Critical Perspectives on Trust and Civil Society. In: Tonkiss, F., Passey, A. (eds.) *Trust and Civil Society*. Houndmills: Macmillan, 151-173.

Fisher, F. (1960). Witness, Testimony. In: Harrison, E. (ed.) *Baker's Dictionary of Theology*. Grand Rapids: Baker Book House, 555-556.

Fort, T. (1999). 'The First Man and the Company Man: The Common Good, Transcendence, and Mediating Institutions.' *American Business Law Journal* 36(3), 391-435.

Frey, D. (1998). 'Individualist Economic Values and Self-interest: The Problem in the Puritan Ethic.' *Journal of Business Ethics* 17(14), 1573-1580.

Friedman, M. (1970). 'The Social Responsibility of Business is to Increase its Profits.' *The New York Times Magazine* 32-33, 122-126.

Gaffin, R. (1988). Kingdom of God. In: Ferguson, S., Wright, D. (eds.) *New Dictionary of Theology*. Leicester: Intervarsity Press, 367-369.

Geldard, M. (1992). Protestant Work Ethic. In: Harrison, R. (ed.) *Encyclopedia of Biblical and Christian Ethics*. Nashville: Thomas Nelson Publishers.

Giddens, A. (1984). *The Constitution of Society*. Cambridge: Polity Press.

Giddens, A. (1998). *The Third Way - The Renewal of Social Democracy*. Cambridge: Polity Press.

Gold, L. (2000). Making Space for Sharing in the Global Market: the Focolare Movement's Economy of Sharing. Glasgow: University of Glasgow.

Gorsuch, R., Mcpherson, S. (1989). 'Intrinsic/Extrinsic Measurement: I/E-Revised and Single-Item Scales.' *Journal for the Scientific Study of Religion* 28(3), 348-354.

Greene, M. (2003). Imagine - How We Can Reach the UK. London: London Institute for Contemporary Christianity.

Günterberg, B., Kayser, G. (2004). SMEs in Germany - Facts and Figures. Bonn: Institut für Mittelstandsforschung.

Hall, P. (1999). 'Social Capital in Britain.' *British Journal of Politics* 29, 417-461.

Harré, R., Gillett, G. (1994). *The Discursive Mind*. London: Sage.

Held, D., McGrew, A. (2003). The Great Globalization Debate: An Introduction. In: Held, D., McGrew, A. (eds.) *The Global Transformations Reader*. Cambridge: Polity.

Hems, L., Tonkiss, F. (2000). Introduction. In: Tonkiss, F., Passey, A. (eds.) *Trust and Civil Society*. Houndmills: Macmillan, 1-11.

Hendry, J. (2000). 'Strategic Decision Making, Discourse, and Strategy as Social Practice.' *Journal of Management Studies* 37(7), 955-977.

Hendry, J. (2001). 'After Durkheim - An Agenda for the Sociology of Business Ethics.' *Journal of Business Ethics* 34(3/4), 209-218.

Hendry, J. (2004). *Between Enterprise and Ethics - Business and Management in a Bimoral Society*. Oxford: Oxford University Press.

Herms, E. (1991). Der religiöse Sinn der Moral. Unzeitgemäße Betrachtungen zu den Grundlagen einer Ethik der Unternehmensführung. In: Steinmann, H., Löhr, A. (eds.) *Unternehmensethik*. Stuttgart: Pöschl.

Hicks, D. (1996). 'The Christian Dimensions of Morality.' *Studies in Christian Ethics* 9(2), 22-35.

Hillyer, P. (1988). Stewardship. In: Ferguson, S., Wright, D. (eds.) *New Dictionary of Theology*. Leicester: Intervarsity Press, 661.

Hughes, J., Sharrock, W., Martin, P. (2003). *Understanding Classical Sociology - Marx, Weber, Durkheim*. London: Sage.

Hussey, J., Hussey, R. (1997). *Business Research*. Palgrave: Basingstoke.

Ibrahim, N., Angelidis, J. (2005). 'The Long-Term Performance of Small Businesses: Are there Differences Between 'Christian-Based' Companies and their Secular Counterparts?' *Journal of Business Ethics* 58, 187-193.

Ibrahim, N., Rue, L., McDougall, P., Greene, G.R. (1991). 'Characteristics and Practices of 'Christian-Based' Companies.' *Journal of Business Ethics* 10, 123-132.

Janjuha-Jivraj, S. (2003). 'The Sustainability of Social Capital within Ethnic Networks.' *Journal of Business Ethics* 47(1), 31-43.

Johnson, J. (2002). In-Depth Interviewing. In: Gubrium, J., Holstein, J. (eds.) *Handbook of Interview Research*. Thousand Oaks: Sage, 103-120.

Kennedy, E., Lawton, L. (1998). 'Religiousness and Business Ethics.' *Journal of Business Ethics* 17, 163-175.

Kuhn, T. (1996). *The Structure of Scientific Revolutions*. Chicago and London: The University of Chicago Press.

Lane, C. (1992). European Business Systems: Britain and Germany Compared. In: Whitley, R. (ed.) *European Business Systems - Firms and Markets in their National Contexts*. London: Sage, 64-97.

Lee, K., McCann, D., Ching, M. (2003). 'Christ and Business Culture: A Study of Christian Executives in Hong Kong.' *Journal of Business Ethics* 43(1/2), 103-110.

Lincoln, Y., Guba, E. (2002). Paradigmatic Controversies, Contradictions, and Emerging Confluences. In: Denzin, N., Lincoln, Y. (eds.) *Handbook of Qualitative Research*. London: Sage, 163-188.

London School of Economics - Centre for Civil Society (LSE) (2004). What is Civil Society? http://www.lse.ac.uk/collections/CCS/what_is_civil_society.htm accessed 2/6/2006.

Longenecker, J., McKinney, J., Moore, C. (2004). 'Religious Intensity, Evangelical Christianity, and Business Ethics: An Empirical Study.' *Journal of Business Ethics* 55, 373-386.

Luo, M. (2006). 'Evangelicals Debate the Meaning of 'Evangelical''. *The New York Times* 16/04/2006.

Lutz, M. (1999). *Economics for the Common Good - Two Centuries of Social Economic Thought in the Humanistic Tradition*. London: Routledge.

Lutz, M. (2002). 'Social Economics, Justice and the Common Good.' *International Journal of Social Economics* 29(1/2), 26-44.

MacIntyre, A. (1988). *Whose Justice? Which Rationality?* London: Duckworth.

Microsoft. Standards of Business Conduct http://www.microsoft.com/about/legal/buscond/standards accessed 27/7/06.

Mikolaski, S. (1992). Holiness. In: Harrison, R. (ed.) *Encyclopedia of Biblical and Christian Ethics*. Nashville: Thomas Nelson Publishers, 180-181.

Münkler, H. (1998). 'Civil Society and Civic Virtue. Do Democratically Constituted Communities Require a Socio-moral Foundation?' *International Review of Sociology* 8(3), 425-438.

Münkler, H., Fischer, K. (2002a). 'Gemeinwohl und Gemeinsinn in der modernen Gesellschaft.' *UNIVERSITAS Orientierung in der Wissenswelt* 57(9), 888-896.

Münkler, H., Fischer, K. (2002b). 'Common Good and Civic Spirit in the Welfare State: Problems of Societal Self-Description.' *The Journal of Political Philosophy* 10(4), 416-438.

Nash, L. (1994). *Believers in Business*. Nashville: Thomas Nelson Publishers.

National Statistics (1999). Frequency of Attending Religious Services: by Gender, *Social Trends* 31, http://www.statistics.gov.uk/statbase/datasets.asp accessed 8/9/2006.

National Statistics (2000). Belonging to a Religion, *Social Trends* 32, http://www.statistics.gov.uk/statbase/datasets.asp accessed 8/9/2006.

National Statistics (2001). Belonging to a Religion, *Social Trends* 34, http://www.statistics.gov.uk/statbase/datasets.asp accessed 8/9/2006.
Niebuhr, R. (1951). *Christ and Culture*. New York: Harper & Row.
Offe, C., Fuchs, S. (2001). Schwund des Sozialkapitals? - Der Fall Deutschland. In: Putnam, R. (ed.) *Gesellschaft und Gemeinsinn - Sozialkapital im internationalen Vergleich*. Gütersloh: Verlag Bertelsmann Stiftung, 417-514.
O'Rourke, A. (2003). 'A New Politics of Engagement: Shareholder Activism for Corporate Social Responsibility.' *Business Strategy and the Environment* 12(4), 227-239.
Ostrom, E. (1990). *Governing the Commons - The Evolution of Institutions for Collective Action*. New York: Cambridge University Press.
Pawlas, A. (2000). *Die lutherische Berufs- und Wirtschaftsethik - Eine Einführung*. Neukirchen-Vluyn: Neukirchener Verlag.
Perry, M. (1999). *Small Firms and Network Economies*. London: Routledge.
Portes, A. (1998). 'Social Capital: Its Origins and Applications in Modern Sociology.' *Annual Review of Sociology* 24, 1-24.
Potter, J., Wetherell, M. (1987). *Discourse and Social Psychology: Beyond Attitudes and Behaviour*. London: Sage.
Putnam, R. (2000). *Bowling Alone - The Collapse and Revival of American Community*. New York: Touchstone.
Quinn, J. (1997). 'Personal Ethics and Business Ethics: The Ethical Attitudes of Owner/Managers of Small Business.' *Journal of Business Ethics* 16, 119-127.
Razzell, P. (1977). 'The Protestant Ethic and the Spirit of Capitalism: a Natural Scientific Critique.' *British Journal of Sociology* 28(1), 17-37.
Roels, S. (1997). 'The Business Ethics of Evangelicals.' *Business Ethics Quarterly* 7(2), 109-122.
Rossouw, G. J. (1994). 'Where Have All the Christians Gone?' *Journal of Business Ethics* 13(7), 557-570.
Sandel, M. (1998). *Liberalism and the Limits of Justice*. Cambridge: Cambridge University Press.
Sauser, W. (2005). 'Ethics in Business: Answering the Call.' *Journal of Business Ethics* 58, 345-357.
Scharpf, F. (2003). Globalization and the Political Economy of Capitalist Democracies. In: D. Held, McGrew, A. *The Global Transformations Reader*. Cambridge: Polity Press, 370-378.
Schlender, W. (1982). Countervailing Values in Business Decisionmaking: Exploring Alternatives to Ambiguity. In: Jones, D. (ed.) *Business, Religion and Ethics*. Cambridge, MA: Oelgeschlager, Gunn and Hain, 183-194.
Schmidpeter, R., Spence, L. (2004). SMEs, Social Capital and Civic Engagement in Bavaria and West-London. In: Spence, L., Habisch, A., Schmidpeter, R. (eds.) *Responsibility and Social Capital - The World of Small and Medium Sized Enterprises*. Houndmills: Palgrave Macmillan, 59-76.
Schuppe, G. F. (2002). 'Gemeinwohl - ein schwieriger Begriff.' *UNIVERSITAS Orientierung in der Wissenswelt* 57(9), 911-927.
Seligman, A. (2000). Trust and Civil Society. In: Tonkiss, F., Passey, A. (eds.) *Trust and Civil Society*. Houndmills: Macmillan, 12-30.
Silverman, D. (2000). *Doing Qualitative Research. A Practical Handbook*. London: Sage.
Small Business Service (SBS) (2005). Small and Medium-sized Enterprise (SME) Statistics for the UK 2004, Statistical Press Release URN 05/92, 25th August.
Spence, L. (1999). 'Does Size Matter? The State of the Art in Small Business Ethics.' *Business Ethics - A European Review* 8(3), 163-174.
Spence, L. (2000). *Priorities, Practice and Ethics in Small Firms*. London: The Institute of Business Ethics.
Spence, L. (2004). Small Firm Accountability and Integrity. In: Brenkert, G. (ed.) *Corporate Integrity and Accountability*. Thousand Oaks: Sage, 50-128.
Spence, L., Rutherfoord, R. (2001). 'Social Responsibility, Profit Maximisation and the Small Firm Owner-manager.' *Journal of Small Business and Enterprise Development* 8(2), 126-139.
Stott, J. (1997). *Understanding the Bible*. Scripture Union.

Symon, G., Cassell, C. (1998). Reflections on the Use of Qualitative Methods. In: Symon, G. Cassell, C. (eds) *Qualitative Methods and Analysis in Organizational Research - A Practical Guide*. London: Sage, 3-8.
Tawney, R. (1938). *Religion and the Rise of Capitalism*. Harmondsworth: Penguin Books.
Ulrich, P. (1997). *Integrative Wirtschaftsethik - Grundlagen einer lebensdienlichen Ökonomie*. Bern/Stuttgart: Haupt.
Unilever. Code of Business Principles http://www.unilever.com/ourvalues/purposeandprinciples/ourprinciples/ accessed 27/7/06.
Van Buren, H., Agle, B. (1998). 'Measuring Christian Beliefs that Affect Managerial Decision-Making: A Beginning.' *International Journal of Value-Based Management* 11, 159-177.
Van Wensveen Siker, L. (1989). 'Christ and Business: A Typology for Christian Business Ethics.' *Journal of Business Ethics* 8, 883-888.
Verstraeten, J. (1998). 'From Business Ethics to the Vocation of Business Leaders to Humanize the World of Business.' *Business Ethics - A European Review* 7(2), 111-124.
Watson, T., Harris, P. (1999). *The Emergent Manager*. London: Sage.
Weaver, G., Agle, B. (2002). 'Religiosity and Ethical Behaviour in Organizations: A Symbolic Interactionist Perspective.' *Academy of Management Review* 27(1), 77-97.
Weber, M. (1930). *The Protestant Ethic and the Spirit of Capitalism*. London: Allen & Unwin.
Webley, S. (1999). Values Inherent in the Interfaith Declaration of International Business Ethics. In: Enderle, G. (ed.) *International Business Ethics - Challenges and Approaches*. Notre Dame: The University of Notre Dame Press, 96-108.
Weick, K. (1995). *Sensemaking in Organizations*. Thousand Oaks: Sage.
Wengraf, T. (2001). *Qualitative Research Interviewing*. London: Sage.
Wittgenstein, L. (1953). *Philosophical Investigations*. Oxford: Blackwell.

If not otherwise noted the biblical quotations are from the Holy Bible, New International Version (1973) London: Hodder and Stoughton.

Appendix I – Profiles of the participants in the study

Note: Not all respondents provided very detailed information about their biographies. Therefore the individual profiles vary in terms of detail and depth.

German respondents

D1	Pharmacy	10 employees
After having worked for a large pharmaceutical company, he started the business in 2003. Bought a second shop in 2004.		
Age (at time of first interview): 41		
Denominational affiliation[180]: United State Church (evangelical) Christian upbringing		
1st interview: 5 April 2004 (40 mins)[181] 2nd interview: 25 August 2004 (70 mins)		

D2	Property Management	4 employees
He joined the business in 1998 and bought it from the previous owners in 1999 (established in 1950). Has a degree in business administration.		
Age (at time of first interview): 45		
Denominational affiliation: Pietistic Church Fellowship Made a commitment to the Christian faith in his adult life		
1st interview: 6 April 2004 (55 mins) 2nd interview: 31 August 2004 (45 mins)		

D3	Mobile Home Rental	Sole trader
After having worked for a larger organisation, he started the company in 1991 as a 'lifestyle' business. Holds a PhD.		
Age (at time of first interview): 55		
Denominational affiliation: United State Church (evangelical) Made a commitment to the Christian faith in his adult life (after he had started the business)		
1st interview: 7 April 2004 (40 mins) 2nd interview: 23 August 2004 (50 mins)		

[180] 'Evangelical' is only denoted where the respondents explicitly pointed out that their church was evangelical.
[181] These are approximate times.

D4	Heating and Plumbing Installation and Service	65 employees
Bought the business from the founder in 1980 (established in 1935).		
Age (at time of first interview): 60		
Denominational affiliation: Pentecostal Made a commitment to the Christian faith in his adult life		
1st interview: 8 April 2004 (65 mins) 2nd interview: 8 September 2004 (50 mins)		

D5	Printing	20 employees
Took over the family business in 1987 (established in 1833). Has a degree in graphic design.		
Denominational affiliations[182]: Independent Free Church, Moravian Christian upbringing		
Age (at time of first interview): 55		
1st interview: 14 April 2004 (90 mins) 2nd interview: 9 September 2004 (80 mins)		

D6	Decorating and Special Surface Coatings	3 employees
Took over the family business in 1973 (established in 1899). Apart from being a qualified decorator, he also has a vocational qualification in business administration.		
Age (at time of first interview): 57		
Denominational affiliation: United State Church (evangelical) Christian upbringing		
1st interview: 17 April 2004 (130 mins) 2nd interview: 28 August 2004 (155 mins)		

D7	Optician	7 employees
Took over the family business in 1998 (established in 1964).		
Age (at time of first interview): 44		
Denominational affiliation: United State Church (evangelical) Made a commitment to the Christian faith in his adult life		
1st interview: 19 April 2004 (65 mins) 2nd interview: 24 August 2004 (45 mins)		

D8	Industrial Building Services (specialising in demolition work)	20 employees
After having trained as a bricklayer and completed an engineering degree, he took over the family business in 1973 (established in 1960).		
Age (at time of first interview): 54		
Denominational affiliation: United State Church Christian upbringing		
1st interview: 20 April 2004 (110 mins) 2nd interview: 31 August 2004 (120 mins)		

[182] Some respondents claimed affiliation to more than one denomination. The first denomination mentioned denotes their main or current affiliation.

D9	Safety Analysis Projects and Software Development	10 employees
Started the business together with two other academics as a spin-off of a university based project group in 1990. Holds a PhD.		
Age (at time of first interview): 48		
Denominational affiliations: Pietistic Church Fellowship, United State Church Made a commitment to the Christian faith as an undergraduate student		
1st interview: 21 April 2004 (50 mins) 2nd interview: 1 September 2004 (50 mins)		

D10	Manufacture of Measuring Instruments	11 employees
After having worked in vocational education, he started the business in 1988.		
Age (at time of first interview): 44		
Denominational affiliation: Lutheran State Church Made a commitment to the Christian faith in his adult life		
1st interview: 29 April 2004 (80 mins) 2nd interview: 6 September 2004 (40 mins)		

UK respondents

UK1	Project Management in the Ceramics Industry and Manufacture of Birthpool Liners	1 employee
Used to be primarily involved in his family's business (manufacture of kiln furniture) until it was sold off. The Project Management business (established in 1985) was a spin-off of the family business. Had also taken over his son's birthpool liner business.		
Age (at time of first interview): 62		
Denominational affiliation: Anglican (stated he was also influenced by Methodism and the Quakers) Christian upbringing		
1st interview: 17 May 2004 (120 mins) 2nd interview: 18 January 2005 (90 mins)		

UK2	Manufacture of Metal Parts	70 employees
Having trained and worked as an accountant, he founded the business in 1966. He is also the director of the holding company that owns the premises of the metal parts factory as well as two other factories.		
Age (at time of first interview): 65		
Denominational affiliation: Anglican Christian upbringing		
1st interview: 24 May 2004 (105 mins) 2nd interview: 12 January 2005 (90 mins) 3rd interview: 12 May 2005 (75 mins)		

UK3	Estate Agent	4 employees
After having worked for a large estate agency firm he started the business in 1989.		
Age (at time of first interview): 57		
Denominational affiliation: Anglican (evangelical) Made a commitment to the Christian faith in his adult life.		
1st interview: 7 July 2004 (65 mins) 2nd interview: 9 February 2005 (50 mins) 3rd interview: 10 May 2005 (45 mins)		

UK4	Car and Van Rental	18 employees
He bought the business in 1997 after having run the company on behalf of the founder for 15 years (established in 1959).		
Age (at time of first interview): 51		
Denominational affiliation: Pentecostal Christian upbringing		
1st interview: 12 July 2004 (60 mins) 2nd interview: 8 February 2005 (45 mins)		

UK5	Heating Installation and Service	5 employees
He started the business in 1989 after having worked as an engineer for a larger company.		
Age (at time of first interview): 43		
Denominational affiliation: Anglican (evangelical) Made a commitment to the Christian faith when he was a young adult.		
1st interview: 3 August 2004 (65 mins) 2nd interview: 18 January 2005 (45 mins)		

UK6	Civil Engineering	100 employees
Used to work in a senior position for the founder of the company (established in 1980). Conducted a management buy-out together with three colleagues in 2000.		
Age (at time of first interview): 50		
Denominational affiliation: Anglican Christian upbringing		
1st interview: 4 August 2004 (70 mins) 2nd interview: 11 March 2005 (70 mins)		

UK7	Engineering	25 employees
After having held a number of senior posts in large engineering companies as well as in SMEs, he co-founded the business in 2001 together with someone who used to run a similar company. Also runs a sustainability consultancy business.		
Age (at time of first interview): 54		
Denominational affiliations: Anglican, Pentecostal Christian upbringing		
1st interview: 4 August 2004 (65 mins) 2nd interview: 15 February 2005 (55 mins)		

<table>
<tr><td>UK8</td><td>Industrial Design</td><td>14 employees</td></tr>
<tr><td colspan="3">Founded the company in 1996. Shares ownership with another person.</td></tr>
<tr><td colspan="3">Age (at time of first interview): 49</td></tr>
<tr><td colspan="3">Denominational affiliation: Baptist
Made a commitment to the Christian faith as an undergraduate student</td></tr>
<tr><td colspan="3">1st interview: 4 August 2004 (40 mins)
2nd interview: 15 February 2005 (45 mins)
3rd interview: 24 May 2005 (40 mins)</td></tr>
</table>

<table>
<tr><td>UK9</td><td>Building Services</td><td>2 employees</td></tr>
<tr><td colspan="3">Founded the company in 1989, turning his hobby into a business.</td></tr>
<tr><td colspan="3">Age (at time of first interview): 55</td></tr>
<tr><td colspan="3">Denominational affiliation: Anglican (evangelical)
Made a commitment to the Christian faith in his adult life (after having started the business).</td></tr>
<tr><td colspan="3">1st interview: 22 September 2004 (55 mins)
2nd interview: 23 February 2005 (50 mins)</td></tr>
</table>

<table>
<tr><td>UK10</td><td>Pharmacy</td><td>7 employees</td></tr>
<tr><td colspan="3">After having worked for a hospital pharmacy and managed a pharmacy on behalf of someone else, he started his own business in 1989. Started with one shop and later opened another.</td></tr>
<tr><td colspan="3">Age (at time of first interview): 43</td></tr>
<tr><td colspan="3">Denominational affiliations: Methodist, Congregational
Christian upbringing</td></tr>
<tr><td colspan="3">1st interview: 10 November 2004 (75 mins)
2nd interview: 27 April 2005 (90 mins)</td></tr>
</table>

<table>
<tr><td>UK11</td><td>Optician</td><td>7 employees</td></tr>
<tr><td colspan="3">The only female respondent. She started her own business in 1998 after having worked for a large optical chain.</td></tr>
<tr><td colspan="3">Age (at time of first interview): 42</td></tr>
<tr><td colspan="3">Denominational affiliations: Independent Free Church, Methodist
Christian upbringing</td></tr>
<tr><td colspan="3">1st interview: 3 December 2004 (45 mins)
2nd interview: 4 March 2005 (40 mins)</td></tr>
</table>

Appendix II – An account of a 'Christian code of conduct'

UK2's account of his Christian code of conduct

My my code of conduct basically is a Christian code of conduct. So I'm um I think the difficulty is when in business um you you have to um, the the whole things of of being a business is about target setting. ... *But I I'm I'm much happier that um you get a process, which, an outcome of which is is the goal. But everybody is then involved with. ... So we examine each quarter how we think the business is going to be across each customer in 18 months time. And we do that with all the all the, well all the interested people, and managers.* Um, and that gets them all involved sort of all the time in um the forecasting, budgeting and it makes that a normal question, when people go out selling, you know, 'Can you tell me what you think your order books will be like in 18 months time?' [pause] 'Why do you want to know?' 'Well, you know, we need to plan our own resources.' Et cetera, et cetera. Um so invariably people will tell us and will show us um, you know, what they're planning for in 18 months. And um that that saves, you know, management a l- quite a lot of headache. Really. 'Cause I think some of the real difficulties of business come, you know, into this area of bonus. And, you know, there there is a bonus on sales and there is a bonus on profit. So whose role is it to give me as a salesman a chance of a bonus? Um, has the boss set the target so far away and I'm never likely to reach it. Is the business likely to yield what level of, a a realistic level so that I'm likely to get a bonus um or not? *And so I think if you've got a process there, which produces something that management and the people generating the um the performance can actually see there is a reasonable a reasonable goal. Then we can all say 'Ok, we go for it.' And that will be um, the basis for our budget. And therefore for our bonus. 'Is that fair?' Everyone says that's fair, so that's what we go for. And then we don't get, you know, people who are very agitated and or who will always be um sly with the deal in order to try and get a bigger bonus.* We don't we don't get that in that case. And it's still exciting.
(UK2a, manufacture of metal parts)

Printed in the United States
134514LV00005B/12/P

9 781599 426754